CONDUCTING
SOCIAL RESEARCH

CONDUCTING SOCIAL RESEARCH

NAN LIN

Department of Sociology
State University of New York at Albany

RONALD S. BURT

National Opinion Research Center
University of Chicago

JOHN C. VAUGHN

Department of Sociology
State University of New York at Albany

McGRAW-HILL BOOK COMPANY

New York   St. Louis   San Francisco   Auckland
Düsseldorf   Johannesburg   Kuala Lumpur   London
Mexico   Montreal   New Delhi   Panama   Paris
São Paulo   Singapore   Sydney   Tokyo   Toronto

CONDUCTING
SOCIAL RESEARCH

1 2 3 4 5 6 7 8 9 0 K P K P 7 9 8 7 6

This book was set in Times Roman by Maryland Composition Incorporated.
The editors were Lyle Linder and Michael Gardner;
the cover was designed by Nicholas Krenitsky;
the production supervisor was Sam Ratkewitch.
Kingsport Press, Inc., was printer and binder.

Library of Congress Cataloging in Publication Data
Lin, Nan.
    Conducting social research.
    Companion vol. and worktext for the author's Foundations of social research.
    1. Sociological research. I. Burt, Ronald S., joint author. II. Vaughn, John C., joint author.
III. Title.
[HM48.L53   301'.01'8   75-25630
ISBN 0-07-037868-1

Contents

Preface

This volume has been prepared for the general reader. No assumptions are made regarding the reader's substantive or methodological training in social science. The reader, however—whether undergraduate student, graduate student, or practicing social scientist—is assumed to be curious about aspects of explaining social phenomena. The parts of the forthcoming discussion the reader finds relevant will depend on his or her past experience.

This volume has been written in conjunction with Nan Lin's introductory text on research methods, *Foundations of Social Research*. It can also be used as an independent resource or with other discussions of theory construction and social research. Given the basically practical focus of this volume, references to other works have been kept to a minimum. Certain works have been cited, however, which present more detailed or different treatments of important issues raised at various points in the book.

The volume is based on two beliefs of the authors, which have been reinforced with experience: (1) the primary reason for practicing social research is to construct, modify, and accumulate explanations of social phenomena, and (2) the best method of learning the practice of explaining social phenomena is through experience—through the practice of social research. The emphasis in this volume is therefore on the *practice* of social research. Each laboratory session can be approached as a simulation experience with an aspect of social research.

The volume is written to treat the mundane problems involved in the practice of social research and to relate these steps to the larger task of constructing and refining theoretical explanations. All the chapters describe laboratory sessions which allow the reader to actually "practice" a major aspect of social research.

Each laboratory session is a controlled simulation. It has been our experience that learning is not maximized when individuals are grouped together in order to produce a questionnaire that is the product of group consensus, or are given a pad of paper and told to go out and observe. We believe that it is essential that individuals have a relatively clear understanding of the logical underpinnings of the method of research in which they are engaged.

There are four sections of discussion in each laboratory session:

1.   An *introduction* briefly defining the research emphasis and outlining its ties to previous research steps.

2.   The *objectives* of the laboratory session, intended to state concisely the kinds of learning the lab attempts to facilitate.

3.   An explanation of the *assignment*. The assignment is designed to provide experience and develop confidence in undertaking and successfully completing an important phase of the research process.

4.   *Instructions* for the completion of the lab session. This material includes background information, cookbook-type instructions, and sufficient supplementary detail so that learning and technical proficiency on the part of the student with little or no prior research experience are maximized.

The laboratory sessions are intended to be conducted with data gathered during the first session. For those individuals in small classes, data on respondents are provided in the Appendixes at the end of the manual.

While all three authors collaborated throughout the volume, Vaughn concentrated on Chapters 1, 2, 3, 4, 5, 8, 9, and 10, and Burt devoted his efforts to Chapters 6, 7, 10, 11, 12, 13, and 14. We are grateful to many colleagues who read various versions and portions of the manuscript, and to our students who used and commented on these materials.

Nan Lin
Ronald S. Burt
John C. Vaughn

Chapter 1

Questionnaire Response

OBJECTIVES

This first lab session initiates the research process (as you, the student, experience it) with the collection of data—the individual items of information derived by means of a questionnaire. Technically, the collection of data is not the first stage of the research process. By initiating our research task with the collection of data, however, concrete examples will be made available with which other phases of the research process can be illustrated.

The first objective of this lab session is to generate data for use in the course as an example analysis.

It is hoped that, since the data will in part reflect your own views, the analysis of the data collected in this first lab session will be of greater interest to you than if an external set of data were provided.

Before you become too enmeshed in the research process in the role of a social researcher, it is desirable for both humanitarian and professional reasons to ensure the researcher's empathy with the respondents' feelings. The humanitarian reason is obvious. It is undesirable to produce social scientists who have no respect for respondents as human beings. The professional reasons revolve around the interpretation of the data and the formulation of the questionnaire. A social scientist who has empathy for the group of people being studied—in contrast to the researcher who views respondents only as units in a random sample—will not only be better able to ask appropriate questions, but will also be in a better position to explain the relationships found to exist.

Our reasons for asking each question may not be apparent to you. You may feel that the questionnaire is an invasion of privacy which cannot be easily avoided. Or you may feel that the questionnaire as presented is inadequate to express your true situation or full feelings. In short, you may find yourself placed in the traditional "lack of control" situation of a respondent who is faced with a specific number of questions arranged in a preset order, phrased in a particular manner, and often allowing a particular range of responses.

A second general objective of this session, therefore, is to sensitize you to the role of the respondent.

Your role is that of an increasingly common kind—respondent to the self-administered questionnaire. As such, the research instrument (the questionnaire) will present you with both ease and frustration as you attempt to answer the questions. Some questions are factual, straightforward items you can quickly answer. Other questions may present you with an issue or a set of alternatives you may wish to reword, rephrase, or even totally reconstruct—although there are no provisions allowing this. For example, none of the available categories for describing your grade point average may precisely express your assessment. You may then find yourself taking the following questions much less seriously. Some questions, such as that referring to the number of persons in your family of origin, may be ambiguous or confusing. You may not, for example, be certain whether to include yourself or not. This uncertainty may lead you to answer hastily, carelessly, or seek further advice.

As a third objective, filling out the questionnaire—acting in the role of respondent—will expose you to the necessity for developing a research instrument that provides the information you need.

The questionnaire should provide a means for you to assess your own feelings about being placed in the role of the respondent under a certain set of conditions. This experience will hopefully increase your desire and stimulate your thinking about how to construct a viable instrument that accurately, reliably, and precisely taps the events, feelings, and attitudes of people that are of theoretical interest to you.

ASSIGNMENT

Fill in the questionnaire during the lab session.

THE LAB SESSION

Please do not mark the questionnaire until your lab instructor tells you to do so. Carefully follow the instruction sheet below with your lab instructor. After the instructor has gone through the instruction sheet with you and answered all questions that have arisen, you may begin to fill in your responses.

Instruction Sheet

You are being asked to respond to a series of questions designed to generate data on various aspects of your general experiences as a family member and as a university student. All answers will be confidential. Your identity will not be known to anyone. The completed questionnaires will be analyzed collectively, so that only group answers will be discussed in class.

Please give accurate answers to the best of your ability and knowledge. The data gathered from these questionnaires will be used as a source of examples for the problems and ideas discussed throughout this course.

Circle only *one* appropriate number for each question.

Please write only on the left-hand side of the questionnaire sheet.

When you have completed your questionnaire, turn it in to your instructor, so that it may be combined with the other questionnaires.

Let me emphasize again: This questionnaire is intended to be an anonymous product when it is completed. Do *not* write your name on the questionnaire. Answer questions by circling the appropriate number or by filling in the blank lines provided following the question. Do not use the right-hand column which is headed, "CODE," for writing down responses. This column will be used for other purposes in another session. Do you have any questions? Begin filling in the questionnaire.

DENTIFICATION NUMBER_____

LABORATORY SESSION _____

Conducting Social Research Questionnaire

Please respond to the following items to the best of your ability and knowledge. Your identity will not be known to anyone. Circle only *one* appropriate response number for each item.

	COLUMN	CODE
1 Sex		
1 Female		
2 Male	6	_____
2 In what year and month were you born?		
Year_____	7–8	_____
Month_____	9–10	_____
3 What is your current registered student status?	11	_____
1 Freshman		
2 Sophomore		
3 Junior		
4 Senior		
5 Graduate student		
6 Nondegree student		
7 Other (please specify)_____		

_____

COLUMN   CODE

4 What academic program are you currently enrolled in?   12   _____
   1   General program
   2   Teacher education program
   3   Other (please specify)_____

   _____

5 Are you registered as studying toward a degree?   13   _____
   1   No
   2   Yes, bachelor of arts
   3   Yes, bachelor of science
   4   Yes, advanced degree (please specify)_____

   _____

6 What is your major or intended major?   14–15   _____

   _____

7 What is your minor (or second major)?   16–17   _____

   _____

8 What do you consider your predominant ethnic origin
   (ancestors) to be?   18–19   _____
   1   American Indian   20–21   _____
   2   Black   22–23   _____
   3   Latin American
   4   Oriental
   5   White, northern or western Europe
   6   White, southern or eastern Europe
   7   Other (please specify)_____

   _____

   A   If you circled two or more above, which *one* of these do you
       feel closer to?   24–25   _____
       1   American Indian
       2   Black
       3   Latin American
       4   Oriental
       5   White, northern or western Europe
       6   White, southern or eastern Europe
       7   Other (pleast specify)_____

       _____

9 What is your religious preference at the present time? Is it
   Protestant, Catholic, Jewish, some other religion, or no religion?   26–27   _____
   1   Protestant
   2   Catholic
   3   Jewish
   4   None
   5   Other (please specify)_____

   _____

   A   If *Protestant*, what specific denomination is that, if any?   28–29   _____
       1   Baptist
       2   Methodist
       3   Lutheran
       4   Presbyterian

    5 Episcopalian
    6 Other (please specify)_____

_____

10 How often do you attend religious services during the school
    year?   30   _____
    1 Never
    2 Less than once a year
    3 About once a year
    4 Several times a year
    5 About once a month
    6 Two or three times a month
    7 Nearly every week
    8 Every week
    9 Several times a week

11 Are your parents currently—married, widowed, divorced, or
    separated?   31   _____
    1 Married
    2 Widowed
    3 Divorced
    4 Separated
    5 Never married

12 What is the highest grade in elementary school, high school, or
    college that your father finished and received credit for?   32–33   _____
     0 No formal schooling
     1 1st grade
     2 2nd grade
     3 3rd grade
     4 4th grade
     5 5th grade
     6 6th grade
     7 7th grade
     8 8th grade
     9 9th grade
    10 10th grade
    11 11th grade
    12 12th grade
    13 1 year of college
    14 2 years of college
    15 3 years of college
    16 4 years of college
    17 5 years of college
    18 6 years of college
    19 7 years of college
    20 8 years of college

13 Generally speaking, does your father think of himself as a
    Republican, Democrat, Independent, or what?   34   _____
    1 Republican
    2 Democrat
    3 Independent
    4 Other (please specify)_____

_____

COLUMN   CODE

14   Is your father presently employed?   35   _____
    1   Full time
    2   Part time
    3   Unemployed
    4   Disabled
    5   Retired
    6   Deceased

15   What kind of work does (did) your father normally do? That is,
    what is (was) his job called?   36–40   _____
    Occupation_____

    _____

16   In which of these groups does (did) your father's total income,
    from all sources, fall last year (or the last year he worked full
    time)—before taxes?   41–42   _____
    1   Under $1,000
    2   $1,000 to $2,999
    3   $3,000 to $3,999
    4   $4,000 to $4,999
    5   $5,000 to $5,999
    6   $6,000 to $6,999
    7   $7,000 to $7,999
    8   $8,000 to $9,999
    9   $10,000 to $14,999
    10 $15,000 to $19,999
    11 $20,000 to $29,999
    12 $30,000 or over
    98 Don't know

17   What is the highest grade in elementary school, high school, or
    college that your mother finished and received credit for? 43–44   _____
    0   No formal schooling
    1   1st grade
    2   2nd grade
    3   3rd grade
    4   4th grade
    5   5th grade
    6   6th grade
    7   7th grade
    8   8th grade
    9   9th grade
    10 10th grade
    11 11th grade
    12 12th grade
    13 1 year of college
    14 2 years of college
    15 3 years of college
    16 4 years of college
    17 5 years of college
    18 6 years of college
    19 7 years of college
    20 8 years of college

COLUMN   CODE

18 Generally speaking, does your mother think of herself as a
Republican, Democrat, Independent, or what?   45   _____
    1 Republican
    2 Democrat
    3 Independent
    4 Other (please specify)_____

_____

19 Is your mother presently employed?   46   _____
    1 Full time
    2 Part time
    3 Unemployed
    4 Disabled
    5 Retired
    6 Deceased

20 What kind of work does (did) your mother normally do? That
is, what is (was) her job called?   47–51   _____
Occupation_____

_____

21 In which of these groups does (did) your mother's total income,
from all sources, fall last year (or the last year she worked)—
before taxes?   52–52   _____
    1   Under $1,000
    2   $1,000 to $2,999
    3   $3,000 to $3,999
    4   $4,000 to $4,999
    5   $5,000 to $5,999
    6   $6,000 to $6,999
    7   $7,000 to $7,999
    8   $8,000 to $9,999
    9   $10,000 to $14,999
   10 $15,000 to $19,999
   11 $20,000 to $29,999
   12 $30,000 or over
   98 Don't know

22 How many brothers and sisters did you have? (Count those
born alive, but no longer living, as well as those alive now. Also
include stepbrothers, stepsisters, and children adopted by your
parents.)   54–55   _____

_____

23 How many brothers and sisters are still alive?   56–57   _____

24 During the last semester or quarter, how much time did you
spend watching television during an average day?   58–59   _____
_____hours

25 How many credit hours of course work did you complete during
the last semester or quarter?   60–61   _____
    1 None
    2 1–3
    3 4–6
    4 7–9

5   10–12
6   13–15
7   16–18
8   19–21
9   22 or more

26   How would you describe your academic performance last
semester or quarter, as compared to that of your fellow
students?   62   _____
1   Outstanding
2   Above average
3   About average
4   Below average
5   Poor
6   Not applicable

27   At the present time, what is your educational goal?   63   _____
1   Undecided
2   Bachelor's degree
3   Master's degree
4   Doctoral degree
5   Other (please specify)_____
_____

28   At the present time, what is your occupational goal?   64–68   _____
1   Undecided
2   To become a_____
_____

29   Generally speaking, do you think of yourself as a Republican,
Democrat, Independent, or what?   69   _____
1   Republican
2   Democrat
3   Independent
4   Other (please specify)_____
_____

30   How many children do you want to have altogether, counting
those you may have now?   70–71   _____
_____

31   How would you rate the food service here on campus? (circle one)   72   _____
Good   Bad
1----2----3----4----5----6----7
9   Does not apply

32   How would you rate the bookstore here on campus? (circle one)   73   _____
Good   Bad
1----2----3----4----5----6----7
9   Does not apply

33   How would you rate the library service here on campus?
(circle one)   74   _____
Good   Bad
1----2----3----4----5----6----7
9   Does not apply

COLUMN   CODE

34 What is your attitude toward the community where this
    campus is located? (circle one)   75   _____
    Good   Bad
    1----2----3----4----5----6----7

35 What is your attitude toward this school? (circle one)   76   _____
    Good   Bad
    1----2----3----4----5----6----7

Chapter 2

Coding Observations

INTRODUCTION

After data have been collected, it is necessary to arrange them in a form that reflects the situation and meanings of the respondent, and provides answers to our prior research questions. These objectives emphasize the importance of the data-collection process we ourselves experienced when we responded to the questionnaire items. The objective and subjective factors of the respondent that are pertinent to the research purpose need to be described by the data we have gathered as accurately and unambiguously as possible. These factors should be recorded in such a fashion during the data-collection process, so that their commonalities and uniquenesses can be discerned during the coding process.

Broadly speaking, coding is the construction, according to some criteria, of a set of symbols (often a series of numbers) which indicates or stands for a particular item or class of information, and the assignment of the constructed symbols to a set of data. The coding process thus involves symbol construction and the assignment of symbols to data.

We may sometimes find ourselves in a research situation in which most of the symbols have been established prior to data collection. That is, the data-collection instrument (e.g., the questionnaire) has been precoded. In such a case, the coding process is reduced to assigning each particular response to one of the preestablished codes. This is the case with the data we are using in our lab sessions.

OBJECTIVES

The general objectives of this lab session are to acquaint you with some of the coding requirements, techniques, and problems associated with this phase of the research process. The major emphasis will be on developing the skill of accurately designating a code symbol to represent a particular activity or meaning as reported by the respondent.

This will involve the transformation of responses given to questionnaire items into a set of numbers specified by the Master Code Book. An important part of this experience will be making coding decisions that are accurate, and producing a coded product that is complete. This will require careful and sometimes tedious effort. It will also require scrupulous fulfillment of coding instructions as specified in the Master Code Book, as well as logical analysis in order to ascertain the meaning of the respondent's answer to each questionnaire item. It is essential that you learn to do this work so that coding error can be reduced to an absolute minimum.

ASSIGNMENT

Code questionnaire.

Transfer codes to code sheets (Supplement 2, pp. 35 and 36).

THE LAB SESSION

During the last session, we filled in a questionnaire. In doing this, we took an important step in the research process: We secured data. In this case, our medium for data collection was the questionnaire. After securing data, the next step is the processing of data.

In many cases of doing research, the sample of the population from which data are obtained is very large, numbering hundreds and even thousands of cases. In such instances it is common practice to precode a large proportion of the questionnaire. Precoding is done for those items of information for which the range of response is known, and for which the set of codes is not so complicated or cumbersome as to impede data collection.

A simple example of precoding is the specification of the numeral "1" to signify a person of the female sex, and the numeral "2" to indicate a person of the male sex. Certain objective or factual items such as income are particularly amenable to the precoding procedure. Some attitude, belief, or opinion statements or questions lend themselves to precoding operations when the range of the parameters is known and can be specified. Thus a good deal of behavior that is of sociological interest and can be observed or elicited may be preclassified in mutually exclusive and exhaustive categories. These data are generally known as *quantitative* data.

There is another group of behaviors that do not readily disclose their entire range of values within a population. Such behaviors are often linked to the internal perceptual and cognitive structures of persons who may not be able or willing to articulate them readily, or the behaviors may shift under varying conditions. Some examples are motivations, opinions, plans of action, and the nature of worry or concern. These phenomena are sometimes referred to as *qualitative* data. The boundaries of these data are frequently difficult to identify. The characteristics exhibiting the presence of these data are not generally agreed on. It is therefore difficult to assign an unambiguous definition to them. It is also a problem to differentiate them from other similar or overlapping phenomena. Such material can often be coded only after all the data have been collected. Such codes sometimes result in general and broad categories that are relatively easy to code, but are of limited usefulness for detailed analysis.

In sum, coding is the transformation of a group of behaviors or answers into symbols that can be more readily manipulated for purposes of data analysis. A code set can be constructed before and/or following data collection. The broad criteria informing the development of a code is the known range of response and the stated purpose of the research.

Concepts and Terms

One of the criteria which will govern our coding procedures is the preparation of data so that they may be analyzed by an electromechanical device such as a sorter and/or an electronic-magnetic device such as a computer.

There are a number of terms commonly used in the practical activity of coding data for machine use. These terms are part of the language of the coding process and should be part of the social researcher's vocabulary. They are:

1 *Character:* Any letter, number, or other symbol such as a period, comma, or plus sign

2 *Field:* One or more letters, numbers, or other characters comprising a discrete or unique unit; a variable such as "student status," "years of schooling," or "month of birth"

3 *Data record:* All the pertinent fields containing data information on a single respondent; respondent information from the point of view of a machine

4 *Observation:* All the data information regarding a single respondent; respondent information from the point of view of the social researcher

There are five terms which are commonly used in the actual coding procedure. They are:

1 *High-order position:* The left side of a field. For example, in the three-column field containing the student identification number 123, the 1 is in the high-order position.

    2 *Low-order position:* The right side of a field. For example, in the eleven-column field containing the code MONTH/BIRTH, the H in BIRTH is in the low-order position.

    3 *Right justified:* When two or more columns are allocated to an item, then all codes should be placed as far to the right as possible, and the remaining columns (to the left) filled in with zeroes or left blank. This frequently occurring instruction is generally used when a field is coded in numbers. For example, the informational item, "March," in the two-column field denoting Month of Birth is coded as "03."

    4 *Left justified:* A name field is to be written in a designated number of columns, beginning with the left-most column allocated to the field. The unused columns to the right are usually left blank. This instruction is generally used when a field is coded in letters. For example, in a thirteen-column field denoting a student's last name, the name "SMITH" would appear in the first five columns of the field, and the succeeding eight columns would remain empty.

    5 *Illegal code:* When a code does not exist for a particular item of information, and the researcher sees no reason for creating an additional category to include it, an illegal code is generally expressed by using the highest possible digit in the pertinent column or columns. If all the numbers of a field have been exhausted in creating a classification for coding, it is an efficient practice to expand the field by one column in order to express the code in numbers consistently, rather than in letters or other symbols. The reason for using high numbers is that, in the eventual analysis, they can easily be eliminated. For example, in a two-column field, three symbols frequently used to express an illegal code are:

    97 No answer (blank)
    98 Does not know
    99 Does not apply

For example, on the first page of the Master Code Book (p. 16), it can be noted in column 11 denoting Student Status that codes 8 and 9 are available for utilization as illegal codes.

Kinds of Information

Two kinds of information are recorded on the questionnaire. They are:

    1 Identification of the observation. Minimally, this will identify a particular respondent by a number, usually from "1" to the total number in the sample. The identification of the observation is a useful informational item because, if something is wrong with some field of information, in future analysis the researcher can trace it back to the raw data (e.g., the original questionnaire), identify the source of error, and make the correction.

The identification may also include a research study number, a card and/or deck number, and other information which identifies the respondent such as name and residence or lab session number.

2   The main body of the data. In our case, the data comprise questions 1 through 35.

Coding Instruments

Besides the questionnaire, there are two other media which the coder frequently uses in the coding process. They are:

1   The Master Code Book which is the product of the researcher's decisions resulting in a set of codes that are either preliminary or complete. A complete Master Code Book is one in which all categories are in a form directly usable for data analysis. A preliminary Master Code Book is one in which some or (less likely) all categories provide a separate code for a larger number of diverse statements or behaviors than is feasible in fulfilling the stated purposes of the research. A preliminary Master Code Book may be further reduced in number of categories by revising it at a second stage of data coding or, as is often done, by collapsing items into fewer categories during the data analysis phase.

The Master Code Book with which you will be working may be primarily regarded as a complete Master Code Book in that most items may be collapsed under preexisting general categories suitable for data analysis. An outstanding exception are major and minor fields of study. You, as researcher, may wish to develop a secondary set of codes more appropriate to your acquired data, your own theoretical interests, or both.

The Master Code Book contains the codes representative of each informational item a respondent may give. The main task of the coder under these circumstances is to decide under which coded category a particular item of information may be subsumed. Most of the time this decision-making process is routine. There are occasions, however, when this decision is not so clear-cut. The problem may be resolved by the team of coders consulting with each other, with the social researchers, or both.

2   The code sheet is a summary sheet on which are entered all valid and reliable codes from the original questionnaires. The codes are listed in a sequential order on the code sheets. This order is easy to follow when transferring code symbols to punched cards. The code sheet, therefore, expedites key punching and increases the speed and accuracy of data preparation for purposes of data analysis.

Coding Operations

When symbols have been preestablished, as is the case for our data, the coding operations may be described as physically consisting of three fundamental steps. These are:

1 Editing the data. This consists of scanning the responses recorded in a set of questionnaires to assess whether data are missing and ambiguous. Editing will increase the likelihood of accurate and complete coding procedures. It is sometimes necessary at this step to recontact a respondent in order to improve data quality.

2 Coding directly on the questionnaire itself. The information provided by the respondent in the body of the questionnaire is transformed by the coder into symbols which are transferred to the right-hand column headed CODE. These codes may then be checked and verified for accuracy by a research supervisor or by other coders in order to achieve a high degree of reliability. We are more confident that the codes reflect the intended answer of the respondent when two or more researchers concur in the assignment of a code to a response.

3 Transferring codes to the code sheet. After maximum reliability and accuracy have been achieved, the symbols are transferred from the CODE column of the questionnaire to the code sheet.

It should be kept in mind that each handling of the data increases the likelihood of coding errors. This may be offset and minimized by continual checking for accuracy by coding supervisors.

The Laboratory Task: Questionnaire Coding

Two things are needed to code the questionnaire. These are:

1 The completed questionnaire. Some of the codes to be used in data analysis are written directly on the questionnaire.

2 The Master Code Book. This instrument provides instructions and symbols for the coding of each field or piece of information.

For questionnaire coding, use a pencil. This will allow corrections to be made more easily. Begin coding procedures. All codes are written on the right-hand column headed CODE on the questionnaire.

Next Assignment

The assignment for the next lab session is to transfer the coded information on the questionnaire to the code sheet.

Look at your code sheet. Put your name on the line headed, Programmer. You will use only the first row of the code sheet, since all the coded data can be reduced to a single row of symbols. The symbols you have listed in the column of the questionnaire headed CODE will be transferred to the first row of the code sheet and entered sequentially across the first row in each column of the code sheet, beginning with column 1 and ending with column 76. The assignment is due at the next lab session.

MASTER CODES

Study:

Date:

Card	Column	Code	Description
1	01–03		Student Identification Number
	04		Laboratory Session (day and time)
			Examples:
		1	Monday, 11:10
		2	Tuesday, 1:00
		3	Wednesday, 9:15
	05	1	Deck Identification Number
	06		Sex
		1	Female
		2	Male
	07–08		Month of Birth
	09–10		Year of Birth
	11		Student Status
		1	Freshman
		2	Sophomore
		3	Junior
		4	Senior
		5	Graduate Student
		6	Nondegree Student
		7	Other
	12		Academic Program Enrolled in
		1	General Program
		2	Teacher Education Program
		3	Other
		4	
		5	
		6	
	13		Degree Sought
		1	None
		2	Bachelor of Arts
		3	Bachelor of Science
		4	Master's Degree
		5	Ph.D.
		6	Other Advanced Degree
		7	
	14–15		Study Major
			Bachelor of Arts—General Program
		01	Afro-American Studies
		02	American Studies
		03	Anthropology
		04	Art
		05	Biology
		06	Comparative Literature
		07	Economics

MASTER CODES

Study:

Date:

Card	Column	Code	Description
		08	English
		09	French
		10	Geography
		11	German
		12	Greek
		13	History
		14	Inter-American Language and Area Studies
		15	Italian
		16	Latin
		17	Mathematics
		18	Music
		19	Philosophy
		20	Political Science
		21	Psychology
		22	Rhetoric and Public Address
		23	Russian
		24	Sociology
		25	Spanish
		26	Speech
		27	Theatre
		28	Other
		29	Undecided
		30	
		31	
			Teacher Education
		40	English
		41	French
		42	German
		43	History
		44	Italian
		45	Latin
		46	Mathematics
		47	Russian
		48	Social Studies
		49	Spanish
		50	Other
		51	
		52	
		59	Undecided
			Bachelor of Science—General Program
		60	Astronomy and Space Science
		61	Atmospheric Science
		62	Biology
		63	Chemistry

MASTER CODES

Study:

Date:

Card	Column	Code	Description
		64	Economics
		65	Geology
		66	Mathematics
		67	Physics
		68	Science
		69	Science—Medical Technology
		70	Speech Pathology and Audiology
		71	Public Accounting
		72	Business Administration
		73	Nursing
		74	Other
		75	
		76	
		79	Undecided
			Teacher Education
		80	Biology
		81	Chemistry
		82	Mathematics
		83	Physics
		84	Science
		85	Speech Pathology and Audiology
		86	Business Education
		87	Other
		88	
		89	Undecided
	16–17		Study Minor (see codes for columns 14–15)
	18–19		Ethnic Origin
		01	American Indian
		02	Black
		03	Latin American
		04	Oriental
		05	White, Northern or Western Europe
		06	White, Southern or Eastern Europe
		07	Other
		08	
	20–21		Ethnic Origin (if a second entry is recorded, use codes for columns 18–19)
	22–23		Ethnic Origin (if a third entry is recorded, use codes for columns 18–19)
	24–25		Ethnic Origin—Subjective Identification (use codes for columns 18–19)
	26–27		Religious Preference
		00	None
		01	Protestant

MASTER CODES

Study:

Date:

Card	Column	Code	Description
		02	Catholic
		03	Jewish
		04	Other
		05	
		06	
	28–29		Specific Protestant Denomination
		01	Baptist
		02	Methodist
		03	Lutheran
		04	Presbyterian
		05	Episcopalian
		06	Other
		07	
		08	
		09	
		10	
	30		Religious Service Attendance
		01	Never
		02	Less than once a year
		03	About once a year
		04	Several times a year
		05	About once a month
		06	Two or three times a month
		07	Nearly every week
		08	Every week
		09	Several times a week
	31		Parent's Marital Status
		01	Married
		02	Widowed
		03	Divorced
		04	Separated
		05	Never Married
	32–33		Father's Education
		00	No formal schooling
		01	1st grade
		02	2nd grade
		03	3rd grade
		04	4th grade
		05	5th grade
		06	6th grade
		07	7th grade
		08	8th grade
		09	9th grade
		10	10th grade

MASTER CODES

Study:

Date:

Card	Column	Code	Description
		11	11th grade
		12	12th grade
		13	1 year of college
		14	2 years of college
		15	3 years of college
		16	4 years of college
		17	5 years of college
		18	6 years of college
		19	7 years of college
		20	8 years of college
	34		Father's Political Party Preference
		1	Republican
		2	Democratic
		3	Independent
		4	Other
		7	No answer (blank)
		8	Don't know
		9	Does not apply
	35		Father's Employment
		1	Full time
		2	Part time
		3	Unemployed
		4	Disabled
		5	Retired
		6	Deceased
		7	No answer (blank)
		8	Don't know
		9	Does not apply
	36–40		Father's Occupation (use codes listed in Supplement 1, pages 23–34)
	41–42		Father's Income
		01	Under $1,000
		02	$1,000 to $2,999
		03	$3,000 to $3,999
		04	$4,000 to $4,999
		05	$5,000 to $5,999
		06	$6,000 to $6,999
		07	$7,000 to $7,999
		08	$8,000 to $9,999
		09	$10,000 to $14,999
		10	$15,000 to $19,999
		11	$20,000 to $24,999
		12	$25,000 or over
		97	No answer (blank)
		98	Don't know

MASTER CODES

Study:

Date:

Card	Column	Code	Description
		99	Does not apply
	43–44		Mother's Education (see codes for columns 32–33)
	45		Mother's Political Party Preference (see codes for column 34)
	46		Mother's Employment (see codes for column 35)
	47–51		Mother's Occupation (use codes listed in Supplement 1, pages 23–34)
	52–53		Mother's Income (see codes for columns 41–42)
	54–55		Number of Siblings
		00	No siblings
		01	One sibling
		02	Two siblings
	56–57		Number of Siblings Still Alive
		00	No siblings
		01	One sibling
		02	Two siblings
		97	No answer (blank)
		98	Don't know
		99	Does not apply
	58–59		Television Watching
		00	No time
		01	Less than 1 hour
		02	1 hour to 2 hours
		03	2 hours to 3 hours
		04	3 hours to 4 hours
		05	4–5 hours
		06	5–6 hours
		07	6–7 hours
		08	7–8 hours
		09	8 hours or more
		97	No answer (blank)
		98	Don't know
		99	Does not apply
	60–61		Credit Hours
		00	None
		01	1–3 hours
		02	4–6 hours
		03	7–9 hours
		04	10–12 hours
		05	13–15 hours
		06	16–18 hours
		07	19–21 hours
		08	22 or more
		97	No answer (blank)
		98	Don't know

MASTER CODES

Study.

Date:

Card	Column	Code	Description
		99	Does not apply
	62		Comparative Academic Performance
		1	Outstanding
		2	Above average
		3	About average
		4	Below average
		5	Poor
		7	No response (blank)
		9	Does not apply
	63		Educational Goal
		1	Undecided
		2	Bachelor's degree
		3	Master's degree
		4	Doctoral degree
		5	Other
		6	
		7	No response (blank)
		9	Does not apply
	64–68		Occupational Goal (use codes listed in Supplement 1, pages 23–34)
		997	No answer (blank)
		998	Does not know
		999	Does not apply
	69		Political Party Preference (use codes for column 34)
	70–71		Number of Children Desired (use codes for columns 50–51)
	72		Campus Food Service
		1	Good
		2	
		3	
		4	Average
		5	
		6	
		7	Bad
		9	Does not apply
	73		Campus Bookstore
		1	Good
		2	
		3	
		4	Average
		5	
		6	
		7	Bad
		9	Does not apply
	74		Campus Library
		1	Good

MASTER CODES

Study:

Date:

Card	Column	Code	Description
		2	
		3	
		4	Average
		5	
		6	
		7	Bad
	75		Attitude toward Community
		1	Good
		2	
		3	
		4	Average
		5	
		6	
		7	Bad
		9	Does not apply
	76		Attitude toward School
		1	Good
		2	
		3	
		4	Average
		5	
		6	
		7	Bad

SUPPLEMENT 1

OCCUPATIONAL CLASSIFICATION*	1970 Census Code†	United States Prestige Score‡	International Score§
PROFESSIONAL AND TECHNICAL WORKERS			
Accountants	001	57	55
Architects	002	71	72
Computer Specialists			
Computer programmers	003	51	51
Computer systems analysts	004	51	51
Computer specialists, n.e.c.	005	51	51
Engineers			
Aeronautical and astronautical engineers	006	71	67
Chemical engineers	010	67	66
Civil engineers	011	68	70
Electrical and electronic engineers	012	69	65

OCCUPATIONAL CLASSIFICATION*	1970 Census Code†	United States Prestige Score‡	International Score§
Industrial engineers	013	54	54
Mechanical engineers	014	62	66
Metallurgical and materials engineers	015	56	60
Mining engineers	020	62	63
Petroleum engineers	021	67	
Sales engineers	022	51	51
Engineers, n.e.c.	023	67	55
Farm management advisors	024	54	54
Foresters and conservationists	025	54	48
Home management advisors	026	54	
Lawyers and Judges			
Judges	030	76	76
Lawyers	031	76	73
Librarians, Archivists, and Curators			
Librarians	032	55	55
Archivists and curators	033	66	55
Mathematical Specialists			
Actuaries	034	55	
Mathematicians	035	65	67
Statisticians	036	55	55
Life and Physical Scientists			
Agricultural scientists	042	56	58
Atmospheric and space scientists	043	68	71
Biological scientists	044	68	69
Chemists	045	69	67
Geologists	051	67	67
Marine scientists	052	68	69
Physicists and astronomers	053	74	77
Life and physical scientists, n.e.c.	054	68	72
Operations and systems researchers and analysts	055	51	51
Personnel and labor relations workers	056	56	57
Physicians, Dentists, and Related Practioners			
Chiropractors	061	60	63
Dentists	062	74	71
Optometrists	063	62	62
Pharmacists	064	61	64
Physicians, including osteopaths	065	82	78
Podiatrists	071	37	
Veterinarians	072	60	61
Health practitioners, n.e.c.	073	51	50
Nurses, Dieticians, and Therapists			
Dieticians	074	52	52
Registered nurses	075	62	54
Therapists	076	37	52
Health Technologists and Technicians			
Clinical laboratory technologists and technicians	080	61	58
Dental hygienists	081	61	44

SUPPLEMENT 1

OCCUPATIONAL CLASSIFICATION*	1970 Census Code†	United States Prestige Score‡	International Score§
Health record technologists and technicians	082	61	
Radiologic technologists and technicians	083	61	58
Therapy assistants	084	37	
Health technologists and technicians, n.e.c.	085	47	
Religious Workers			
Clergymen	086	69	60
Religious workers, n.e.c.	090	56	39
Social Scientists			
Economists	091	57	61
Political scientists	092	66	
Psychologists	093	71	66
Sociologists	094	66	67
Urban and regional planners	095	66	
Social scientists, n.e.c.	096	66	69
Social and Recreation Workers			
Social workers	100	52	56
Recreation workers	101	49	
Teachers, College and University			
Agriculture	102	78	78
Atmospheric, earth, marine, and space	103	78	78
Biology	104	78	78
Chemistry	105	78	78
Physics	110	78	78
Engineering	111	78	78
Mathematics	112	78	78
Health specialists	113	78	78
Psychology	114	78	78
Business and commerce	115	78	78
Economics	116	78	78
History	120	78	78
Sociology	121	78	78
Social science, n.e.c.	122	78	78
Art, drama, and music	123	78	78
Coaches and physical education	124	78	78
Education	125	78	78
English	126	78	78
Foreign language	130	78	78
Home economics	131	78	78
Law	132	78	78
Theology	133	78	78
Trade, industrial, and technical	134	78	78
Miscellaneous, college and university	135	78	78
Teachers, college and university, subject not specified	140	78	78
Teachers, Except College and University			
Adult education	141	43	
Elementary school	142	60	57

SUPPLEMENT 1

OCCUPATIONAL CLASSIFICATION*	1970 Census Code†	United States Prestige Score‡	International Score§
Prekindergarten and kindergarten	143	60	49
Secondary school	144	63	61
Teachers, except college and university, n.e.c.	145	43	62
Engineering and Science Technicians			
Agriculture and biological, except health	150	47	47
Chemical	151	47	46
Draftsmen	152	56	55
Electrical and electronic engineering	153	47	46
Industrial engineering	154	47	
Mechanical engineering	155	47	46
Mathematical	156	47	
Surveyors	161	53	58
Engineering and science, n.e.c.	162	47	46
Technicians, except Health, Engineering, and Science			
Airplane pilots	163	70	67
Air traffic controllers	164	43	
Embalmers	165	52	34
Flight engineers	170	47	67
Radio operators	171	43	49
Tool programmers, numerical control	172	47	
Technicians, n.e.c.	173	47	
Vocational and educational counselors	174	51	55
Writers, Artists, and Entertainers			
Actors	175	55	52
Athletes and kindred workers	180	51	50
Authors	181	60	62
Dancers	182	38	45
Designers	183	58	56
Editors and reporters	184	51	56
Musicians and composers	185	46	45
Painters and sculptors	190	56	57
Photographers	191	41	45
Public relations men and publicity writers	192	57	57
Radio and television announcers	193	51	50
Writers, artists, and entertainers, n.e.c.	194	51	
Research workers, not specified	195	51	
Professional, technical, and kindred workers—allocated	196	51	51

MANAGERS AND ADMINISTRATORS, EXCEPT FARM

Assessors, controllers, and treasurers, local public administration	201	61	
Bank officers and financial managers	202	72	76
Buyers and shippers, farm products	203	41	39
Buyers, wholesale and retail trade	205	50	48
Credit men	210	49	49
Funeral directors	211	52	34
Health administrators	212	61	

SUPPLEMENT 1

OCCUPATIONAL CLASSIFICATION*	1970 Census Code†	United States Prestige Score‡	International Score§
Construction inspectors, public administration	213	41	
Inspectors, except construction, public administration	215	41	61
Managers and superintendents, building	216	38	47
Office managers, n.e.c.	220	50	59
Officers, pilots and pursers, ship	221	60	54
Officials and administrators, public administration, n.e.c.	222	61	65
Officials of lodges, societies, and unions	223	48	50
Postmasters and mail superintendents	224	58	58
Purchasing agents and buyers, n.e.c.	225	48	47
Railroad conductors	226	41	39
Restaurant, cafeteria, and bar managers	230	39	37
Sales managers and department heads, retail trade	231	50	47
Sales managers, except retail trade	233	50	
School administrators, college	235	61	86
School administrators, elementary and secondary	240	60	68
Managers and administrators, n.e.c.	245	50	59
Managers and administrators, except farm—allocated	246	50	63

SALES WORKERS

Advertising agents and salesmen	260	42	42
Auctioneers	261	32	39
Demonstrators	262	28	28
Hucksters and peddlers	264	18	22
Insurance agents, brokers, and underwriters	265	47	45
Newsboys	266	15	14
Real estate agents and brokers	270	44	49
Stock and bond salesmen	271	51	·56
Salesmen and sales clerks, n.e.c.	280	34	28
Sales representatives, manufacturing industries	281	49	46
Sales representatives, wholesale trade	282	40	
Sales clerk, retail trade	283	29	34
Salesmen, retail trade	284	29	32
Salesmen of services and construction	285	34	42
Sales workers—allocated	296	34	28

CLERICAL AND KINDRED WORKERS

Bank tellers	301	50	48
Billing clerks	303	45	42
Bookkeepers	305	48	49
Cashiers	310	31	31
Clerical assistants, social welfare	311	36	
Clerical supervisors, n.e.c.	312	36	55
Collectors, bill and account	313	26	27
Counter clerks, except food	314	36	
Dispatchers and starters, vehicle	315	34	37
Enumerators and interviewers	320	36	
Estimators and investigators, n.e.c.	321	36	

SUPPLEMENT 1

OCCUPATIONAL CLASSIFICATION*	1970 Census Code†	United States Prestige Score‡	International Score§
Expediters and production controllers	323	36	44
File clerks	325	30	31
Insurance adjusters, examiners, and investigators	326	48	49
Library attendants and assistants	330	41	41
Mail carriers, post office	331	42	33
Mailhandlers, except post office	332	36	29
Messengers and office boys	333	19	26
Meter readers, utilities	334	36	21
Office Machine Operators			
Bookkeeping and billing machine operators	341	45	45
Calculating machine operators	342	45	45
Computer and peripheral equipment operators	343	45	53
Duplicating machine operators	344	45	
Key punch operators	345	45	45
Tabulating machine operators	350	45	
Office machine operators, n.e.c.	355	45	
Payroll and time-keeping clerks	360	41	42
Postal clerks	361	43	39
Proofreaders	362	36	41
Real estate appraisers	363	43	48
Receptionists	364	39	38
Secretaries			
Secretaries, legal	370	46	59
Secretaries, medical	371	46	
Secretaries, n.e.c.	372	46	
Shipping and receiving clerks	374	29	29
Statistical clerks	375	36	
Stenographers	376	43	42
Stock clerks and storekeepers	381	23	31
Teacher aides, except school monitors	382	36	50
Telegraph messengers	383	30	26
Telegraph operators	384	44	45
Telephone operators	385	40	38
Ticket, station, and express agents	390	35	37
Typists	391	41	42
Weighers	392	36	
Miscellaneous clerical workers	394	36	38
Not specified clerical workers	395	36	37
Clerical and kindred workers—allocated	396	36	44
CRAFTSMEN AND KINDRED WORKERS			
Automobile accessories installers	401	47	
Bakers	402	34	33
Blacksmiths	403	36	35
Boilermakers	404	31	31
Bookbinders	405	31	33
Brickmasons and stonemasons	410	36	34

OCCUPATIONAL CLASSIFICATION*	1970 Census Code†	United States Prestige Score‡	International Score§
Brickmasons and stonemasons, apprentices	411	36	
Bulldozer operators	412	33	32
Cabinetmakers	413	39	40
Carpenters	415	40	37
Carpenter apprentices	416	40	
Carpet installers	420	47	
Cement and concrete finishers	421	32	34
Compositors and typesetters	422	38	47
Printing trades apprentices, except pressmen	423	40	
Cranemen, derrickmen, and hoistmen	424	39	34
Decorators and window dressers	425	37	
Dental laboratory technicians	426	47	
Electricians	430	49	45
Electrician apprentices	431	41	
Electric power linemen and cablemen	433	39	36
Electrotypers and stereotypers	434	38	42
Engravers, except photoengravers	435	41	41
Excavating, grading, and road machine operators, except bulldozer	436	33	32
Floor layers, except tile setters	440	40	
Foremen, n.e.c.	441	45	46
Forgemen and hammermen	442	36	35
Furniture and wood finishers	443	29	28
Furriers	444	35	35
Glaziers	445	26	26
Heat treaters, annealers, and temperers	446	36	38
Inspectors, scalers, and graders, log and lumber	450	31	31
Inspectors, n.e.c.	452	31	
Jewelers and watchmakers	453	37	40
Job and die setters, metal	454	48	
Locomotive engineers	455	51	43
Locomotive firemen	456	36	33
Machinists	461	48	43
Machinists apprentices	462	41	
Mechanics and Repairmen			
Air conditioning, heating, and refrigeration	470	37	43
Aircraft	471	48	50
Automobile body repairmen	472	37	
Automobile mechanics	473	37	43
Automobile mechanic apprentices	474	37	
Data processing machine repairmen	475	34	
Farm implements	480	33	
Heavy equipment mechanics, including diesel	481	33	
Household appliance and accessory installers and mechanics	482	33	
Loom fixers	483	30	30
Office machines	484	34	

SUPPLEMENT 1

OCCUPATIONAL CLASSIFICATION*	1970 Census Code†	United States Prestige Score‡	International Score§
Radio and television	485	35	42
Railroad and car shop	486	37	
Mechanic, except automobile, apprentices	491	41	
Miscellaneous mechanics and repairmen	492	35	
Not specified mechanics and repairmen	495	35	30
Millers, grain, flour, and feed	501	25	33
Millwrights	502	40	40
Molders, metal	503	39	38
Molders, apprentices	504	39	
Motion picture projectionists	505	34	34
Opticians, lens grinders, and polishers	506	51	57
Painters, construction and maintenance	510	30	34
Painter apprentices	511	30	
Paperhangers	512	24	24
Pattern and model makers, except paper	514	39	39
Photoengravers and lithographers	515	40	46
Piano and organ tuners and repairmen	516	32	33
Plasterers	520	33	31
Plasterer apprentices	521	33	
Plumber and pipe fitters	522	41	38
Plumber and pipe fitter apprentices	523	41	
Power station operators	525	39	43
Pressmen and plate printers, printing	530	40	41
Pressmen apprentices	531	40	
Rollers and finishers, metal	533	36	36
Roofers and slaters	534	31	31
Sheetmetal workers and tinsmiths	535	37	34
Sheetmetal apprentices	536	37	
Shipfitters	540	36	
Shoe repairman	542	33	28
Sign painters and letterers	543	30	29
Stationary engineers	545	35	34
Stone cutters and stone carvers	546	33	39
Structural metal craftsmen	550	36	44
Tailors	551	41	40
Telephone installers and repairmen	552	39	35
Telephone linemen and splicers	554	39	36
Tile setters	560	36	
Tool and die makers	561	42	40
Tool and die maker apprentices	562	41	
Upholsterers	563	30	31
Specified craft apprentices, n.e.c.	571	41	
Not specified apprentices	572	41	
Craftsmen and kindred workers, n.e.c.	575	47	
Former members of the armed forces	580	47	46
Craftsmen and kindred workers—allocated	586	47	
Current members of the armed forces	590	47	46

SUPPLEMENT 1

OCCUPATIONAL CLASSIFICATION*	1970 Census Code†	United States Prestige Score‡	International Score§
OPERATIVES, EXCEPT TRANSPORT			
Asbestos and insulation workers	601	28	28
Assemblers	602	27	30
Blasters and powdermen	603	32	
Bottling and canning operatives	604	23	35
Chainmen, rodmen, and axman, surveying	605	39	
Checkers, examiners, and inspectors, manufacturing	610	36	39
Clothing ironers and pressers	611	18	22
Cutting operatives, n.e.c.	612	26	34
Dressmakers and seamstresses, except factory	613	32	39
Drillers, earth	614	27	45
Dry wall installers and lathers	615	27	
Dyers	620	25	25
Filers, polishers, sanders, and buffers	621	19	27
Furnacemen, smeltermen, and pourers	622	33	45
Garage workers and gas station attendants	623	22	18
Graders and sorters, manufacturing	624	33	
Produce graders and packers, except factory and farm	625	19	22
Heaters, metal	626	33	38
Laundry and dry cleaning operatives, n.e.c.	630	18	22
Meat cutters and butchers, except manufacturing	631	32	32
Meat cutters and butchers, manufacturing	633	28	18
Meat wrappers, retail trade	634	19	
Metal platers	635	29	28
Milliners	636	33	32
Mine operatives, n.e.c.	640	26	34
Mixing operatives	641	29	
Oilers and greasers, except automobile	642	24	
Packers and wrappers, n.e.c.	643	19	
Painters, manufactured articles	644	29	29
Photographic process workers	645	36	36
Precision Machine Operatives			
Drill press operatives	650	29	
Grinding machine operatives	651	29	27
Lathe and milling machine operatives	652	29	36
Precision machine operatives, n.e.c.	653	29	40
Punch and stamping press operatives	656	29	
Riveters and fasteners	660	29	
Sailors and deckhands	661	34	35
Sawyers	662	28	31
Sewers and stitchers	663	25	26
Shoemaking machine operatives	664	32	28
Solderers	665	29	
Stationary firemen	666	33	33
Textile Operatives			
Carding, lapping, and combing operatives	670	29	29

SUPPLEMENT 1

OCCUPATIONAL CLASSIFICATION*	1970 Census Code†	United States Prestige Score‡	International Score§
Knitters, loopers, and toppers	671	29	29
Spinners, twisters, and winders	672	25	34
Weavers	673	25	30
Textile operatives, n.e.c.	674	29	26
Welders and flame cutters	680	40	39
Winding operatives, n.e.c.	681	29	
Machine operatives, miscellaneous specified	690	32	38
Machine operators, not specified	692	32	38
Miscellaneous operatives	694	32	35
Not specified operatives	695	32	35
Operatives, except transport—allocated	696	32	
TRANSPORT EQUIPMENT OPERATIVES			
Boatmen and canalmen	701	37	23
Bus drivers	703	32	32
Conductors and motormen, urban rail transit	704	28	28
Deliverymen and routemen	705	28	28
Fork lift and tow motor operatives	706	29	29
Motormen, mine, factory, logging camp, etc.	710	27	27
Parking attendants	711	22	24
Railroad brakemen	712	35	29
Railroad switchmen	713	33	29
Taxicab drivers and chauffeurs	714	22	28
Truck drivers	715	32	33
Transport equipment operatives—allocated	726	29	28
LABORERS, EXCEPT FARM			
Animal caretakers, except farm	740	29	
Carpenters' helpers	750	23	23
Construction laborers, except carpenters' helpers	751	17	15
Fishermen and oystermen	752	30	28
Freight and material handlers	753	17	20
Garbage collectors	754	17	13
Gardeners and groundskeepers, except farm	755	23	21
Longshoremen and stevedores	760	24	21
Lumbermen, raftsmen, and woodchoppers	761	26	19
Stockhandlers	762	17	
Teamsters	763	12	18
Vehicle washers and equipment cleaners	754	17	
Warehousemen, n.e.c.	770	20	20
Miscellaneous laborers	780	17	19
Not specified laborers	785	17	18
Laborers, except farm—allocated	796	17	19
FARMERS AND FARM MANAGERS			
Farmers (owners and tenants)	801	41	40

OCCUPATIONAL CLASSIFICATION*	1970 Census Code†	United States Prestige Score‡	International Score§
Farm managers	802	44	54
Farmers and farm managers—allocated	806	41	40
FARM LABORERS AND FARM FOREMEN			
Farm foremen	821	35	41
Farm laborers, wage workers	822	18	21
Farm laborers, unpaid family workers	823	18	34
Farm service laborers, self-employed	824	27	30
Farm laborers, farm foremen, and kindred workers— allocated	846	19	22
SERVICE WORKERS, EXCEPT PRIVATE HOUSEHOLD			
Cleaning Service Workers			
Chambermaids and maid, except private household	901	14	14
Cleaners and charwomen	902	12	17
Janitors and sextons	903	16	21
Food Service Workers			
Bartenders	910	20	23
Busboys	911	22	
Cooks, except private household	912	26	31
Dishwashers	913	22	
Food counter and fountain workers	914	15	16
Waiters	915	20	23
Food service workers, n.e.c., except private household	916	22	25
Health Service Workers			
Dental assistants	921	48	44
Health aides, except nursing	922	48	
Health trainees	923	36	
Midwives	924	23	47
Nursing aides, orderlies, and attendants	925	36	42
Practical nurses	926	42	44
Personal Service Workers			
Airline stewardesses	931	36	50
Attendants, recreation and amusement	932	15	20
Attendants, personal service, n.e.c.	933	14	
Baggage porters and bellhops	934	14	17
Barbers	935	38	30
Boarding and lodging house keepers	940	22	22
Bootblacks	941	09	12
Child care workers, except private households	942	25	
Elevator operators	943	21	24
Hairdressers and cosmetologists	944	33	35
Personal service apprentices	945	14	
Housekeepers, except private households	950	36	33
School monitors	952	22	
Ushers, recreation and amusement	953	15	

SUPPLEMENT 1

OCCUPATIONAL CLASSIFICATION*	1970 Census Code†	United States Prestige Score‡	International Score§
Welfare service aides	954	14	
Protective Service Workers			
Crossing guards and bridge tenders	960	24	25
Firemen, fire protection	961	44	35
Guards and watchmen	962	22	22
Marshals and constables	963	46	60
Policemen and detectives	964	48	40
Sheriffs and bailiffs	965	55	47
Service workers, except private household—allocated	976	25	31
PRIVATE HOUSEHOLD WORKERS			
Child care workers, private household	980	23	23
Cooks, private household	981	18	
Housekeepers, private household	982	25	28
Laundresses, private household	983	18	
Maids and servants, private household	984	18	17
Private household workers—allocated	986	18	22

* n.e.c. = not elsewhere classified.

† U.S. Bureau of the Census, *1970 Census of Population: Alphabetical Index of Industries and Occupations*, U.S. Government Printing Office, Washington, D.C., 1971.

‡ Paul M. Siegel, "Prestige in the American Occupational Structure," unpublished Ph.D. dissertation, University of Chicago, 1971.

§ Donald J. Treiman, "A Standard International Occupational Prestige Scale," in *Occupational Prestige in Comparative Perspective*. Certain categories were not available.

Source: Occupational titles, census codes, and prestige scores are from *National Data Program for the Social Sciences*, Codebook for the Spring 1972 General Social Survey, National Opinion Research Center, University of Chicago, Chicago, appendix F, pp. 88–102.

SUPPLEMENT 2:   CODING SHEET

SUPPLEMENT 2:   CODING SHEET

41	50	60	70	80

Chapter 3

Keypunching and Duplicating Data Cards

INTRODUCTION

After data have been encoded on summary code sheets, they are ready to be transferred to a common-language medium that can be fed into various machines which allow rapid arithmetic and logical manipulations. One such vehicle permitting machine processing is the punched card. Once the encoded data are recorded on such cards, no additional referrals to the original questionnaires are generally required. By transferring the codes to a punched card, the codes are transformed into a language that is recognizable to a variety of machines. This transformation into machine-readable language can be accomplished by the key punch machine.

OBJECTIVES

This session will involve you in the research procedure of transferring coder's symbols to a machine-readable medium. In order to do this, you must become familiar with the key punch machine and generally adept at its operation.

ASSIGNMENT

Transfer coded data to a machine-readable medium: Keypunch a punched card. Using the data on your code sheet, transfer these codes to a punched card. Make three copies of these data.

THE LAB SESSION

The Punched Card

A commonly used medium for processing data is the punched card. Perhaps the most popular punched card is the *Hollerith card*. Let us introduce you to the Hollerith card. The face of the card is covered with a series of numbers. The card is numbered at the top and bottom across its face from left to right into eighty columns. The card is divided into twelve rows. There are ten numbered rows, from "0" through "9." There are two unnumbered rows above the "0," identified as the "11" row and the "12" row. So the "12-edge" of the card is the top edge, and the "9-edge" is the bottom edge of the card. There is a total of 960 locations on a single card (80 columns times 12 rows).

The punched card has been a popular medium for recording social research data. There are five major reasons for this. First, it reduces random error. Once an item of information is accurately recorded, subsequent reports will usually be correct. Second, it is a relatively permanent form of data storage. The cards do not deteriorate quickly, and can be used over and over with a very high probability of successful performance. Further, the cards can be used to transfer data to even more compact, portable, and durable media, such as magnetic tapes or disks. Third, it provides access to a computer system which can perform a wide variety of commonly used arithmetic and statistical operations at an exceedingly rapid rate. Fourth, it expedites the completion of a large-scale study involving hundreds and even thousands of persons. Fifth, large quantities of punched cards can be obtained at a nominal cost.

The Key Punch Machine

A major means of transforming coded symbols into a machine-readable language is the key punch machine. The key punch machine is like a typewriter with a keyboard plus some additional features. Most of these additional features relate to the punched card. All card machines have a place to insert cards for punching, and to stack cards after punching. These are called the *hopper* and the *stacker*, respectively. Cards are processed through the machine on a frame called a *card bed*.

There are many keypunches on the market. Since most have features similar to those of the IBM 29, we will use this machine as an illustration for proper keypunch operation. The operation steps are:

   1   Turn the machine on (the ON-OFF switch is on the side, under the desk).

2   Turn on the toggle switches (located on the top center of the keyboard. They should be *up*).

3   But turn off the AUTOMATIC FEED switch. This will simplify the key punch operation by presenting you with a single card at a time. It will also reduce card wastage.

4   Remove any cards in the card bed by pressing the CLEAR switch *up* (this is the toggle switch on top right-hand side of the keyboard).

5   Remove any cards from the card stacker (upper left-hand side of the machine).

6   Place a new deck of cards in front of the old deck that you have just removed from the key punch machine. Fan the cards in order to prevent the sticking of one card to another.

7   Insert the deck of cards into the card hopper: (*a*) Straighten *very* carefully the deck of cards to be inserted in the card hopper; (*b*) push back the sliding pressure plate in the card hopper; (*c*) place the deck of cards in the hopper (printed side facing you, 9-edge down), taking care that the deck remains straight; (*d*) let the plate fall back against the cards. Do not remove cards from the card hopper. Place the cards you wish to use in front of those already there.

8   Position a card in the card bed for keypunching: (*a*) Depress the FEED key; (*b*) depress the REGISTER key.

The column indicator shows the column number that is about to be punched. It should be at column 1. (The column indicator is the window in the center of the machine above the READ station).

9   Punch the first card, using the keyboard like a typewriter. Follow regular touch typing procedure. Since our questionnaire contains only numbers, you will depress the NUMERIC key with your left forefinger during the entire operation. You can advance to any column without punching by using the space bar (this is the long blue bar at the bottom of the keyboard).

10   When you have transferred all codes to the card, check the column indicator in order to verify that you have punched the required number of columns. In this project involving seventy-six columns, the column indicator should read "77." This is an important accuracy check.

11   When the first card has been completed: (*a*) Depress the RELEASE key; (*b*) depress the FEED key; (*c*) depress the REGISTER key. You are now ready to punch your next card.

Duplicating a Data Card

An important feature of the key punch machine is its ability to duplicate punched cards. The DUPLICATOR key enables you to reproduce identical cards. This is done as follows:

1   Complete one card *accurately*.
2   Depress the RELEASE key.
3   Depress the FEED key.

4   Depress the REGISTER key. You are now in a position to duplicate your original, error-free card.

5   Depress the DUPLICATE key. Hold the key down until the column indicator shows that the required number of columns has been duplicated. You may wish to continue the duplicating operation several columns beyond the required number in order to ensure that all numerals are recorded on the punched card. The duplicating procedure is now complete, and may be repeated, beginning with step 2.

Error Correction

Another feature which is an offshoot of the duplication ability is error correction. If an error has been made in the keypunching process, an efficient correction procedure is as follows:

1   Check the column indicator to determine the column number at which the error occurred (recall that the indicator points to the column which is about to be punched).

2   Depress the RELEASE key.

3   Depress the FEED key.

4   Depress the REGISTER key.

5   Depress the DUPLICATE key until the key punch approaches the column error vicinity.

6   Observing the column indicator, press the DUPLICATE key with discrete strokes until the card is positioned exactly at the error column. For example, if the column number containing an error is "38," the DUPLICATE key will be utilized until the column indicator points to "38."

7   Punch in the correct number.

8   Complete the card.

Key Punch Completion

When you have finished your punching job, the last card is released by pushing the CLEAR switch *up*.

You should check your card against your code sheet in order to verify the identity of the two sets of codes. This is another important accuracy check. The key word in the entire coding transferral process is *accuracy.* You must check and recheck your work in order to ensure error-free data transfer to a machine-readable medium.

Handling Punched Cards

It is a truism of great importance that punched cards must never be bent, folded, stapled, spindled, or mutilated. It is particularly important to observe this caution when handling only two or three cards. A few cards are especially susceptible to being slightly creased in handling, or receiving other damage scarcely visible to the naked eye. This can result in arithmetic and logical errors during machine processing, or cause a card to be chewed up or damaged by a machine. Such conditions require the expenditure of additional time because of the necessity for reproducing damaged cards, and also become a source of frustration to the researcher seeking to complete a necessary phase of the research process as rapidly as possible.

Having produced a set of data in machine-readable form, we are now in a position to engage in the initial phase of data analysis by means of a variety of machines. During the next two sessions, we will introduce you to two machines frequently used for purposes of data analysis: the counter/sorter machine and the General Purpose Stored Digital Computer (GPSDC). The former was particularly popular during the 1950s when machine-readable devices were beginning to be widely adopted as an aid in the data analysis phase of social research. The latter is more widely used today, since it eliminates a large portion of human intervention when obtaining statistical results, allows the acquisition of more complex statistical measures, and provides the needed measures more rapidly.

Chapter 4

Counting/Sorting Fields

INTRODUCTION

The transfer of data to a machine-readable medium such as a punched card is an important preliminary step toward data analysis, because it provides access to a group of machines that comprises a complete data processing system. The use of punched cards and the machines designed to handle them in a system of data processing is sometimes called *punched-card data processing*. Because of the central role of the punched card in the data processing phase, it is absolutely crucial that the social researcher verify the accuracy of each punched card. Further, it is important that a second deck of punched cards be reproduced so that punched cards too worn to be reliably used in the machine or damaged by a machine can be easily and immediately replaced. The efficient researcher will always retain a second card on every respondent no matter how many times a card must be replaced.

After securing data and placing them on a machine-readable medium, the researcher now needs to obtain information as to the frequency with which each type of response occurs. This is a basic and fundamentally essential first step toward building a foundation for analysis and interpretation of the data. The distribution of frequencies of different kinds of responses or social facts among the entire group of persons included in the study provides the first overview of where responses cluster, spread out, or both. It provides the first crude basis for assessing where responses occur as anticipated or differ from what was expected. It yields a profile of group characteristics not only with respect to standard demographic traits, but also areas of problematic responses. In sum, frequency distributions for the total group of persons participating in a study can begin to suggest strategies for data analysis. The researcher needs to examine the distribution of responses for each item in order to acquire some notion of the identification of those items which ought to receive special analytical attention because of their patterns of distribution. This is especially helpful when the researcher is seeking to identify important explanatory variables of observed phenomena, or to generate clues as to which variables are importantly related to one another in the development, expansion, or both, of theoretical statements regarding a certain behavior. For example, a researcher may wish to see if it is possible to identify specific demographic attributes such as age or father's occupation, and correlate these with a subcategory of attitudes toward certain aspects of institutional experience such as library service or meals served within the confines of an institution. In order to carry out such an analysis, the researcher must first be sure that there is some spread or differences in response with respect to these items. Otherwise no comparison of differences and the sources and consequences of these differences is possible.

It is then crucial to obtain a distribution of frequency of responses for each item for the entire group of respondents as the first step of data analysis. The utilization of punched-card data processing is simply an expedient means of facilitating the data analysis phase. The frequency distributions obtained are sometimes called *marginal distributions*, because they represent the total for each different kind of response and are placed at the end (i.e., in the margin) of the column or row of tallies.

OBJECTIVES

This session will involve you in the research procedure of obtaining marginal distributions by way of a machine-readable medium, namely, the punched card. This will require a working knowledge of two machines associated with this research activity, the card reproducer and the counter/sorter. Minimally, you should achieve sufficient mechanical competence so that you will be able to obtain the desired marginal distributions by machine utilization. You should also be able to see that such distributions are an essential means of gaining initial familiarization with the data prior to any higher-order analysis.

ASSIGNMENT

1   Using the reproducing punching machine, reproduce a second deck of punched cards.

2 Using the counter/sorter machine, count frequencies on the following one-column, two-column, and three-column fields:

One-Column Fields

Question	Column	Description
1	6	Sex
10	30	Religious Attendance
11	31	Parent's Marital Status
29	69	Political Loyalty
35	76	School Rating

Two-Column Fields

2	7–8	Year of Birth
12	32–33	Father's Education
22	54–55	Number of Siblings
24	58–59	Television Watching
30	70–71	Number of Children Desired

Three-Column Fields

| 15 | 36–38 | Father's Occupation |
| 28 | 64–66 | Occupational Aspiration |

---

3 Using a calculator, compute percentages for each of the above categories in these fields.

4 Display results in the following format:

Variable Name (e.g., Sex)

Sex	Frequency (*n*)	Percent (%)
Female	27	58
Male	19	42
Unknown	0	0
Total	46	100

THE LAB SESSION

In order to engage in punched-card data processing, you will need to acquire a familiarity with, and a working ability to use, two machines associated with the punched card. We will provide you with a set of instructions appropriate for a machine commonly used in each type of activity. Other machines have similar devices and principles. Your instructor will acquaint you with the ways in which the machines you will use differ.

Reproducing Punch Machine Instruction Sheet

The IBM 514 reproducing punch machine feeds at the rate of 100 cards per minute. Its operation is relatively easy.

1 *Lightly* place an "X" mark on the front of the first card and the back of the last card of the deck to be reproduced. This will provide you with verification that the entire deck has actually been reproduced.

2 Turn on the MAIN LINE switch. This switch is located on the right side of the machine.

3 Remove the card weight from the read unit feed, located at the left side of the top of the machine.

4 Make certain that the cards are *carefully* stacked so that they exhibit a smooth symmetric surface.

5 Place the punched-card deck in the read unit feed. The cards are to be placed *face down* with the 12-edge (top of card) facing the throat of the machine.

6 Make certain that the cards lie *flat* and are not buckled. This is most important, because the machine will likely jam if this condition does not exist. Place the card weight on top of the card deck.

7 Remove the card weight from the punch unit feed, located to the right of the read unit feed.

8 Obtain a deck of clean, unpunched cards. Fan the cards in order to prevent the sticking of one card to another.

9 Place a clean, *un*punched, carefully stacked deck of cards in the punch unit. The cards are placed face down, with the 12-edge facing toward the throat of the machine. Make certain that the cards lie flat. Place the card weight on top of the card deck.

10 Press the START key and hold it down for three or four seconds. The machine will automatically stop at the last card to be punched.

11 When the machine stops, check the read unit feed and verify that there is only a single punched card remaining in the throat of the machine. If this is the case, then remove all unpunched cards from the punch unit feed.

12 Press the START key and hold it down for three or four seconds. When the machine stops, the job is complete.

13 Remove the decks from the card stackers by lowering the elevator platform on the ceiling of the card stacker.

14 Make certain that the first and last cards of the original deck contain the "X" marks you placed there.

15 Compare the first and last cards of the original deck with the first and last cards of the new deck.

16 Turn off the MAIN LINE switch.

How to Handle a Malfunction

1 If the machine stops during the reproducing operation, check to see if the signal light (located to the left of the START key) has come on.

2 If the signal light is on, check the comparing indicator unit, located just below the card stackers, and note the column number at which a punch error has occurred.

3 Remove both decks of punched cards from the card stackers and compare the last several (the two or three cards on the top of each deck) cards, particularly the column or columns at which the comparing indicator revealed a discrepancy.

4 Discard the newly reproduced punched card that reveals an error after comparison with the original card. Repunch the original card on the key punch machine (duplicating up to the column or columns at which discrepancy occurred).

5 Place the corrected card in the read unit feed.

6 Push up on the restoring lever, located on the right side of the comparing indicator unit.

7 Press the START key, holding it down for three or four seconds.

In the event that you encounter a machine difficulty you cannot handle, your instructor will provide you with the name of a person who can help you.

Counter/Sorter Instructions for Operation

The IBM 83 Sorter can sort 650 cards per minute; its card feed hopper can hold approximately 1,200 cards.

1 Turn on the MAIN LINE switch, located on the top front panel of the machine. You must *wait 60 seconds* before the machine warms up adequately and becomes operable.

2 Turn on (push up) the COUNTER switch. Turn off (push down) the COUNT ONLY switch and SORT SUPPRESS switch. These three switches are located at the bottom of the front control panel.

3 Push all SELECTION switches (including the red switch) toward the *outside* of the cylinder. The SELECTION switches are located just above the MAIN LINE switch.

4 Set the column indicator at the column number for which sorting is desired. The column selector handle is located just above the SELECTION switches. An efficient means of moving the column selector over many columns is as follows:

a Move the column selector handle one-half an arc so that it is positioned at the uppermost point of its circular orbit (i.e., so that it is closest to the ceiling).

b Pull down the finger lever of the column indicator and slide it to the desired column. The column indicator finger lever is the circular button attached to the outside portion of the column indicator. (When counting over more than one column, start with the last column of the field farthest to the right and proceed one column to the left after each sorting sequence until the total field has been sorted.)

5 Set all numbers on the counter to zero. The counter is located just above the thirteen pockets. To set the counter at zero for all locations, push the CLEAR switch down and turn the counter crank *clockwise*, making *two* full revolutions. The CLEAR switch is located on the top right side of the counter.

6 Remove the card weight from the card feed hopper. Fan the cards to ensure that none of them will stick together.

7 *Carefully* stack cards so that they exhibit a smooth symmetric surface.

8 Place the punched cards *face down* with the *9-edge* toward the machine in the card feed hopper. Place the card weight on top of the cards.

9 Press the START switch. The cards will now sort according to punches (categories). The counter will tabulate frequencies according to categories and register the deck total. The sorter will stop automatically.

10 Write down the frequency information.

    a Recall that, according to the codes we have specified for some fields,

> Pocket 7 = No answer (blank)
> Pocket 8 = Don't know
> Pocket 9 = Does not apply

    b Pocket R ("reject") should contain those cards whose column is blank, that is, which contain no number. Our coding system does not permit a blank to occur in any field. No cards, therefore, should appear in pocket R.

11 Remove the cards from the card pockets in the following sequence:

    a First remove the cards from pocket 0 without changing their position (i.e., do not turn the cards over or around).

    b Remove the cards from pocket 1 and place them on *top* of the cards from pocket 0.

    c Continue this procedure through pocket 9.

    d Remove the cards from pocket R and place them on top of pocket 9.

The card deck is now in correct numerical order, beginning with the lowest number and ending with the highest number. Illegal codes and blanks are on the bottom of the deck.

12 Reset the counter to zero before continuing the next frequency-count operation.

13 Reset the column indicator at the desired column number.

14 You are now ready to do your next operation. Remember that, with this particular machine model, you must wait *60 seconds* between each operation.

Counting on Multiple-Column Fields

Once the researcher begins to gather information located on more than a one-column field, then one must distinguish between *counting* and *sequencing*.

Counting involves tallying the frequency of occurrence of each category (values) for a given field. Sequencing involves arranging punched cards in numerical order from high to low of mutually exclusive categories.

Counting and sequencing entail opposite starting points in actual machine operation. When one wishes to count the frequency of occurrence of each category in a multiple-column field, one starts with the lowest column number and proceeds to the highest column number. When one wishes to sequence the data according to some datum such as Respondent Identification Number (e.g., 001 to 099), and wishes to make certain that one and only one number exists for each record, than the researcher starts with the highest column number and proceeds to the lowest column number.

Our research task will focus on the counting operation. One example of the procedure of counting multiple-column fields grouped by categories is the Month of Birth (columns 7 and 8 of the questionnaire).

1   The possible coding categories are:

01	January	07	July
02	February	08	August
03	March	09	September
04	April	10	October
05	May	11	November
06	June	12	December

2   Using the counter/sorter, place the column indicator on the lowest column number of the field (namely, column 7).

3   For this variable (field), column 7 may take on two values: "0" or "1." "0" represents those persons born in the months of January through September. "1" represents those persons born in the months of October through December.

4   Sort on column 7.

5   Remove the cards from pocket 1 and place them in the reserve card tray located above the machine in the slot marked "1."

6   Remove the cards from pocket 0 and place them in the card feed hopper.

7   Set the column indicator on the next highest number of the field for Month of Birth (column 8).

8   Sort and count on column 8 for cards with "0" in column 7.

9   Write down the frequency information.

10   Remove the cards from pockets and place them in the reserve tray in slot 0.

11   Remove the cards from slot 1 of the reserve tray.

12   Sort and count on column 8 for cards with "1" in column 7.

13   Write down the frequency information.

14   You may now remove the cards from the pockets and from the reserve tray slot 0, reintegrate the deck, and place the cards in the card feed hopper. You are now ready to count and sort the next field.

How to Handle a Machine Malfunction

By far the most frequent cause of machine trouble is the card jam. When this occurs, you may take the following steps:

1   Remove all the remaining cards from the card feed hopper.

2   Remove the damaged card by turning the hand feed wheel, located just behind the card feed hopper.

3   Duplicate the damaged card on the key punch machine, using the identical card from the duplicate deck.

4   Return one card to the duplicate deck; place the newly duplicated card in the working deck. You are now ready to continue the counting and sorting operation.

If a machine difficulty occurs that you cannot handle, your instructor will provide you with the name of a person who can help you.

Improper handling of cards is the cause of most of the difficulties that occur in sorting operations. The most common cause of card jams is the sticking together of adjacent cards within the deck. Fanning the cards will help prevent this. Cards must be carefully stacked and properly positioned in the machine hopper, and they must lie *flat* in the feed hopper. Be sure there is no bend or buckle when the cards are positioned in the feed hopper.

Chapter 5

Using the Computer

INTRODUCTION

The computer enables the social researcher to handle a large amount of data in a relatively short period of time. *Computer* is a generic term. Not all computers are electronic, and the analog computer does not compute at all. It is the digital computer which is of special interest to the social researcher, and it is primarily this system that is referred to when one speaks of the computer revolution. The chief advantages of the computer are its rapid operation and its high-capacity storage. It is these advantages which extend the researcher's ability to manipulate data for practical and theoretical purposes. The utility of the computer for the social researcher has been further enhanced by the development of standardized programs, which vastly simplifies the often lengthy and complex procedures of programming.

The General Purpose Stored Digital Computer (GPSDC) is a set of five separate machines which are combined and interrelated so that their coordinated functions constitute a system. The five machines are:

1 The *input unit* which transfers information to the computer.

2 The *storage unit* (memory) which contains information pertinent to the problem for which a solution is sought.

3 The *control unit* which directs the flow of information and the sequence of operations.

4 The *arithmetic/logical unit* which performs mathematical manipulations on information sets and subsets.

5 The *output unit* which transfers information out of the computer.

The computer components and their interrelations may be illustrated as follows:

General Purpose Stored Digital Computer
(GPSDC)

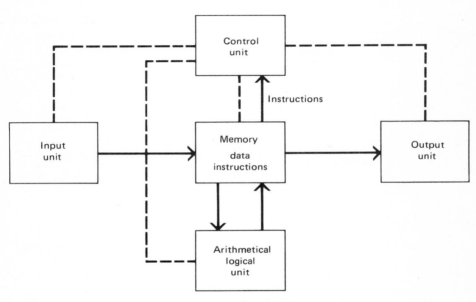

Logical Structures of Machine
Logical Flow of Information Through System

Information paths = solid line
Control paths = dotted line

Two particularly important characteristics of the computer are as follows. First, the computer differs from a mechanical calculator in that the sequence of operations is not directed by a human operator, but by the control unit. Second, the point of contact between the computer and its environment is located at the input/output units. These important features are illustrated in the following simplified diagram:

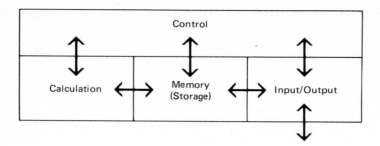

Standardized Programs

A standardized program is a series of prewritten machine-language statements specifying the sequence of steps to be followed by the computer in order to manipulate data in repeated and routine research analysis. This is also called a *canned* or *prepared* program. Such a program is stored in the computer's memory and may be retrieved for utilization by a small number of instructions to the computer.

A standardized program provides a singularly important advantage to the social researcher, namely, it saves a considerable amount of time by electronically performing arithmetic operations, thereby permitting the utilization of more sophisticated statistical analyses and allowing a greater proportion of the researcher's time to be devoted to data interpretation.

Some examples of commonly used standardized programs are: Biomedical Computer Programs (BMD), Statistical Package for the Social Sciences (SPSS), Princeton standardized routines (P-STAT), STAT-PAK, MATH-PACK, STATJOB.

These previously written programs will perform a number of useful and frequently needed mathematical routines such as frequency counts, central tendency, variability, cross-tabulation, bivariate correlation analysis, correlation, multiple regression, and factor analysis.

SPSS is a standardized program that you will be using during this lab session. Although the assignment is restricted to obtaining frequency counts, SPSS is also able to provide all the statistics mentioned in the above paragraph. If, in the future, you need to obtain any of these other statistics, you may generate them by following the instructions provided in Norman H. Nie et al., *Statistical Package for the Social Sciences*, 2d ed., McGraw-Hill, New York, 1975.

OBJECTIVES

This session is intended to acquaint you with utilization of the computer in the social science research process. It will introduce you to the advantages of standardized programs in doing social research. Finally, it will enable you to develop a familiarity with and competence in handling some basic procedures and problems encountered in obtaining the desired calculations through a standardized computer program.

ASSIGNMENT

Using the standardized computer program SPSS, secure the marginal distributions for the various fields of the questionnaire. This involves:

1 Creating an *accurate* set of instruction cards
2 Keypunching the instruction cards
3 Combining the instruction cards with the data cards
4 Submitting the deck of cards to the computer center
5 Successfully securing the desired calculations

THE LAB SESSION

In order to obtain the desired arithmetic manipulations, a small number of instruction cards is required. These instruction cards are called *control cards*. The instructions and the data cards are all that the computer needs to perform the necessary operations.

Thirteen separate instructions are needed to acquire frequencies for certain fields, using the SPSS. In preparing these instructions on computer cards, three important facts need to be kept in mind. First, the sequence of the cards is fixed. The cards, therefore, must be placed in a particular order. Second, all instructions are necessary in order to obtain all the desired information. No instruction card may be omitted. Third, the format is fixed. Therefore, any deviation whatsoever, such as the omission or inclusion of a space or a comma, is highly likely to produce an error message from the computer, and the job will be terminated before the necessary calculations are obtained.

Introduction to Control Cards

1 The initial card or cards are for the purpose of gaining entry into the computer system. Your instructor will provide you with the necessary system-related cards.

2 All control cards are keypunched beginning at column 1, i.e., are left-justified.

3 The first word or words on a control card are *control words*. These words inform the system about the kind of information that is on the card. The control words are written in columns 1 through 15 only, unless otherwise specified.

4 Specific instructions are placed in columns 16 through 80. These words or symbols are called the *specification field*.

It is important to distinguish between control words and specification fields, since each is positioned in a different portion of the punched card.

General Symbols

1 The "7/8" punch is an uppercase "C" on the key punch keyboard. Sometimes the character "@" replaces this symbol.

2   The symbol "−" = space.
3   The symbol "∅" = the letter "O."
    The symbol "0" = the number zero.
4   The symbols needed to identify the specification field of the input format card (no. 8) are:

   a   "X" = skip space(s); e.g., 4X = skip four spaces, and 1X = skip one space
   b   "A" = number of columns in a field; e.g., A2 = a two-column field, and A1 = a one-column field
   c   If there are several fields in sequence which consist of the same number of columns, then this may be indicated by placing the exact number of fields of the same number of columns which follow each other, before the symbol "A"; e.g., 2A1 = two consecutive fields of one column each, and 5A2 = five consecutive fields of two columns each

5   The input format card specifies to the standardized program all the specific fields for which the researcher desires to obtain arithmetic manipulations. Those fields for which the researcher does not desire any operation will be omitted by using the "X" symbol. For example, if the researcher wishes to ignore the first two fields of his or her data occupying columns 1 through 5, then the researcher will indicate this by the specification "5X", which signifies: "Skip the first five columns on the punched card."

Control Card Sequence and Format

Card no.	Column 1	Column 16
1	(Access to computer. Instructor will give information)	
2	⅞SPSS∗SPSS.SPSS/V5	
3	RUN-NAME_____CLASS DATA	
4	FILE-NAME_____INTR∅-T∅-S∅CIAL-RESEARCH	
5	VARIABLE-LIST_____VAR001-T∅-VAR043	
6	INPUT-MEDIUM_____CARD	
7	N∅-∅F-CASES_____46	
8	INPUT-F∅RMAT_____FIXED(A1, 4X, A1, 2A2, 3A1 . . . . A2, A1, A2, 5A1)	
9	PRINT-F∅RMATS_____VAR001-T∅-VAR043-(A)	
10	MARGINALS_____VAR001-T∅-VAR043	
11	READ-INPUT-DATA	
	(PLACE DATA DECK HERE)	
12	FINISH	
13	(Exit from computer. Instructor will give information)	

Interpretation of Control Cards

The control cards provide the researcher with a means of communicating with the computer and its systems. The control cards converse with the computer and its systems as follows:

Card 1 (computer access) : "I'm coming in, computer. Hope you have room for me."

Card 2: "Oh yes, computer, please use SPSS to calculate my data."

Card 3 (run name) : "Hello SPSS. Please identify my job as 'Class Data'."

Card 4: "Also, SPSS, please identify my file as 'Intro to Social Research.' Now I'm sure we'll get along fine."

Card 5 (variable list) : "I have forty-three variables requiring calculations."

Card 6 (input medium) : "I'm using punched cards in order to enter my data with you."

Card 7 (number of cases) : "I have forty-six observations I'd like you to include in all your calculations."

Card 8 (input format) : "I have forty-three variables for which I would like information. I have a couple more variables than this, and I'll tell you where they are so you can omit them from your calculations. Some of my variables consist of one column and some consist of two or three columns. I'll tell you which is which, and also give you their order."

Card 9 (print formats) : "Please print out the values which each variable assumes, so I'll be able to identify them quickly and easily."

Card 10 (marginals) : "The only calculations I need from you right now are the frequency distributions for the forty-three variables. Will you give me that now?"

Card 11 (read input data) : "I've given you all the information you need to get started, so now why don't you look over the data, file them away in your mind for future use, and carry out the instructions I have given you."

Card 12 (finish) : "That's all I need for now, SPSS. Thanks for a job well done."

Card 13 (computer sign-off) : "I've got all my business done here, computer. Thanks for getting me to the right system."

Sampling and Inference

INTRODUCTION

Some elaboration of the concepts and rationale involved in random sampling and statistical inference is presented in Chapter 10. This session will illustrate some important characteristics traditionally associated with sampling and inference.

Some basic concepts you need to know are as follows. A *population* is the total group of cases which share one or more characteristics. These characteristics are specified by the researcher. For example, a population could be all people attending college, all tape recorders with black cases, or all students enrolled in a social research class. A *population parameter* is any numeral or index describing the population. For example, the *percentage* of car buyers who purchased a foreign-made car last year is a parameter. A *sample* is a portion of the population taken from a complete population. We often draw a sample because it is not possible or practical to obtain information from the complete population. Characteristics of the sample are used to infer characteristics of the population. A *sample statistic* is any numeral or index describing the sample. In order to make statements about the population on the basis of information gathered from a sample, the relationship between the population and the sample of the population must be made explicit. Each person or object in the population must have a known probability of appearing in the sample. Such samples are known as *probability samples*. One important kind of probability sample is one in which every member of the population has an equal chance of appearing in the sample. This type of sample is called a *random sample*. If a researcher wishes to increase his or her confidence that the sample value truly approximates the population value, he or she can draw additional random samples from the population. Thus, a researcher could draw two random samples and average the values of the two random sample statistics. This would give a better estimate of the population parameter. Following this logic, an infinite number of random samples could be drawn, and the average value of the sample statistic for the samples would provide an even better estimate of the population parameter. By drawing an infinite number of samples and computing the statistic for each sample, the researcher could create a sample of values of a statistic. This sample of values is commonly known as a *sampling distribution* of a statistic.

OBJECTIVES

1   To familiarize you with the use of a table of random numbers and the selection of respondents for a random sample
2   To illustrate the effect of sample size on the accuracy of inference from a sample statistic to a population parameter
3   To illustrate the effect of the range of values a population can assume on the accuracy of inferring percentages in the population.

ASSIGNMENT

Complete the exercise included at the end of chapter:

1   Draw three random samples consisting of ten respondents each (three samples of five respondents each will be drawn in the lab).
2   Find frequency distributions and percentages for each random sample on the selected variables.
3   Find frequency distributions and percentages for the two sampling distributions on the selected variables.
4   Compare the sample values and sampling distribution values to the population values of the selected variables.

THE LAB SESSION

The lab session will have four phases:

1   Defining the population parameters
2   Drawing a random sample of respondents from the population
3   Computing the values of sample statistics for each random sample

4 Comparing the computed values of a statistic to known values of its corresponding population parameter.

Defining the Population Parameters

The population to be considered is the entire group of students enrolled in the class (or the completed data set included in Table A.6). The variables to be considered in the present lab session are:

Sex (column 6)

1 Female
2 Male

Student Status (from column 11)

1 Freshman
2 Sophomore
3 Junior
4 Senior
5 Graduate student

Father's Occupation (from column 35)

1 Full time
2 Part time
3 Unemployed
4 Disabled
5 Retired
6 Deceased

Occupational Goal (from columns 64–66)

0 Undecided
1 Decided (combination of all occupational codes)

Notice that some of the previously separate categories have been collapsed into combined categories in order to simplify the assignment. For example, instead of treating each student occupational goal separately, respondents have been separated into only two groups: 0—those who have not yet decided on an occupational goal, and 1—those who have decided on an occupational goal.

With the entire class being treated as the population, the population parameters for this lab will be the frequency distributions and percentages of the above variables based on the entire set of data gathered in the first lab session.

Consider the second page of the sampling and inference assignment included in the workbook. The first line identifies the variable being considered on each page. On the second page, the variable "sex" is being considered. Continuing down the page, the next line lists the possible values the variable being considered can assume. On the second page, for the variable "sex," there are two possible values or codes: "1"—female or "2"—male. Beneath each possible code you will find a blank space labeled Frequency and a blank space for a percentage labeled %. To the left of each row of blank spaces is a sample size labeled n. To the left of each sample size is a reference to the type of sample from which the blanks under Frequency and % are computed.

Locate the row labeled Population. The blanks in any row labeled Population will be filled with frequency counts and percentages computed for the full population—the entire class of students. The population size n then becomes the number of students enrolled in the Introduction to Social Research class. You found the population values of the frequency counts and percentages in lab sessions 4 and 5. Your lab instructor will give you the correct values for each population parameter. Each population parameter will be written on a page twice, once in the upper row labeled Population and once in the lower row labeled Population. When you have entered all the population parameters, there should not be any blank spaces left in any of the rows labeled Population. Check each page to be sure you have recorded all the population parameters. You will need these parameters to complete the assignment outside the lab.

Drawing a Random Sample from the Population

The population has been defined as the students enrolled in this Introduction to Social Research class. Each member of the population is referenced by his or her identification number. A random sample can be drawn from the population, therefore, by taking random identification numbers from the table of random numbers included in your workbook. The range of valid numbers will correspond to the range of respondent identification numbers. For purposes of illustration, an example class of 90 students will be used. Thus, any number taken from the table of random numbers between 01 and 90 refers to a member of the population being considered.

Turn to the table of random numbers in your workbook, close your eyes, and put your finger down on the table. The block of numbers where you placed your finger will be the block of numbers where you will begin to draw respondents for your first sample. If there are more than 100 students in your social research class, start with the first three numbers in the upper left-hand corner of the block of numbers you chose to begin drawing a sample. If there are fewer than 100 students in your social research class, start with the first two numbers in the upper left-hand corner of your chosen block of numbers. The choice of the upper left-hand corner as an initiation point is arbitrary, but it gives some degree of closure to your first experience with a table of random numbers. The number in the upper left-hand corner of your chosen block of numbers will be the first member of your random sample.

Using the example of a ninety-student class size, and an initiation point of the block of numbers in the second row and ninth column of the table of random numbers, the first respondent of a random sample is respondent number 43.

The remaining respondents in this first sample will be found by continuing down the column of digits until the researcher has drawn a sufficient number of respondents. For this first sample, five respondents are desired. Thus, continuing down, if a number is drawn for which there is no corresponding respondent in the population (e.g., if the number refers to a respondent who failed to complete the questionnaire or if the number is larger than the number of students enrolled in the social research class), the useless number is discarded and another number is drawn.

Using the example of a ninety-student class size introduced above, the first respondent in the random sample is 43. The number below 43 is 87, so the second respondent is number 87. The third respondent is 06. The fourth respondent is number 96; however, since there are only 90 respondents in the population, there is no respondent number 96 and another number needs to be drawn. The fourth respondent is, therefore, number 02. The fifth and final respondent is then number 27. The first sample in this example then consists of respondents 43, 87, 06, 02, and 27.

Your lab instructor will go through this procedure of drawing random samples with you by drawing three random samples consisting of five respondents each. The respondent identification numbers of the respondents in each sample are to be written in the blank spaces on the first page of the sampling exercise in your workbook. As you follow your lab instructor in drawing the three samples, write the respondent identification numbers he or she reads out to you in the blank spaces on page 1. When all three samples have been drawn, there will be no blank spaces to the right of samples 1, 2, or 3 on page 1 of the exercise.

After the sample respondents have been identified, take the data card corresponding to each respondent out of the total deck of data cards and separate them according to the sample. Thus, for example, using the five-person sample drawn from the ninety-student example class above, five data cards would be extracted from the entire ninety-card deck of cards. The five data cards comprising sample 1 are the card with respondent 43's responses, the card with respondent 87's responses, the card with respondent 06's responses, the card with respondent 02's responses, and the card with respondent 27's responses. When you have extracted all the cards corresponding to the sample respondents in the three samples, you will have four separate piles of data cards in front of you: one pile containing five data cards for the respondents in sample 1, a second pile containing five data cards for the respondents in sample 2, a third pile containing five data cards for the respondents in sample 3, and a fourth pile consisting of cards for the respondents who were not selected to serve as sample respondents (this fourth pile of cards will be of no further use during this lab session). Since it is possible for one respondent to be in two separate samples, you may have fewer than fifteen cards in front of you.

Computing the Values of the Sample Statistics for the Sample Observations

The three samples of data will be used to compute frequency distributions and percentages for each sample and for the sample distribution on the variables "sex" and "student status." The remainder of the exercise will be due at the next lab session.

Turn to the second page of the sampling and inference exercise. Following your lab instructor, look at column 6 of the five data cards contained in sample 1. Write the number of females (coded "1") under Frequency in the first column and first row. Write the number of males in sample one (coded "2") under Frequency in the second column and first row. Thus, if in our example sample there were three 1s and two 2s in column 6 of the five data cards (43, 87, 06, 02 and 27), the first row of the exercise would appear as:

Sample	n	Frequency	%	Frequency	%
1	5	3		2	

The percentages can be filled in by dividing the observed frequency by the total sample size. For example, in the above row, the percentage of females in sample 1 equals $\frac{3}{5} = .60 = 60\%$. Similarly, the percentage of males in sample 1 equals $\frac{2}{5} = .40 = 40\%$.

Repeat the above steps for each of the other two random samples. When you have completed this step, there should be no blank spaces to the right of samples 1, 2, or 3 on page 2 of the exercise.

For the example of a ninety-student class, the sample statistics for the three random samples on the variable "sex" appeared as follows:

Sample	n	Frequency	%	Frequency	%
1	5	3	60	2	40
2	5	4	80	1	20
3	5	1	20	4	80
Sampling distribution	5	—	—	—	—

The values for a limited sampling distribution can be found by averaging the values of the sample statistics into a single estimate of the population parameter. The usual definition of a sampling distribution involves an extremely large number of samples. However, three samples are sufficient to illustrate the idea of sampling distributions. The values for the sampling distribution will be written in the row labeled Sampling Distribution which appears immediately underneath sample 3.

Values for the sampling distribution are calculated by summing the individual frequencies and percentages found for each separate sample and dividing the sum by the number of samples considered. Using the ninety-student class as an example, the sample size being considered in the sampling distribution will equal $(5 + 5 + 5)$ divided by 3, which is 5. The number 5 has been entered on your exercise sheet already. The number of females in the sampling distribution for the example data equals $(3 + 4 + 2)$ divided by 3, which is 2.67.

Similarly, the number of males in the sampling distribution for the example data equals $(2 + 1 + 4)/3$, which is 2.33. The values of the percentages for the sampling distribution can be found either by averaging the individual values of the sample statistics or by dividing the sampling distribution value of a frequency count by the sample size. For example, the percentage of females in the sampling distribution equals $(60\% + 80\% + 20\%)/3$, which is 53.33 percent. The percentage of females in the sampling distribution could alternatively be found as 2.67/5, which equals 53.33 percent. Similarly, the percentage of males in the sampling distribution equals 2.33/5, which equals 46.67 percent. Write the values of the sampling distribution in the blank spaces in the row labeled Sampling Distribution.

The same procedure used to compute values for the sample statistics and values for the sampling distribution of the variable "sex" will yield sample statistics and values for the sampling distribution of the variable "student status."

Comparing the Computed Values of a Statistic to the Known Value of Its Corresponding Parameter

Once the values of the sample statistics have been computed and the values of the sampling distribution have been identified, the only remaining task in the lab session (and in the process of observation) is to compare these values to the known values of the population parameters. A comparison of sample and population values is made here in the interest of demonstrating some of the basic ideas of inference; however, the many statistical methods of inference are not introduced.

By following through the two examples worked out in this lab session and in discussion with your lab instructor, the following points should be demonstrated:

1 *Inference of population parameters from sample statistics is more accurate when large samples are used than when small samples are used.* As the sample size increases, the level of confidence in inferring the population parameter from its sample statistic increases. As sample size increases, in other words, the confidence interval around the estimated population parameter decreases. A related point is that inference is more accurate when several independent samples are combined to provide a sampling distribution for a parameter than when the several samples are considered separately.

2 *The more detailed the distinctions made by population parameters among characteristics of a population, then the lower the accuracy of inferring those parameters from sample statistics.* When estimating percentages and frequency distributions as population parameters, this second point will be illustrated by the fact that inferences are most accurate when there are few possible categories of a variable and many persons or objects in each category. For example, inference should be more accurate for the variable "sex" than for the variable "father's occupation."

Conducting Social Research

Chapter 6 SAMPLING and INFERENCE

NAME _____ LAB SESSION _____

(Self) _____

(Other
members
of work
group) _____

RESPONDENT IDENTIFICATION NUMBERS

Sample 1 _____
Sample 2 _____
Sample 3 _____
Sample 4 _____
Sample 5 _____
Sample 6 _____

Variable: *Sex* (column 6)

CODES

Sample	n	1 (Female)		2 (Male)	
		Frequency	*%*	*Frequency*	*%*
1	5				
2	5				
3	5				
Sampling Distribution	5				
Population	—				

63

Sample	n	Frequency	%
4	10		
5	10		
6	10		
Sampling Distribution	10		
Population	—		

Variable: *Student Status* (column 11)

CODES

Sample	n	1 Freshman Frequency	%	2 Sophomore Frequency	%	3 Junior Frequency	%	4 Senior Frequency	%	5 Graduate Frequency	%
1	5										
2	5										
3	5										
Sampling Distribution	5										
Population	—										

Sample	n	Frequency	%	Frequency	%	Frequency	%	Frequency	%	Frequency	%
4	10										
5	10										
6	10										
Sampling Distribution	10										
Population	—										

Variable: *Father's Occupation* (column 35)

CODES

	n	1 (Full time)		2 (Part time)		3–5 (Other–3 or 4)	
		Frequency	%	Frequency	%	Frequency	%
Sample							
1	5	___	___	___	___	___	___
2	5	___	___	___	___	___	___
3	5	___	___	___	___	___	___
Sampling Distribution	5	___	___	___	___	___	___
Population		___	___	___	___	___	___
Sample		Frequency	%	Frequency	%	Frequency	%
4	10	___	___	___	___	___	___
5	10	___	___	___	___	___	___
6	10	___	___	___	___	___	___
Sampling Distribution	10	___	___	___	___	___	___
Population	—	___	___	___	___	___	___

Variable: *Occupational Goal* (columns 64–66)

	n	Decided (codes 001–986)		Undecided (000)	
		Frequency	%	Frequency	%
Sample					
1	5	___	___	___	___
2	5	___	___	___	___
3	5	___	___	___	___

Sampling
Distribution 5 —— —— —— ——
Population — —— —— —— ——
                Frequency   *%*   *Frequency*   *%*

Sample	*n*	*Frequency*	*%*	*Frequency*	*%*
4	10	——	——	——	——
5	10	——	——	——	——
6	10	——	——	——	——

Sampling
Distribution 10 —— —— —— ——
Population — —— —— —— ——

Relational Variables

OBJECTIVES AND INTRODUCTION

Most of the discussion in this volume focuses on the characteristics of individuals as the values of simple concepts and variables. We ourselves have gathered data on a number of variables which describe characteristics associated with individuals: sex, student status, number of years of education completed, and dollars of income received. In this chapter, the focus of interest is shifted to the relations *between* individuals as the values of simple concepts. The values of variables and concepts will still concern individuals. However, they will concern individuals in terms of their relationships with other individuals. For example, variables frequently used as relational variables are "frequency of interaction with other group members," "popularity in the eyes of the other group members," "prestige," "power," and "similarity to other group members."

This lab session is a transition point from the earlier labs, which dealt with methods of observing and recording elements of a population, to the forthcoming lab sessions which deal with methods of analyzing the observations previously recorded. In this lab, special methods of observing and recording are required. Values of relational variables are usually computed from several aspects of the interactions involving an individual. The computation of values of relational variables therefore involves both observation and a preliminary form of data analysis. As a reflection of this nature of relational variables, this lab session has objectives concerning both the observation and analysis of data:

1   To introduce the conceptualization of variables which measure the nature of the relations among individuals as opposed to variables which measure the nature of the characteristics of individuals themselves

2   To introduce the possible need for procedures of sampling other than strict random sampling

3   To illustrate the concept of different group structures and one way of distinguishing separate groups

4   To illustrate the transformation of variables measured at the nominal level (the sociogram) to variables measured at the interval or ratio level of measurement.

We will begin by providing a brief introduction to relational variables before actually conducting the lab session.

SAMPLING SOCIOMETRIC DATA

When the theorist is interested only in observing characteristics of individuals such as education, age, sex, etc., some variation of a random sampling procedure is optimal, since it lays the best foundation for inference of population parameters from sample statistics. When the theorist is interested in the relationships among individuals, on the other hand, he or she must draw sample elements from the population such that groups of elements appear together in the sample. Instead of drawing a random sample of elements therefore, the theorist will frequently draw random groups of interconnected elements, or *clusters* of elements, from the population. Since the clusters of elements have been selected so as to represent the population of elements, the theorist can still infer values of relational parameters from values of relational statistics (see Coleman,[1] for a good summary description of procedures for sampling clusters of elements from a population). In the present lab session, all the members of the lab session will be considered a cluster of elements from the population of class members. During this lab and in the assignment, the structure of relations among the members of the lab will be observed and recorded in different forms.

An essential aspect of the interpretation of the relations among persons is the reason for the relations. For example, the fact that there is a relationship between two persons will have a different interpretation if the two persons interact for business reasons than if they interact for social reasons. The method of collecting data on the relations among persons therefore deserves careful consideration. The

---

[1] J. S. Coleman, "Relational Analysis: The Study of Social Organization with Survey Methods." *Human Organization*, **17**, 1958, pp. 28–36.

relationships between one individual and the other individuals in a cluster of elements are usually ascertained by asking the individual to give the investigator a list of names of the individuals with whom the respondent interacts for some reason. Particular questions ask the respondent to list the names of those with whom he or she interacts for certain reasons. For example, the respondent could be asked to list the individuals with whom he or she most often interacts for social reasons, for the purpose of getting advice, for the purpose of influencing others, etc. The data gathered from such a method of data collection are described as *sociometric data*. The interpretation, or substance, of the values of a relational variable will depend on the question asked.

Relational Variables

For the purposes of this lab, there are three approaches to the computation of values of relational variables: (1) sociograms, (2) algebraic indices, and (3) probabilistic indices. The first approach generates values at the nominal level of measurement. The last two approaches generate values at the ordinal level and frequently at the interval or ratio level of measurement.

Sociograms—Interpretation of a Visual Presentation of Sociometric Data

A sociogram is a visual picture of the relations among a set of persons or actors who interact with one another (cliques) and persons who interact with no one (isolates).[2]

Clique: A group of actors or persons who interact with one another either directly or indirectly.

Isolate: An actor, person, who does not interact with anyone included in a sample of actors.

Thus, if person A interacts with person B who then interacts with person C,

---

[2] The definition of an isolate given here is a fairly standard one; however, there is no generally accepted definition of a clique in social research. Some definitions insist on a high level of interaction among members of a clique (for example, L. Festinger, S. Schachter, and K. Back, *Social Pressures in Informal Groups*, Harper & Row, New York, 1950). Other definitions ask only that the interaction among clique members be somehow distinct from interactions among nonclique members. These are definitions based on a variety of perspectives. (For example, see review by P. M. Lankford, "Comparative Analysis of Clique Identification Methods," *Sociometry*, **37**, 1974, pp. 287–305; and specific examples by D. MacRae, "Direct Factor Analysis of Sociometric Data," *Sociometry*, **23**, 1960, pp. 360–371; C. H. Hubbell, "An Input-Output Approach to Clique Identification," *Sociometry*, **28**, 1965, pp. 377–399; E. O. Laumann and F. U. Pappi, "New Directions in the Study of Community Elites," *American Sociological Review*, **38**, 1973, pp. 212–230. R. S. Burt, "Positions in Networks," University of Chicago, *Social Forces*, **55** (in press); H. C. White and R. Breiger, "Multiple Networks in Small Populations: Blockmodels," *American Journal of Sociology*, **81**, 1976 (in press). The definition given here is a minimal definition of a clique since, in advanced industrial societies, most individuals are interconnected either directly or indirectly.

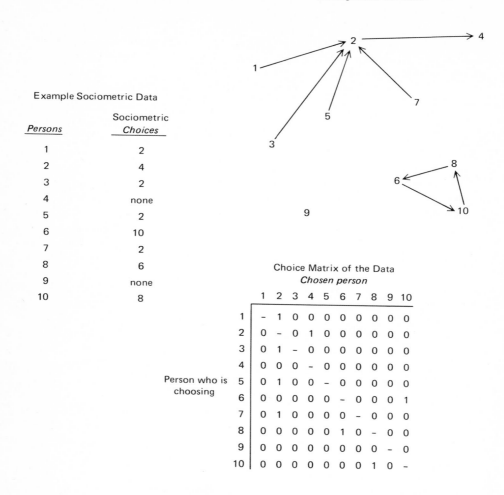

Example Sociometric Data

Persons	Sociometric Choices
1	2
2	4
3	2
4	none
5	2
6	10
7	2
8	6
9	none
10	8

Choice Matrix of the Data

Chosen person

		1	2	3	4	5	6	7	8	9	10
	1	–	1	0	0	0	0	0	0	0	0
	2	0	–	0	1	0	0	0	0	0	0
	3	0	1	–	0	0	0	0	0	0	0
	4	0	0	0	–	0	0	0	0	0	0
Person who is	5	0	1	0	0	–	0	0	0	0	0
choosing	6	0	0	0	0	0	–	0	0	0	1
	7	0	1	0	0	0	0	–	0	0	0
	8	0	0	0	0	0	1	0	–	0	0
	9	0	0	0	0	0	0	0	0	–	0
	10	0	0	0	0	0	0	0	1	0	–

Figure 7.1   Example sociometric data and their visual presentation in a sociogram and a choice matrix.

persons A, B, and C are all in a single clique. A and B interact directly, and B and C interact directly. Actors A and C interact indirectly.

Figure 7.1 presents some example sociometric data generated from the question "Name the person with whom you spoke most frequently during the past week." The sociometric data are listed as two columns of numbers on the left side of Figure 7.1. The first list of numbers consists of the identification numbers of the respondents in a cluster of individuals. The second list of numbers consists of the identification numbers of the persons cited in response to the sociometric question. For example, person 1 cited person 2 as being the person he or she spoke to most frequently during the previous week. Figure 7.1 gives two ways in which sociometric data can be presented visually: the sociogram (top of Figure 7.1), or the matrix (bottom of Figure 7.1). In the sociogram, arrows lead from chooser to chosen. For example, there is an arrow leading from person 1 to person 2 to indicate that person 1 cited person 2 in response to the sociometric question.

In the matrix—termed a *choice matrix*, the rows of numbers represent the choices made by persons, and the columns of numbers represent the choices received by persons. The matrix is composed of ones and zeros. The "1" represents a choice, and the "0" represents the lack of a choice. If person i cites person j in response to a sociometric question, then a "1" appears in the spot where row i and column j meet. Otherwise a "0" is placed in that spot. For example, person 1 cited person 2 in the example data. Therefore the choice matrix has a "1" in the location where row 1 and column 2 meet. Only the choice matrix is presented here, because most analyses of sociometric data currently being used involve choice matrices. It is therefore useful to be able to interpret one when it is presented in the literature. The focus of attention in this lab—in terms of nominal levels of measurement—will be the sociogram.

The sociogram shows that there is one isolate in the cluster of persons sampled—person 9. Further, there are two cliques in the cluster of persons sampled. One clique contains six persons, (1, 2, 3, 4, 5, 7). The other clique contains three persons (6, 8, 10). In addition to demonstrating that there are two cliques in the cluster of elements sampled, the sociogram gives the viewer an idea of the overall structure of the cliques. In the large clique in Figure 7.1, there is one person who receives many citations, while most persons do not receive any. This is person 2. The large clique in Figure 7.1 can therefore be described as having a hierarchical structure.

Hierarchical clique: A clique in which a small percentage of the members of the clique receive a large percentage of the sociometric citations. In contrast to the hierarchical clique in the sociogram, the small clique in the sociogram exhibits a peer structure.

Peer clique: A clique in which the sociometric citations are equally distributed among the members of the clique. The small clique in the sociogram has a peer structure, because each member of the clique receives the same number of citations—one citation each.

Using the information provided in the sociogram, a variable can be constructed at the nominal level of measurement for which values equal the type of clique structure in which the individual exists. The values of this variable are presented in Table 7.1 along with the example sociometric data and values of variables to be explained shortly. The "clique structure" variable assumes three different values in Table 7.1. For every member of the large clique, the variable equals the value "hierarchical." For every member of the small clique, the variable equals the value "peer." For the one isolate, the variable equals the value "isolate." The variable "clique structure" is measured only at the nominal level of measurement, since there is no order among the values of the variable.

Table 7.1   Values of the Relational Variables for the Example Sociometric Data

| Respondents | Sociometric choices | Relational variables | | |
		Clique structure	Choice status	Popularity
1	2	Hierarchical	$(0/9) = 0$	$(0/9–1/9) = -.11$
2	4	Hierarchical	$(4/9) = .44$	$(4/9–1/9) = .33$
3	2	Hierarchical	$(0/9) = 0$	$(0/9–1/9) = -.11$
4	None	Hierarchical	$(1/9) = .11$	$(1/9–1/9) = 0$
5	2	Hierarchical	$(0/9) = 0$	$(0/9–1/9) = -.11$
6	10	Peer	$(1/9) = .11$	$(1/9–1/9) = 0$
7	2	Hierarchical	$(0/9) = 0$	$(0/9–1/9) = -.11$
8	6	Peer	$(1/9) = .11$	$(1/9–1/9) = 0$
9	None	Isolate	$(0/9) = 0$	$(0/9–1/9) = -.11$
10	8	Peer	$(1/9) = .11$	$(1/9–1/9) = 0$

Algebraic Indices   An algebraic index is a combination of two or more aspects of the interactions of an individual (or group). One of the most common algebraic indices is *choice status*. "Choice status" is a variable whose values equal the number of choices received by an individual, divided by the number of choices he or she could have received. Possible citations equal the cluster size minus 1.

$$\text{Choice status} = \frac{\text{number of sociometric choices received}}{\text{number of persons in cluster} - 1}$$

For example, in the sociometric data in Figure 7.1 and Table 7.1, person 2 received four sociometric citations. The number of persons in the cluster equals 10, so the number of persons in the cluster minus 1 equals 9. The choice status of person 2 therefore equals 4/9, or .44. This tells the theorist that person 2 was cited by 44% of the cluster as being the person to whom they spoke most frequently during the past week. A 1 is subtracted from the number of persons in a cluster, since an individual could not cite himself or herself.

Probabilistic Indices   A probabilistic index is a combination of two or more aspects of the interactions of an individual (or group) in comparison to some hypothesized value for that combination of aspects. A probabilistic index can therefore be discussed as a combination of two algebraic indices: one index which quantifies an observed condition and another index which quantifies a hypothetical condition based on the rules of probability. Although it need not be, the most common hypothetical condition used is that of random chance. For example, if it is observed that an individual receives 44 percent of the sociometric choices in a cluster of elements, it is useful to know how this value compares to the percent of citations he or she would be expected to receive simply as a result of random chance. According to random chance, it would be expected that each individual in a cluster of elements would receive one of the available citations (since in the example data each person can only cite one name.[3]) This value will equal the choice status of an individual if citations are distributed among members of the cluster according to random chance.

$$\text{Expected choice status} = \frac{1}{\text{number of persons in cluster} - 1}$$

This value can then be compared to the actually observed value of choice status for an individual to see whether the individual received more citations than would be expected by random chance. This probabilistic index can be discussed as popularity.

$$\text{Popularity} = \text{observed choice status} - \text{expected choice status}$$

$$= \frac{\text{number of sociometric choices received} - 1}{\text{number of persons in cluster} - 1}$$

If popularity is a positive value, then the individual received more citations than would be expected by random chance. For example, person 2 has a popularity score of .33 (see Table 7.1), so that individual received more citations than would be expected by random chance. In contrast, persons 1, 3, 5, 7, and 9 have negative popularity scores, which shows that they received fewer citations than would be expected by random chance. Persons 4, 6, 8, and 10 have popularity scores of zero, which shows that they received the same number of citations as would be expected by random chance—their observed "choice status" equals their "expected choice status." (A point to be noted is the difference in the zero points in "choice status" versus "popularity." The bottom of the scale for "choice status" is zero, whereas "popularity" has negative numbers. The zero point on both variables is meaningful, however, since they each tell the theorist something different. The choice of indices will depend on the interests of the theorist.)

The above three relational variables, "clique structure," "choice status," and "popularity" give the theorist an initial indication of the structure of the interactions in which a respondent is involved. These variables, although of potential utility in social research, ignore many of the more subtle aspects of structure in the relations among respondents which are captured by recent developments in the social sciences (see e.g., references in footnote 1).

MATERIALS

One 3 by 5 card for each member of the lab session.

[3] In general, the numerator in "expected choice status" will equal the number of sociometric citations an individual was allowed to make. In the example data each individual could only make one choice, so the numerator equals "1."

ASSIGNMENT

Using the sociometric data gathered during the lab, a table of values for the three variables discussed above will be completed. This means that the following information will be handed in:

1   The number of isolates in the sociogram
2   The type of clique structure in which each respondent exists
3   The values of the variable "choice status"
4   The values of the variable "popularity."

CONDUCTING THE LAB SESSION

Sampling Sociometric Data

You will be asked to record the name of the member of the lab to whom you spoke most frequently during the last week. Thus, the cluster of elements here is the group of individuals in the lab session. The substance of the relational variables to be computed will therefore be in terms of the social interactions of members of the lab. The recording of this sociometric data will follow six steps:

1   The lab instructor will place a diagram of the class seating arrangement on the blackboard. Each seat will be given a number to identify it as a potential respondent.
2   You will receive a 3 by 5 card from the lab instructor.
3   Place your seat number in the upper left-hand corner of the 3 by 5 card. *Circle* your identification number on the card.
4   The lab instructor will write the question for generating the sociometric data on the blackboard. You will be asked, "Name the person in the lab with whom you spoke most frequently during the past week outside of the lab sessions."
5   Identify this person with whom you spoke most frequently outside of the lab sessions by his or her seating position number as indicated in the diagram on the blackboard. Place this person's number on your 3 by 5 card. *Do NOT circle this person's number.* Your choice is based on your own personal evaluation, so you do not need to confer with others regarding your choice.
6   Hand your card to the lab instructor so that he or she can rearrange the numbers to ensure the anonymity of respondents. This completes the collection of the example sociometric data.

Computing Values for the Relational Variables

The lab instructor will rearrange the respondent identification numbers and list the sociometric choices on the blackboard. Take the sheet at the end of this lab session and write in the sociometric choices next to the respondent identification numbers. The remainder of this lab session will consist of going through the example sociometric data given in the introduction, constructing a sociogram, and computing values for the three variables "clique structure," "choice status," and "popularity." Your assignment will then be to do with the example data gathered above exactly what was done during the lab session with the data from the introduction.

We have now covered such research activities as data collection by means of a self-administered questionnaire and obtaining frequency counts by means of machines. Next we will discuss and practice a number of basic statistical procedures that will enable us to summarize data pertaining to a single variable and to convert it into a simple and convenient form.

CONDUCTING SOCIAL RESEARCH

Chapter 7   Relational Variables

Respondents	Sociometric choices	Relational variables		
		Clique structure	Choice status	Popularity
1				
2				
3				
4				
5				
6				
7				
8				
9				
10				
11				
12				
13				
14				
15				
16				
17				
18				
19				
20				

Chapter 8

Descriptive Statistics of One Variable: Central Tendency

INTRODUCTION

After having gathered a set of observations, the researcher transfers them to a machine-readable medium in order to engage in statistical analysis. There are two important steps in this phase of the research process. The first step is the summarization of data. The second step is making general statements on the basis of summary data. In this session and the next we will be concentrating on the first step, the summarization of data. This step focuses on the reduction of an often large amount of data according to a set of agreed on rules and procedures, so that the essential characteristics of some event or phenomenon can be presented in a more usable and informative manner. An important goal is the description of data in as clear and simple a form as possible. For this reason, this phase of data analysis is often referred to as *descriptive statistics*. We will further confine our analysis to characteristics regarding a variable in this chapter.

OBJECTIVES

Our primary goal is to reduce quantitative data to a descriptive summary measure that provides a readily ascertainable overview of the chief characteristics of the data. In order to do this, you must become familiar with the rules and procedures which facilitate this reduction. Also you will need to be aware of some central assumptions affecting the selection of appropriate summary measures. Certain measures, in order to be meaningful, are applicable under certain conditions, and not under other conditions.

ASSIGNMENT

Find the (1) mode, (2) median, and (3) mean for the following characteristics of your data:

- *a* Father's education (columns 32–33)
- *b* Father's income (columns 41–42)
- *c* Mother's political party (column 45)
- *d* Television viewing (columns 58–59)
- *e* Academic performance (column 62)
- *f* Attitude toward bookstore (column 73)
- *g* Attitude toward library (column 74)

THE LAB SESSION

Data analysis deals with two kinds of cases. The first is analysis of a single variable. The second is analysis of relationships between two or more variables. A special type of multivariable case is the analysis of relationships between two variables only, the *bivariable* case. We will restrict our consideration at this time to the univariable case. There are seven kinds of statistics by which we commonly organize and summarize our data in order to describe the univariable distribution simply and clearly. These are as follows.

The Marginal or Frequency Table

A frequency table consists of a heading identifying its contents. The body of the table includes information with respect to the variable name, the categories of the variable, the frequency of each category, and the total frequency of all categories.

All the categories that comprise a variable are listed in the frequency table. When numerals or numbers are used to express the category, they are listed from low to high. An additional category indicating missing or unknown observations is also included at the end of the category list.

Two common formats of a frequency table are shown in Tables 8.1 and 8.2.

The categories are ordered according to the numerals assigned to them during the earlier coding process (female = 1; male = 2; unknown = 9). The frequency of observations associated with each category of the variable, as well as the total number of observations made with respect to the sex variable, not only forms the frequency distribution of the variable, but also may be regarded as the *marginals* of the variable. It thereby derives its name *marginal* or *frequency*

Table 8.1   Classroom of Students by Sex

Sex	Frequency
Female	27
Male	19
Unknown	0
Total	46

Table 8.2   Classroom of Students by Sex

Female	Male	Unknown	Total
27	19	0	46

table. Each observation has been placed within the appropriate coded category of the variable. We say, then, that these tables consist of grouped data.

The next three types of statistics are indices which make possible simple comparisons among frequencies associated with variables or their categories.

Ratio

A *ratio* expresses the relationship between two sets of numbers in decimal form by dividing one number by another. The ratio of one number (e.g., A) to another number (e.g., B) is defined as A divided by B. In the preceding sentence, the quantity preceding the preposition *to* is placed in the numerator; the quantity following the same preposition is placed in the denominator. The generalized formula for expressing a ratio may be written as:

$$\frac{N_A}{N_B}$$

where N = frequency of an observation, and the subscripts A and B = the specific phenomenon (e.g., variable, category).

Using the same data applied to the frequency table and following customary usage, we may express the ratio of males (N_A) to females (N_B) as:

$$^{19}\!/_{27} = .704$$

This ratio may also be equivalently written as:

19:27

The decimal (.704) is the composite number which expresses the number of males for every female. It literally tells us that there are 704-thousandths of a male for 1 female.

But this is an awkward way of comparing two observations. We can simplify the expression by rounding and stating the ratio in terms of a denominator of unity, so that we may say: There are seven-tenths of a male for every female. Or we can normalize by ten, so that our statement becomes: For every seven males there are ten females. Or we can normalize by 100, which results in the interpretation: For every 70 males, there are 100 females. If we do not wish to sacrifice some of our accuracy, we can eliminate the rounding and express the ratio in thousands: For every 704 males, there are 1,000 females.

The ratio is often used to compare categories of a single variable. The utility of the ratio declines, however, when the denominator is very small and the numerator is very large. For example, if in a social system males $= 5,497$ and females $= 27$, then the ratio is:

$$\frac{5,497}{27} = 203.59$$

The ratio formed by these divergent numbers is scarcely more meaningful than the original data themselves.

Proportion

A *proportion* is a special kind of ratio. The numerator consists of one or more categories; the denominator always represents the total number of observations within which the category or categories of the numerator are nested. The numerator, therefore, is a certain fraction of the total number of cases. The proportion has an added value over the ratio because it ensures us that the denominator will be larger than the numerator. The proportion p may be generally written:

$$p = \frac{N_A}{T_A}$$

where $N =$ frequency associated with each set of observations
    $A =$ subset of observations
    $T_A =$ set of observations of which subset A is a member

Again, using our previous set of data, we may express the proportion of females with respect to the total group as:

$$\frac{\text{Females}}{\text{Total people}} = \frac{\text{females}}{\text{females} + \text{males}} = \frac{27}{46} = .58$$

This composite index informs us that 58-hundredths, or over one-half of the total group, is composed of female members.

Percentage

A *percentage* is a proportion multiplied by 100. Normalizing a proportion by 100 has the great advantage of presenting a summary number that can be easily visualized. You will recall that an important goal of an index is to summarize data in as simple and clear a manner as possible, so that its significance and meaning will be readily apparent. The generalized model for expressing a percentage may be written:

$$100p = (100) \frac{N_A}{T_A}$$

where the notation is the same as that stated for the proportion.

Applying the formula to our previous data on sex distribution, we may ascertain the relative frequency of females:

$$100p = (100) \frac{27}{46} = 58 \text{ percent}$$

We are now able to compare the number of females relative to the number of males with considerable ease both within the classroom under study and with outside classes, regardless of differences in size.

The typical marginal or frequency table of a univariate distribution generally includes three items of information within its body: categories of the variable, frequency of occurrence by category, and relative frequency with which observations are found within each category (percentage). Our data of sex distribution would thus be presented in the form shown in Table 8.3.

When percentages are calculated across categories of a single variable, missing values and illegal responses are eliminated. Thus the total frequency written in the denominator may vary from time to time.

The Mode

Very simply, the mode expresses the value or values of a distribution by specifying the category or categories for which there are more observations than for any other category in the neighborhood. It is possible for a distribution to have more than one modal category. For example, the frequency of females in the United States labor force over their work careers is generally bimodal. The first modal category appears before a woman bears a child (18–24 years old);

Table 8.3 Classroom of Students by Sex

Sex	Frequency (n)	100p (%)
Female	27	58
Male	19	42
Unknown	0	0
Total	46	100

Table 8.4   Number of Children in Family of Origin

Number of children	Frequency (N)	Percentage $100p$
1	8	18
2	12	27
3	12	27
4	6	14
5	4	9
6	0	0
7	2	5
9	12	
Total	56	100

the second modal category occurs after the family no longer requires continuous maternal oversight and responsibility (40–44 years old).

In the data available to us via the class questionnaire, we exclude missing values or illegal responses as a choice of the mode. In our questionnaire, one class of students produced a distribution with respect to Number of Children in Family of Origin (question 22, columns 54–55) shown in Table 8.4.

We note two important things from the above table. First, code 9 (illegal response) is eliminated from the percentage calculation, as well as from the determination of the modal category or categories. The denominator in the percentage formula is 44 (56 − 12). Second, we can see from visual inspection of the frequency distribution that two categories contain the largest number of frequencies. These are, therefore, identified as our modal categories, namely, "two children" and "three children" in families of origin.

Our next two summary indices are called *central tendency measures*. They are used to locate the *single* central value in a distribution of observations across a set of categories pertaining to a single variable.

Median

The median is the point which has an equal number of observations lower and higher than itself. It is a special case of a percentile rank; it is the value at the 50th percentile. The median is meaningful only when the values of the categories can be rank-ordered (ordinal data).

The median is especially useful when the distribution of values is skewed. For example, the distribution of incomes of American families would reveal that while most families have incomes in the "middle" range, a few families will have extremely high or low incomes. Such distribution affects some measures of central tendency—for example, the arithmetic mean, which will be discussed shortly. However, the distribution has little effect on the median. Average incomes of American families, therefore, are frequently expressed by the median which is not susceptible to distortion by extreme values.

There are four different operations which apply to the calculation of the median: three for ungrouped data and one for grouped data.[1] The particular technique to be adopted will be determined first and foremost by whether the data are grouped or ungrouped. If they are ungrouped, then the determining factors are: (1) whether the total frequency of observations results in an odd or even number, and (2) whether or not there are several observations which assume the same value in the category in which the median falls.

The form of the data will first inform our selection of the formula to be utilized. The data may be arranged in (1) an array, (2) an ungrouped frequency distribution, or (3) a grouped frequency distribution. An array is simply the arrangement of a set of observations from low to high values. An ungrouped frequency distribution is the assignment of a set of observations to categories which assume one and only one value. A grouped frequency distribution is constructed by placing a set of observations in a set of categories, each of which encompasses more than one value.

The data from our questionnaire have been coded so that both ungrouped frequency distributions (e.g., Number of Children in Family of Origin) and grouped frequency distributions (e.g., Number of College Credit Hours) will result. Whether you use ungrouped or grouped data formulas for calculating the median on the two kinds of frequency distributions is left to the discretion of your instructor. Following Glass and Stanley, we choose to use the grouped-data formula for both distributions.

Ungrouped Data

The formula for calculating the median is the same for both an array of data and an ungrouped frequency distribution. We will use the array to illustrate three techniques utilized for calculating the median under three different conditions.

Before doing so, we should recall that the true limits of a whole number on a continuous scale are .5, and where the number can take on an infinite number of intermediate values within the range. For example, assuming a continuous scale, the range of values the whole number 3 may assume is 2.5 to 3.5. The midpoint of this range is 3.0, the whole number itself.

Condition 1: where the total frequency of observations results in an odd number. The calculation of the median under this condition is very straightforward. We

---

[1] Glass and Stanley recommend utilization of the grouped-data formula for both grouped and ungrouped data. We will include a discussion of both techniques of calculating the median, since it is an invaluable aid to understanding, and since most statistics texts maintain the distinction. (*See* Gene V. Glass and Julian C. Stanley, *Statistical Methods in Education and Psychology*, Prentice-Hall, Englewood Cliffs, N.J. 1970, pp. 59–60.)

place the median at the value which is the $[(n + 1)/2]$th value from the lowest number of the array or ungrouped frequency distribution. For example, in an array of observations that take on the values 1, 2, 2, 3, 4, 5, 7, the median is calculated as $[(7 + 1)/2] = 4$. Starting at the lowest value and progressing to the fourth value, we locate the median position in this array with an odd number of total observations. The median is 3.

Condition 2: where the total frequency of observations results in an even number. We place the median between the $(n/2)$th value and the $[(n/2) + 1]$th value. For example, given the values 1, 2, 2, 3, 4, 5, the median is calculated from the above formula: $6/2$ and $6/2 + 1$. The median is thus placed at the position between the third and fourth values. Starting at the lowest value and counting to the third and fourth values, we ascertain that these values are 2 and 3, respectively. The median is placed at a position exactly between these two values. The exact position of the median is determined by taking the arithmetic average of the third and fourth values, namely, $[(2 + 3)/2] = 2.5$. Therefore, the median for the given array of values whose total frequency results in an even number is 2.5.

Condition 3: where the median is located at a position which is part of a set of values which are equal. Assume an array with the values 1, 2, 2, 2, 3, 5, 7. Since condition 1 prevails, we locate the median position by the calculation $[(7 + 1)/2] = 4$. The fourth value is 2. This 2 is a member of a set of values which assumes the same quantity. It is the third 2 in a set composed of three 2s. Assuming that these values compose a continuous scale, let us recall that the true limits of 2 are 1.5 to 2.5. If we further assume that each observation is evenly spread throughout this interval, we may precisely locate the position of our third 2. This may be done by using the formula:

$$l + \frac{f_i}{f_n} (w)$$

where l = lowest limit of the category within which the median falls
$\quad\quad f_i$ = rank order within the category in which median falls
$\quad\quad f_n$ = total number of members within the category in which the median falls
$\quad\quad\quad$ falls
$\quad\quad w$ = width of the interval of the category within which the median falls

Applying the formula, we find:

$\quad$ $1.5 + 3/3 \,(1) = 1.5 + 1 = 2.5$.

The median is located at the position of 2.5.

Grouped Data

Condition 3 occurs most commonly with ungrouped or grouped frequency distributions. In fact, one of the reasons data are placed within the framework of a frequency table is to facilitate the summarization of data where numerous observations assume the same values. When data are placed in a grouped frequency distribution, the median may be determined by the formula:

$$l + \frac{(N/2) - cn}{n}(w)$$

where l = lower limit of the category containing the median

N = number of observations with legal codes

cn = cumulative number of observations in the category immediately preceding the median category

n = number of observations within the category in which the median falls

w = width of the category containing the median

We may apply this formula to some data on the frequency of television viewing that one class of undergraduate students reported, and which were initially summarized in a grouped frequency table (see Table 8.5).

$$\text{Median} = 1.0 \frac{45\frac{1}{2} - 20}{13}(1.0)$$

$$1.0 \frac{22.5 - 20}{13}(1.0)$$

$$1.0 \frac{2.5}{13}(1.0)$$

$$1.0 .19 (1.0)$$

$$1.19$$

Table 8.5   Television Viewing per Day

Television viewing time	Frequency (N)	Percentage (100p)	Cumulative frequency (CN)
1 No time	9	20	9
2 1 hour or less	11	24	20
3 1–2 hours	13	29	33
4 2–3 hours	7	16	40
5 3–4 hours	3	7	43
6 4–5 hours	2	4	45
7 No response	1		
Total	46	100	45

We conclude that the median hours of television viewing for our respondents (observations) is 1.19 hours—about 1 hour and 11 minutes (.19 × 60).

The Arithmetic Mean

The mean is a highly useful statistic that is generally defined by its formula. It is meaningful when the values of the categories are continuous; that is, the distance between each pair of values is known. For example, age, income, and years of schooling have continuous values, whereas race, sex, and religious affiliation do not. The *mean* is an average number. It is the sum of values of a set of observations divided by the number of observations in the set. The above statement is a literal expression of the formula:

$$\bar{X} = \frac{\sum X}{N}$$

where $\bar{X}$ = the mean
X = value of each observation
N = total number of observations
$\sum$ = summation of the values for each observation

The mean takes into account each and every value in a set of observations. Therefore the relative weights of extreme values in a set of observations are reflected in the value expressed by the mean. The mean is the value which would occur if the total values of the set were evenly distributed among all observations. It is possible to view the population mean as the true value of the set of observations, and to regard all departures from this true value as random error. From this viewpoint, the mean is the true error-free value of a set of observations. In line with this reasoning is the fact that departures from this true value cancel each other out. This is to say that the net effect of deviations from the mean is zero. This may be written as:

$$\sum (X - \bar{X}) = 0$$

The calculation of the mean is very straightforward. We will review the computation of the mean under three different conditions of data presentation.

1   For any set of values, our original formula can be used. Assume we have a set of six observations on the number of children in the family of origin: 1, 2, 2, 3, 3, 13. The mean for this group is:

$$\bar{X} = \frac{1 + 2 + 2 + 3 + 3 + 13}{6}$$

$$= 24\%_6$$

$$= 4$$

We conclude that the average number of children in the family of origin for

Table 8.6   Student Attitudes toward University Food Service

Rating (v)	Frequency (n)	Cumulative frequency (CN)	Percentage (100p)
1 (Good)	0	0	0
2	2	2	5
3	2	4	5
4 (Average)	16	20	36
5	7	27	16
6	8	35	18
7 (Bad)	9	44	20
9 (Unspecified)	2		
Total (N)	46	44	100

this group of respondents is 4. It should be noted that, since the mean is sensitive to all scores, the single high score increases the value of the mean.

2   When we have an ungrouped frequency distribution, such as the one produced immediately below, then the efficiency for computing the mean can be increased by multiplying the frequency with which a particular choice is made by the value assigned to the choice, thereby speeding up the data-manipulation process when it is being carried out by hand. (See Table 8.6.)

The mean for the above data is:

$$\bar{X} = \frac{(2 \times 2) + (3 \times 2) + (4 \times 16) + (5 \times 7) + (6 \times 8) + (7 \times 9)}{44}$$

$$= \frac{4 + 6 + 64 + 35 + 48 + 63}{44}$$

$$= {}^{220}\!/_{44}$$

$$= 5$$

The procedures for carrying out the above calculations may be generalized as:

$$\bar{X} = \frac{\Sigma\,(vn)}{N}$$

The mean attitude toward the university food service is 5—on the negative side.

3   When we have a grouped frequency distribution, and no additional information is provided which would help us locate the precise position of each score, as in the student questionnaire data reflecting father's income (see Table 8.7), the calculation of the mean may be facilitated by assuming that all values within an interval cluster at the midpoint on the scale of values. The interval midpoint is actually the mean of values within the interval. Thus all values within an interval are treated as midpoint values. This simplifying assumption

Table 8.7   Father's Income for Undergraduate Students

Father's income, $ (v)	Midpoint, $ (v_m)	Frequency (n)
1 Under 1,000	500	0
2 1,000– 1,999	1,500	0
3 2,000– 2,999	2,500	0
4 3,000– 3,999	3,500	0
5 4,000– 4,999	4,500	0
6 5,000– 5,999	5,500	3
7 6,000– 6,999	6,500	0
8 7,000– 9,999	8,500	7
9 10,000–11,999	11,000	9
10 12,000–14,999	13,500	8
11 15,000–24,999	20,000	11
12 25,000–49,999	37,500	3
13 50,000 or more	50,000*	0
99 Unspecified		5
Total		46

* The assignment of the lower limit of this category is an exception to the principle being illustrated by these data. See H. M. Blalock, Jr., *Social Statistics*, McGraw-Hill Book Company, New York, 1972, pp. 61–62, for a discussion of the determination of extreme open-interval values.

produces small distortions when the interval is small. It may produce large distortions at the extreme intervals of a scale. The distorting effects of extreme categories are usually ameliorated by the small number of observations often found there.

This problem of informational loss and its effects on accuracy underscores the simple principle that the presentation of a large amount of data in a form that achieves clarity, economy, and meaningfulness usually entails the collapsing of data into larger categories, producing some informational loss and its negative attendant effect on accuracy of analysis. Such loss of detail need not result in significant distortion. A large number of categories (viz., ten to twenty) with small intervals will reduce this source of error. Further, the extreme categories, which are potentially major sources of error, often contain the smallest number of frequencies.

The formula expressing this simplifying assumption that scores within intervals cluster at the midpoint, and may be assigned the midpoint value is:

$$\bar{X} = \frac{\sum(v_m n)}{N}$$

where v_m = the midpoint of values within each interval.

Calculating the mean of father's income, using the data in Table 8.7,

$$\frac{\begin{array}{l}(5{,}500 \times 3) + (8{,}500 \times 7) + (11{,}000 \times 9) + (13{,}500 \times 8) \\ + \ (20{,}000 \times 11) + (37{,}500 \times 3)\end{array}}{41}$$

$$= \frac{16{,}500 + 59{,}500 + 99{,}000 + 108{,}000 + 220{,}000 + 112{,}500}{41}$$

$$= \frac{615{,}500}{41}$$

$$\bar{X} = \$15{,}012.20$$

We conclude that the mean income of fathers in a class of undergraduate students is $15,012.20.[3] This is considerably more than the mean American *family* income reported by the 1970 census of $10,955. The ratio of students' father's mean income to the average American family income is 1.37 to 1. The proportion of income enjoyed by students' fathers as compared to the average American family is .578.

[3] The *median* income of students' fathers is $12,562.31, thereby indicating that the shape of the distribution is negatively skewed. This is the opposite of the distribution for all American citizens for which the shape is positively skewed.

Chapter 9

Descriptive Statistics of One Variable: Variability

INTRODUCTION

Data may be simply and clearly summarized by ordering them according to the values they assume, and describing them in terms of some typical or representative number, according to its general location along their entire range. This was our goal in the last session when we organized our data by constructing frequency tables and calculating numerals, such as the mode, the median, and the mean, which are useful for comparison purposes and which may serve as typical values representative of the data set.

We will continue this data-summarization process for single variables by presenting a second crucial set of indices—variability.

OBJECTIVES

This session will introduce you to some commonly used variability indices. Not only will you gain experience in calculating variability values, but you will also see the essential importance of this research step in providing you as a data analyst with an index that describes the manner in which a population varies in one or more ways. You will see that this kind of information is not apparent from earlier information you have derived. In other words, it is new information, independently acquired. And, finally, you will begin to perceive that an index of variability makes explicit an important phenomenon that you as a social researcher wish to explain or reduce: uncertainty. Variability, in a sense, is uncertainty. And it is uncertainty that we wish to account for.

ASSIGNMENT

Using grouped data, with categories v and frequencies n as follows:

1 Father's education (columns 32 and 33)
2 Father's income (columns 41 and 42)
3 Rating of university food service (column 72)
4 Rating of university bookstore (column 73)
5 Rating of university library (column 74)

calculate:

1 Sample variance s^2
2 Sample standard deviation s
3 z score for each category of the five variables

For variables 1, 3, 4, and 5, use category values. Assume the values are continuous.

THE LAB SESSION

Variability is not a particular index. It is a general term used to describe a number of different techniques which indicate the relative extent to which a set of data cluster together or spread apart. It is an indication of the distance along which a set of values may be found on the entire scale. The fact that we seek to describe meaningfully distances within a set of data suggests that we assume that our data are at least approximately measured on an interval scale. Although we may not always rigorously meet this criterion, social researchers have found that departures from this stringent requirement nevertheless may yield suggestive and fruitful results.

We will confine ourselves to four summary measures that describe the relative clustering or dispersion of a set of data: (1) the range, (2) the interquartile range, (3) the variance, and (4) the standard deviation. We will use the last-named dispersion measure to provide us with a means of making comparisons within a set of data. We will do this by calculating and utilizing what is known as a *standard score*.

The Range

The total range is the simplest and most straightforward index of variability. It indicates the range of values over which a set of observations occurs. It does this by finding the differences between the largest and smallest values among the observations, thereby revealing the minimum distance necessary to encompass all the observations in a set. The *range*, then, is defined simply as the highest value minus the lowest value:

Range = highest value − lowest value

Its major strength is the speed with which it may be calculated once the extreme values are known, providing a general picture of the total variability of a collection of data. It suffers from serious drawbacks, however. It is based on only two extreme values. Extreme values are often rare or unusual, and may not reflect those aspects of variability in which we are most interested. Second, the pattern of variation between the two extreme values is not described by the total range. The variability that is of more crucial research interest may not show up.

The Interquartile Range

Quartiles are the observations in a collection of observations which divide the distribution into four equal portions or quarters. A quartile indicates the distance between the observation lying at the 25th percentile and the observation lying at the 75th percentile.

The observation below which 25 percent of the cases lie is called the first quartile or Q_1. The observation below which 75 percent of the cases lie is called the third quartile or Q_3. (Q_2 is the median.) The interquartile range is the distance between the first and third quartiles:

$$Q = Q_3 - Q_1$$

The larger value Q_3 is listed first in the formula in order to keep the interquartile value positive.

Quartiles are calculated in a manner similar to the median. The analyst first divides the total frequency by 4, thereby obtaining the number of cases which are to be placed in each quartile of the distribution. Assuming that the data are displayed in grouped format, the analyst may obtain Q_1 by counting up to the category containing the 25th percentile value. As is the case when finding the precise value needed within an interval of continuous numbers, the analyst divides the additional needed observations that will equal the 25th percentile by the number of observations occurring in the interval. This answer is multiplied by the number of values the interval includes. This answer is added to the lower limit of the class interval, and the first quartile is obtained. We will illustrate this procedure by calculating Q_1, using the data taken from the previous lab session (see Table 9.1).

$$Q_1 = l_1 + \left(\frac{N/4 - cn}{n_1} \right) w_1$$

where l_1 = lower limit of category containing Q_1

Table 9.1   Number of Children in Family of Origin

Number of children	Frequency	Cumulative frequency
1	8	8
2	12	20
3	12	32
4	6	38
5	4	42
6	0	42
7	2	44
8	0	44
9	12	56
Total	56	

N = total number of observations with legal codes
cn = cumulative number of observations in the category immediately preceding category containing Q_1
n_1 = number of observations within the category in which Q_1 falls
w_1 = width of the category containing Q_1

$$Q_1 = 1.5 + \left(\frac{14 - 8}{12}\right) 1$$

$$= 1.5 + .5$$

$$= 2$$

Twenty-five percent of the respondents come from families that have 2.0 children or fewer.

The interquartile range is a range-type variability index based on the difference between two points in the distribution which are not located at either extreme of the distribution of values. The two points are sensitive to the basic concentration of the data, since they comprise the middle 50 percent of the observations. Since it avoids the extreme values of the distribution, it is less subject to fluctuation due to chance. Although it is not computed as simply as the range, this lack of simplicity is offset by the gain in sampling stability. Nevertheless this utilization of distance between two percentiles as an index of variability is not frequently used in the social sciences, since quartile deviation does not take into account all the available data. We will now turn to measures of variability that permit more precise interpretation of values occurring within a distribution and that will allow additional mathematical manipulations essential to statistical inference.

The Variance

Since many social phenomena, when measured, tend to cluster around a central area, social researchers often choose some norm or standard somewhere near the middle of that cluster to serve as a baseline for comparing the extent of scatter among a set of data. The central tendency index most frequently used as the norm is the arithmetic mean (unless the distribution is markedly skewed, and then the median is generally preferred). When such a strategy is chosen, data scatter may be fruitfully conceived as the deviation from the norm. Deviation, then, becomes the difference between an individual value and the average value of the entire collection of values. Such a procedure allows us to include every value in this assessment of data scatter. The symbol for deviation is x. The deviation from a norm such as the mean is written as:

$$x = X - \bar{X}$$

Persons who score below the mean receive a negative deviation score; persons who score above the mean receive a positive deviation score. Thus a deviation score represents a distance from the mean on a metric score scale. The sum of the positive and negative deviation values is zero:

$$\sum x = 0$$

If we wish to proceed in the same manner as we did in calculating the mean, then we need to sum the deviation scores and divide by the total number of observations in the set. We are prevented from doing this directly, however, since deviation scores from the mean sum to zero. We can surmount this problem in two ways. (1) We can ignore the negative signs and sum all deviation scores (take the absolute value of the deviation scores); or (2) we can eliminate the negative values by squaring each deviation score.

The second strategy is the most frequently chosen one. By adopting the second strategy of squaring deviations, we arrive at the variance and standard deviation.

The result obtained by summing the squared deviations from the mean is simply called the *sum of squares*, and is expressed as:

$$\sum x^2 = \sum (X - \bar{X})^2$$

Such a squaring procedure now underlines the wisdom in our choice of the mean as the norm for measuring the extent of data scatter. The mean, because it is the point of balance in a distribution, will give us the least amount of error. Given the condition that the deviations are squared, the position of the mean in the distribution of values is such that there is less distance between it and the most extreme score at either end of the distribution than is the case for any other value in the entire collection of data. Choosing the mean for our norm in measuring dispersion results in the least amount of error. Because of this, the strategy of using the mean to measure dispersion is called the *least-squares* solution.

The variance is an application of the least-squares solution. The *variance* describes the scatter of a set of data by calculating the average squared deviation from the mean. When applied to a population, it is symbolized by the Greek letter sigma (σ), and its formula is written as:

$$\sigma^2 = \frac{\sum (X - \mu)^2}{N} = \frac{\sum x^2}{N}$$

where μ is the mean, X is a score, and N is the total number of cases.

The variance is a special kind of mean. It is the mean of the squared deviation scores. It is therefore sometimes called the *mean-square deviation*. Because the variance is derived from squared deviations, it is an area measure rather than a linear measure. Its numerical solution is expressed as squared units on the original scale, that is, as a squared distance. It is, therefore, difficult to visualize and interpret it in everyday applied social research. Because of this, the standard deviation is more frequently used by social researchers.

The Standard Deviation

The standard deviation is simply the square root of the variance. By unsquaring the variance and expressing deviations in terms of the linear scale of the original data, we are able to interpret our findings more easily. When applied to a population, it is symbolized by the Greek letter sigma (σ), and its formula is written as:

$$\sigma = \sqrt{\frac{\sum (X - \mu)^2}{N}} = \sqrt{\frac{\sum x^2}{N}}$$

In theoretical statistics, the variance is more frequently utilized. In applied social research, however, the standard deviation is preferred. The two concepts are so closely related that we will now discuss some of the features they share.

Every Score Affects Their Value

The variance and standard deviation are the primary measures of variability. They are based on every value in the total collection of observations. Therefore, if any single value is changed, the numerical value of these indices will likewise change. If the distance between a particular value and the mean is increased, then the variance and the standard deviation will be larger than before. If the distance between a particular value and the mean is decreased, then the variance and the standard deviation will be smaller than before.

Effects of Squaring

The operation of squaring is a geometric computation that gives greater weight to values as they increase in magnitude. So extreme values that are the greatest distance from the mean will have the greatest weight in determining the size of the variance *and* the standard deviation. Even when we use the standard deviation, the disproportionate influence of extreme scores is still present. Thus a few extreme scores in a small sample can produce misleading results. In such an instance, it is advisable to choose the median for the norm or to use a range type of dispersion measure.

Sample Symbolization and Correction

Sometimes when the data we are using are drawn from considerably less than the total population of our theoretical interest, the sample variance and standard deviation formulas are used. They are represented as s^2 and s, respectively. The formula for the two variability indices are the same, except for a correction factor introduced into the denominator. We subtract 1 from the total sample size. This provides an adjustment for the sample size and results in an unbiased statistic (a value essentially equal to the one we expect to find in the population).

Raw Score Formula

A number of formulas may be derived from the initial expression:

$$s^2 = \frac{\sum (X - \bar{X})^2}{n - 1}$$

We recommend that you use the raw score formula:

$$s^2 = \frac{\sum X^2 - \frac{(\sum X)^2}{n}}{n - 1}$$

$$\text{and } s = \frac{\sqrt{\sum X^2 - \frac{(\sum X)^2}{n}}}{n - 1}$$

This raw score formula is not only quick and easy to use, but also allows greater accuracy since it does not involve rounding errors during the calculation process. Rounding errors are especially unavoidable when the deviation from the mean does not result in a whole number or a simple fraction.

Relationship to Central Tendency Measures

As stated in the section, "Objectives," measures of variability are new information. They cannot be deduced from a knowledge of central tendency. We will illustrate this independence of information by using two sets of data in which a constant is added to each value in the second data set. We shall see that the variances are equal, although the means are unequal:

X_1	X^2	$X_1 + k = X_2$		X^2
1	1	1 3	4	16
2	4	2 3	5	25
3	9	3 3	6	36
4	16	4 3	7	49
5	25	5 3	8	64
$\sum X = 15$	$\sum X^2 = 55$	$\sum X = 30$		$\sum X^2 = 190$
$\bar{X}_1 = 3$		$\bar{X}_2 = 6$		

We see that mean 2 is twice as large as mean 1, or $\bar{X}_2 = \bar{X}_1 + k$.

In order to show the independent effects of the mean when calculating the variance, we will use a different raw score formula:

$$\sigma_1^2 = \frac{\sum X^2}{N} - \mu^2 \qquad \sigma_2^2 = \frac{\sum X^2}{N} - \mu^2$$

$$= {}^{55}\!\!/_5 - (3)^2 \qquad = {}^{190}\!\!/_5 - (6)^2$$

$$= 11 - 9 \qquad\qquad = 38 - 36$$

$$= 2 \qquad\qquad\qquad = 2$$

and $\sigma_1 = \sqrt{2} = 1.44 \qquad \sigma_2 = \sqrt{2} = 1.44$

Thus we see that the means are unequal, but the variances and standard deviations are the same. We cannot, therefore, use either index to predict the other. Both pieces of information must be separately obtained.

We are now in a position to see the importance of the mean, variance, and standard deviation in comparing our data and interpreting our findings.

Standard Score

Standard scores or z scores provide a method to describe individual scores in relation to the group. Their use is associated with a particular type of distribution known as the normal curve, so we will briefly discuss this first.

Many kinds of social phenomena assume a distribution resembling the normal curve, a mathematical function for which the area beneath it is precisely known. This curve has high utility. Many powerful statistical techniques are available for data analysis when this curve is applicable. For this reason, social researchers sometimes transform data (by means of logarithms, exponents, etc.) to fit this distribution.

The normal curve has only one central point which splits the population into two equal halves. This central point is the position where the mode, median, and mean are found. The area under each side of the curve can be partitioned by standard deviations. Therefore the proportion of area for any distance from the mean is known, that is, can be measured. Three standard deviations on either side of the mean include most of all the observations. The percentage of cases associated with each standard deviation may be shown for the normal curve as follows:

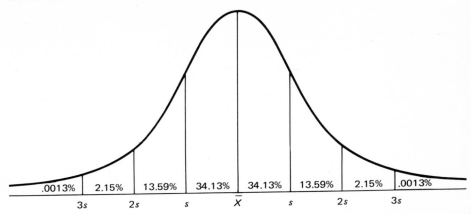

| .0013% | 2.15% | 13.59% | 34.13% | 34.13% | 13.59% | 2.15% | .0013% |

$$3s \qquad 2s \qquad s \qquad \bar{X} \qquad s \qquad 2s \qquad 3s$$

It can be seen that just over 68 percent of the cases lie within 1 standard deviation of either side of the mean. Two standard deviations on either side of the mean should include about 95 percent of all the cases.

When we know or assume that our data are distributed in approximately the form of the normal curve, then we are able to estimate (1) the extent to which our sample is representative of the population, (2) the extent to which our sampled observations deviate from the population average, and (3) the relative distance separating any two observations in the data set.

The last-named ability can be met by the standard score which indicates the relative deviation of the individual from the mean in terms of the standard deviation on the normal curve. The *standard score* is symbolized by z and is defined as the deviation of a value from the mean divided by the standard deviation. The formula is written:

$$z = \frac{X - \bar{X}}{s}$$

When we divide the deviation score by the value of the standard deviation, we are transforming the original value units into standard deviation units. This operation has the effect of setting the mean at zero, and each standard deviation at 1. The original shape of the distribution of X remains the same for the z scores.

The standard score provides us with an indication of the relative position of the individual and the distance of one individual from another. Since any z distribution has a mean of zero, a positive z score indicates it is above the mean, and a negative z score is below the mean. Thus a z score of .5 is ½ standard deviation above the mean. A z score of −1.5 is 1½ standard deviations below the mean. If one person has a z score of .5 and another person has a z score of 1.5, we know that both scores are above the mean, that one score is greater than another, and, in fact, that one score is 1 standard deviation greater than the other. When we consult a normal curve table, we see that the person with a z score of .5 has 69.15 percent of the people below him, and that the person with 1.5 has 93.62 percent of the people below her.

When converting to z scores, we have a new metric scale. z scores are valuable because they provide clarity in making comparisons among observations, are a convenient form for discussing findings, and have wide application.

One way to display the results obtained from z scores is shown below. They are from our questionnaire.

Attitude toward College Proportion Rounded from Mean

	v	x	$z = x/s$	Percent from mean	Percent ahead	Percent behind
Good	1	−3	−2.016	−.4783	97.83	2.17
	2	−2	−1.344	−.4099	90.99	9.01
	3	−1	−0.672	−.2486	74.86	25.14
Neutral	4	0	0	0	50.00	50.00
	5	1	0.672	.2486	25.14	74.86
	6	2	1.344	.4099	9.01	90.99
Bad	7	3	2.016	.4783	2.17	99.83

Keep in mind that the normal curve is composed of two equal halves, and that the normal curve table gives you only area proportions for one-half of the total area. This means you must note the sign associated with the z score. This will tell you, when calculating relative distances of two observations from each other, whether the 50 percent of the area belonging to the other half of the total curve will be added or subtracted from the percentage or proportion you are finding.

We have now developed an acquaintance with and facility for calculating a group of summary measures, especially the mean and the standard deviation. We are now ready to move into the second stage of data analysis. We will use statistical inference to make statements about the population on the basis of the data from the sample when particular sampling methods are used (e.g., random). Statistical inference will also enable us to test ideas of hypotheses about the population values when we have some already developed theory. That is, we will engage in hypothesis testing. This is our task in the next session.

Chapter 10

Introduction to Statistical Inference: *t* Test

INTRODUCTION

An important objective of the scientific method is the formulation, by means of explicit procedures in the face of uncertain conditions, of a general statement existing among the widest possible variety of phenomena. The phenomena about which social and behavioral scientists seek to make statements often consist of far more elements than they are practically able to observe. They are forced to study some portion (the sample) of the total cases (the population) and then draw conclusions on the basis of evidence derived from the sample, which are applicable to the entire population of interest. The goal, then, is to observe a sample in order to obtain an accurate estimate of the actual or true value in the population. An estimate becomes an inference when the value—obtained from observed cases assumed to possess characteristics similar to those of the larger group of unobserved cases—is applied to the population.

Such an inferential process presents the researcher with a problem: How accurate is the estimate, and how close is it to the actual population value?

OBJECTIVES

This lab session will introduce you to the procedures of assessing population values by means of statistical inference. For this purpose we will require an acquaintance with several important concepts and techniques.

1 Randomness and probability theory will be briefly discussed in order to illustrate their contribution to the construction of a theoretical distribution that may be mathematically described, particularly the standard normal curve.

2 The crucial role of the standard normal curve in hypothesis testing will be presented. This will involve such concepts as critical regions, levels of confidence, null and alternative hypotheses, and types of error.

3 Hypothesis testing when sample size is small will be illustrated by presenting a research problem and testing a hypothesis about a single mean by using a *t* test.

ASSIGNMENT

Familiarize yourself with the concepts and techniques of statistical inference. Be prepared to discuss them in class. The principles discussed in this session provide a foundation for more elaborate research endeavors in subsequent chapters.

THE LAB SESSION

A Quick Review

A major interest of social research is explaining why social phenomena behave, interact, and change as they do. This means that we are often interested in a large group of elements that share similar characteristics. Such a group is called a *population*. A population, you will recall, consists of all the cases that have one or more common characteristics. These cases may be people or objects. A characteristic describing the population is called a *parameter*. A sample is a part of the whole group of cases and is collected or selected in order to make statements or draw conclusions about the population from which it came. A characteristic describing the sample is called a *statistic*.

You will recall that in Chapter 6 we drew samples of varying sizes from a population of known parameters and compared the sample statistics with the population parameters. While engaged in this procedure we sought to ascertain the effects of sample size as a determinant of accurate estimation of population values. That exercise comprised an important part of the task of statistical inference. We learned at that time that inference from sample statistics to population parameters is more accurate when sample size is increased. Accuracy was also enhanced when we drew several samples and took their average as an estimate of the population value. We thereby achieved greater confidence that our sample statistics indeed represented the true value of the population. We will now look briefly at some of the theoretical underpinnings on which inference rests. We first look at probability theory and randomness.

Probability Theory

Probability theory provides us with a way of establishing the extent to which we risk being wrong when making a decision regarding the outcome of an event. Probability theory is based on a priori theoretical distributions rather than those we normally observe in everyday life. This means that probability theory is completely based on logical considerations of the nature of the random process. Therefore each event may be considered as equally likely, and no other source of variation need be considered—such as a worn coin or loaded dice. Despite its origins in the pure, unadulterated world of logic, probability theory furnishes the principles and procedures of statistical inference whereby we may know the characteristics of the theoretical distribution of a sample statistic, and thereby assess the extent to which the statistic is likely to represent the population parameter.

A probability is basically a proportion. Theoretically it is the proportion of times we may expect an outcome of an event to take place during an infinite number of occurrences that happen in the same way and under the same conditions.

For our purposes, there are two important rules or theorems of probability. The first is the rule of addition. A simple application of the addition rule states that the probability of either a heads (event A) or tails (event B) appearing on a single flip of a coin is $P(A) + P(B)$. Since there are only two possible outcomes that can occur in the single flip of a coin, and since we have in mind a hypothetical perfect coin, a perfect coin flipper, and a perfect surface on which the coin will land, the probability of the coin landing with the heads side up is one-half. The same applies to the tails side of the coin. We derive the probable occurrence of each outcome by placing in the numerator the number of times each outcome in which we are interested may occur, and by placing in the denominator the number of possible outcomes that can occur. In our example this is shown as:

$$\tfrac{1}{2} + \tfrac{1}{2} = 1.0$$

In general, the addition rule states that the probability of the occurrence of all outcomes is the sum of the probabilities associated with each outcome of interest. This rule has the further requirement that each possible outcome must be mutually exclusive. That is, if one outcome occurs, another outcome cannot occur. In our example the number of possible outcomes was two, heads or tails. They were mutually exclusive. If the coin landed with the heads side up, then the tails side could not also be up.

The second important rule of probability is the rule of multiplication. Using our hypothetical coin, coin flipper, and surface again, we are able to ascertain the probability of two or more events occurring jointly. One form of the multiplication rule states that the probability of heads (outcome A) appearing on the first flip of a coin followed by the probability of heads (outcome A) occurring on the second flip of the coin is $P(A)P(A)$. In this case the two outcomes are independent. The first outcome does not affect the outcome of the second. Heads *or* tails are as likely to occur on the second outcome as they were on the first event.

In both of these cases either heads or tails has an equal chance of appearing. Although we cannot know in advance what a particular outcome will be, we can determine the likelihood of any possible combination of occurrences when the coin is flipped any known number of times. This suggests that random occurrences can be displayed in a known pattern.

For example, suppose our hypothetical flipper tosses our hypothetical coin twice—just as she did before. This time we want to know the probabilities associated with every possible outcome. That is, we want to know how likely it is that in two flips of the coin the outcome will be two heads, one heads and one tails, and two tails. One of the ways we can obtain this information is to use the general binomial expression:

$$(p + q)^n$$

where p = probability of heads

q = probability that heads will not occur (i.e., that tails will occur instead)

n = number of times the event will be repeated

Since we want to know the probabilities associated with every possible outcome of two tosses $(n = 2)$ of our coin, we can write our expression as:

$$(p + q)^2$$
$$= (p + q)(p + q)$$
$$= p^2 + 2pq + q^2$$

This equation will give us the form of the probabilities when perfect randomness exists—that is, when each outcome has an equal chance of occurring every time the event occurs. In our case we know that heads is likely to occur one-half of the time. Likewise for tails. Applying the expansion of the binomial expression we have:

$$(½)^2 + 2(½)(½) + (½)^2$$
$$= ¼ + ½ + ¼$$

This tells us that the relative frequency with which two heads (p) will occur is ¼—or once every four times that two coins are flipped. One heads and one tails (pq) will occur once in every two occurrences in which two coins are tossed. Two tails (q) will occur once in every four occurrences in which two coins are flipped. Each of these probabilities holds under the condition of perfect randomness.

When we increase the number of coin flips, the number of possible outcomes also increases. If we decide to flip the coin ten times, the expression expands to:

$$(p + q)^{10}$$

$$= (p + q)(p + q)(p + q)(p + q)(p + q)(p + q)(p + q)(p + q)(p + q)$$

$$(p + q)$$

$$= p^{10} + 10p^9q + 45p^8q^2 + 120p^7q^3 + 210p^6q^4 + 252p^5q^5 + 210p^4q^6 + 120p^3q^7$$

$$+ 45p^2q^8 + 10pq^9 + q^{10}$$

$$= \frac{1 + 10 + 45 + 120 + 210 + 252 + 210 + 120 + 45 + 10 + 1}{1,024}$$

This expression informs us that there is one chance in 1,024 occurrences that ten coin flips will produce either all heads or all tails. (Keep in mind that ten coin flips constitute a single occurrence.) There are ten chances in 1,024 occurrences that the same side of the coin will appear nine times in ten flips. The most likely occurrence (252 chances in 1,024) is that ten flips of the coin will result in five heads and five tails. In order to grasp the probable outcomes of each possible combination of events, we can display the theoretical outcomes in the following table:

Number of heads	Probability ($p = .5$)
0	$1/1024 = .001$
1	$10/1024 = .010$
2	$45/1024 = .044$
3	$120/1024 = .117$
4	$210/1024 = .205$
5	$252/1024 = .246$
6	$210/1024 = .205$
7	$120/1024 = .117$
8	$45/1024 = .044$
9	$10/1024 = .010$
10	$1/1024 = .001$

We can readily see from the above table that about 65 percent of the time we may expect an equal or nearly equal number of heads and tails to occur. You may recall from the last chapter in the discussion of standard scores and the standard normal curve that the occurrence of certain values 65 percent of the time is very close to the values we expect to obtain in the normal curve about 68 percent of the time when they are no farther than $\pm\sigma$ from the mean. The similarities between our theoretical distribution and the normal curve can be readily seen when we plot the frequencies with which we expect each possible set of outcomes to occur. When we do this we obtain the results shown in Figure 10.1.

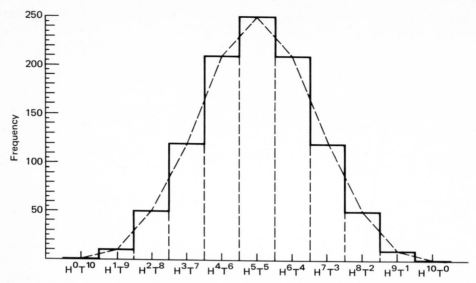

Figure 10.1   The histogram and frequency polygon of theoretical frequencies of heads and tails of 10 coins tossed 100 times. (*From Kenneth R. Hamond and James E. Householder*, Introduction to the Statistical Method, *Knopf, New York, 1962. Used by permission of the publisher.*)

The midpoints of the histogram have been joined. The resulting frequency polygon is remarkably similar to the standard normal curve. This is no accident. The more we increase the number of coin flips which constitute a single set, the more closely the expected outcomes resemble the normal curve. This fact highlights the relationship between concrete random events and a mathematical function. Because a large number of random events may be described by a specified number of theoretical outcomes whose frequency is known, we are able to use this theoretical knowledge to make statements about the confidence we have that the values we randomly obtain from a portion of the population resemble the values that exist in the population as a whole. Let us therefore turn to one of these theoretical distributions and look at a few of its salient features.

Sampling Distributions of the Mean

The theoretical distribution provides us with two important concepts based on logic and procedures of the probability distributions which may be derived by means of the binomial expression. The first is known as the *central-limit theorem*. Stated in terms of its practical implications for our research, the theorem tells us that, if a large number of random samples is drawn from a population, then the sample statistic (e.g., the mean) will usually be distributed normally when all the means are plotted in the form of a histogram or frequency polygon with a mean equal to the population mean and a variance equal to σ^2/N. This distribution, in the case of sample means, is called the *sampling distribution* of the mean. Furthermore, the mean of this distribution of means will be identical or nearly identical to the mean of the population. Applying our knowledge about normal distributions, we know that about 68 percent of these sample means will lie $\pm\sigma$ from the true mean. Thus any sample mean randomly obtained is more likely than not to represent a value resembling the true population value.

The second characteristic of the theoretical distribution of means is closely related to the first. It is called the *law of large numbers*. Essentially, it states that the larger the sample size, the more closely the statistic shall resemble the parameter value of the population, regardless of the shape of the distribution from which the samples were drawn. Thus, the larger the sample size, the greater our confidence that the sample value will represent the actual population value.

The formula for calculating the standard deviation of the random sampling distribution of means is

$$\sigma_{\bar{x}} = \frac{\sigma}{\sqrt{n}}$$

where $\sigma_{\bar{x}}$ = standard error of the mean
  σ = standard deviation of the population
  n = sample size

The formula is called the standard error of the mean. The variance of the sampling distribution of the mean $\sigma_{\bar{x}}^2$ is approximately equal to the variance of the population divided by n (the sample size): σ^2/n.

When we deal with randomly drawn samples of large size (e.g., 100 or more), we assume that the sampling distribution of the mean approximates the normal curve. Since the sampling distribution has a mean approximating the population mean, we utilize the normally distributed curve in estimating the extent to which the sample is representative of the population and the sample observations deviate from the population average.

The normal curve is an important mathematical distribution by which we can determine the probability that any given random event will occur. Before we apply a derivative of the normal curve to a hypothetical problem, let us make explicit a few observations regarding the concept of randomness.

Randomness

As we have already noted, a series of occurrences may be considered as random when one event does not affect subsequent ones. This was our definition of independence. Another important characteristic associated with randomness is that each member of the set or population has an equally likely chance of occurring.

The fulfillment of these two conditions is crucial for statistical inference. When they are met, we are then able to generalize the findings of our sample to a specific population with a known degree of risk of error. We are also able to utilize the rules of probability when our sample has been selected by random procedures. We did exactly this during our lab session as described in Chapter 6.

Hypothesis Testing

The availability of the sampling distribution provides a theoretical distribution whose area is virtually completely known. This provides us with a means to utilize statistical tests in research. The purpose of research is to determine whether hypotheses derived from theory or suggested by prior observations are acceptable or not. Data collected from observations provide information for making the decision of hypothesis acceptability.

Before data collection, we engage in a number of activities that facilitate the decision-making process. First, on the basis of our theory, we formulate a series of theoretical possibilities that could conceivably characterize the population of interest. We specify that one of these possibilities is true. We call this the statistical (null) hypothesis. The statistical hypothesis is a statement about an expected parameter value. Frequently the statistical hypothesis is formulated for the explicit purpose of being rejected (nullified). It is symbolized as H_0.

Suppose the chairman of an Anthropology department knows that the grade point average of students majoring in Anthropology is 2.9. He suspects that the department's majors who are specializing in Physical Anthropology have scores superior to this since they have taken additional courses in math and science. The chairman reasons that persons who take additional courses in these areas are academically superior students. In order to test his impressions, he states his null hypothesis as H_0: $\mu_{A_1} = 2.9$. He states his theoretical hypothesis as H_A: $\mu > 2.9$. In order to account for the possibility that Physical Anthropology majors who have taken a number of courses in science and math are also the students who receive the lowest grades in these courses, the chairman adds an additional alternative hypothesis, H_A': $\mu < 2.9$. A test of the null hypothesis (namely, H_0: $\mu_{A_1} = \mu_{A_2}$, where A_1 = Physical Anthropology majors and A_2 = all other anthropology majors) can result in information indicating whether Physical Anthropology majors are academically equivalent, superior, or inferior to students who major in other facets of Anthropology. Whatever the outcome, he has stated in advance of data collection that he expects the null hypothesis that Physical Anthropology majors achieve the same grade point average as other Anthropology majors. When the obtained value is greater than the expected value (2.9), and it is noted that this difference is extremely rare on the basis of chance alone, then the chairman may decide to take the risk in accepting the theoretical hypothesis that indeed the difference observed is due to the intrinsic academic superiority of the Physical Anthropology majors to other majors.

Let us test the null hypothesis for the chairman. Since we are short of time available to help the chairman, let us set the sample size of Physical Anthropology majors to be drawn at 25. The null hypothesis and the sample size we set will determine the sampling distribution of the statistic. We are now in a position to specify the level of significance which will inform us whether the obtained value a propos the null hypothesis is probable or improbable.

The level of significance specifies how much risk we are willing to take that our conclusions are wrong. The level of significance refers to a small portion of the area on either one end or both ends of a sampling distribution. If the sample value falls within this small area, we will consider it an improbable statistic and therefore reject the null hypothesis and accept the appropriate alternative hypothesis as a credible theoretical statement. Because these areas provide an objective means of rejecting H_0, we refer to them as the critical areas of rejection. Social researchers often select either 5 percent (.05 level) or 1 percent (.01 level) of the extreme areas of the distribution as reasonable cause for rejecting the null hypothesis. These small areas specifying the level of significance are symbolized as α. To set $\alpha = .05$ means that we are willing to bet that, 95 times out of 100, the obtained values will reflect true parameter characteristics, and that we will be wrong 5 times out of 100. When we recognize that a value may occur in either direction of the value we hypothesize, we use both tails of the distribution. When we use both tails of the distribution, the .05 level is 1.96 standard deviations to the left and to the right of the mean. The statistical test is a conservative one. It allows only the presence of extreme values to be used as evidence of real parameter differences not attributable to chance alone.

Setting the significance level plays a crucial role in our likelihood of making an erroneous decision regarding the acceptance or rejection of the null hypothesis. Thus if we set α too high (e.g., .10 or .20), then we increase the probability that we will reject a true null hypothesis. We are thereby more likely to call something different when it really is not. You will recall that, when we sample, we seldom obtain the same results each time. We expect most random samples to provide us with values relatively close to the center of the distribution and therefore to represent the true population value. We expect to draw a few random samples that will approximate values which lie in the extreme tails of the distribution. When we draw one of these extreme values, we may say it is a value that represents a different population when it does not. This is called a *type I error*— to reject the null hypothesis when it is true. The higher the α, the more likely we are to make a type I error.

Conversely, if we select a very low significance level (for example, .01 or .001), we increase the probability that we will not find differences even when they are there. This is a *type II error.*

As we have mentioned, the .05 and .01 levels of significance are most often selected in social research. In order to test the hypothesis advanced by the Anthropology chairman we will choose the .05 level of significance.

t Distributions

Since we have decided to randomly select 25 Physical Anthropology majors, we should acquaint ourselves with the *t* distribution. When we deal with small sample sizes and the population variance is not known (which is often the case), then we need to resort to another set of distributions known as the t distributions. The t test provides us with a way of handling two difficult problems: small sample size and an unknown standard deviation. We have seen that sample estimates introduce error into the inference process and that amount of error is a function of sample size; the smaller the sample size, the greater the likelihood of error. Similarly, when the population standard deviation is unknown, we are unable to calculate directly the standard error of the mean. We must estimate it on the basis of sample data.

The t distribution is similar in certain ways to a normal distribution (Chapter 9). It has a symmetric shape, a single peak, and a mean of zero. The t distribution differs from the normal distribution in certain respects. It has more of its area in the tails of the distribution. Because of this, the standard deviation is larger. For the normal distribution, 95 percent of the area is encompassed within 1.96 standard deviations; for the t distributions the same areal proportion requires a greater number than 1.96.

The t distribution, unlike the normal distribution, has a different shape for each sample size or, more exactly, for each degree of freedom. The *degrees of freedom* are the number of values that are free to vary under the condition that some minimum number of values is fixed. Under the particular constraints with which we are dealing, $n - 1$ will give us the degrees of freedom. As the degrees of freedom drop below 100, the t distribution undergoes changes in shape, becoming increasingly different from a normal distribution. The formula for obtaining the t value when testing a hypothesis about a single mean is:

$$t = \frac{\bar{X} - \mu}{s_{\bar{X}}}$$

where $s_{\bar{X}} = s_x / \sqrt{n - 1}$

Applying this formula to our chairman's problem requires a knowledge of the mean and standard deviation of our sample. We find that our random sample of 25 Physical Anthropology students had a grade point average of 3.1 and a standard deviation of .5. We want to find out if a grade point average of 3.1 obtained by our sample of students is significantly different from what might be expected by chance alone from a population whose grade point average is 2.9. Using our formula for the t test about a single mean, we find:

$$t = \frac{3.1 - 2.9}{.5/\sqrt{25}} = \frac{.2}{.1} = 2.00$$

Our t value is 2 standard deviations from the mean. In order to determine whether this value lies in the critical region at the .05 level or lower, we need to check the distribution of t with 24 degrees of freedom $(25 - 1)$. This is available to us in Table A.4. We find that the critical value is 2.064. Our obtained value is less than this. We therefore retain the null hypothesis and conclude that the difference between the grade point average of Physical Anthropology majors and that of other Anthropology majors is not significant.

It may be seen that t distributions allow us to estimate with a known degree of risk of error whether an obtained sample value significantly differs from other sample or population values. It is particularly useful with small sample sizes and an unknown population standard deviation σ. There are other nonnormal sampling distributions such as F and χ^2. We will discuss these in subsequent chapters.

Cross-tabulation of Two Variables in Contingency Hypotheses

Variables do not exist by themselves as social phenomena, as would be expected from the discussion in the previous three chapters. Rather, the empirical characteristics of a social phenomenon occur in patterns of relationships among variables. Thus, the distribution of values of a single variable is usually associated with the distribution of values of other variables. For example, the occupation held by an individual is associated with the educational level completed by the individual, the social life of an individual is affected by the maturity and appearance of the individual, the grades received by an individual are affected by the individual's ability to study class material, etc. This interrelated nature of the characteristics of social phenomena leads to the subsequent step in data analysis—the analysis of the relationship between distributions of values of two or more variables. Instead of analyzing the distribution of values of a single variable as has been done in the previous three chapters, from this point forward, distributions of values of a single variable are analyzed in relation to the distributions of values of other variables.

Cross-tabulation and the Types of Hypotheses

In discussing the distribution of values of a single variable, a range of possible values was specified and an analysis performed. For example, for the variable "race," two possible values can be discussed: "white" and "nonwhite." An analysis of this variable would then consist of observing samples from a population in order to determine the frequency with which "white" occurs and the frequency with "nonwhite" occurs. Similarly, an analysis of the variable "sex" would seek the frequency with which "male" occurs and the frequency with which "female" occurs. A cross-tabulation of the two variables "race" and "sex" presents the frequency with which each combination of possible values occurs. In this example there are four combinations of possible values: "white-male," "white-female," "nonwhite-male," and "nonwhite-female." In essence therefore, a cross-tabulation of two variables presents the frequency or probability with which joint occurrences of the possible values of the variables have been, or should be, observed.

Joint occurrence: The simultaneous observation of values of different variables or empirical events together.

For example, consider the two variables discussed above and the population of the United States in 1820. An analysis of the two variables would present the frequency count for each value of the variables and the percent of all observations which had that value (frequencies are given in thousands of persons):

RACE			SEX		
Value	Frequency	Percent	Value	Frequency	Percent
White	7,867	81.6	Male	4,897	50.8
Nonwhite	1,772	18.4	Female	4,742	49.2
Total	9,639	100.0	Total	9,639	100.0

The cross-tabulation of the two variables then presents the frequency for each combination of the possible values and the precent of all observations which had that combination of values (again, frequencies are given in thousands of persons):

CROSS-TABULATION OF RACE AND SEX IN 1820

Joint Occurrence of Values	Frequency	Percent
White-male	3,998	41.5
White-female	3.869	40.1
Nonwhite-male	899	9.3
Nonwhite-female	873	9.1
Total	9,639	100.0

Notice that the total number of observations is constant for both the one- and the two-variable analysis, but the distribution of observations is considered in a different perspective in a two-variable analysis. A two-variable analysis is based on the frequencies of the joint occurrence of values of different variables, and an analysis of a single variable is based on the frequencies of the occurrence of values of a single variable.

A preferred manner of presenting a cross-tabulation is to combine a one- or two-variable analysis into a single table of squares. The rows of the table correspond to the possible values of one variable (traditionally this is the dependent variable when such a distinction is applicable) and the columns of the table correspond to the possible values of the second variable (the independent variable). The squares where a row meets a column are described as the *cells* of the table. For each possible joint occurrence of values between the two variables there will be one cell in the table. The frequency with which a joint occurrence of values is observed will then appear in the cell of the table corresponding to that joint occurrence. Table 11.1 presents the logical form of the rows, columns, and cells for the example data given above. Table 11.2 presents the cross-tabulation and univariate distributions of the example data.

There are four cells in Tables 11.1 and 11.2, corresponding to the four combinations of possible values for the two variables "race" and "sex." Notice that, in the table presentation of a cross-tabulation (Table 11.2), the two-variable analysis appears in the cells of the table, and the one-variable analysis for each variable appears in the margins of the table. The row margins (marginals) correspond to the frequencies with which the values of the variable (race in this case) distributed over the rows of the table are observed. The column marginals correspond to the frequencies with which the values of the variable (sex in this case) distributed over the columns of the table are observed. Notice further that each column of frequencies and percentages in the cells of the table adds up to the frequency and percentage in the column marginal (e.g., 3,998 + 899 = 4,897, and 3,869 + 873 = 4,742). Similarly, each row of frequencies and

Table 11.1   Cells in a Cross-tabulation of the Variable "Race" versus the Variable "Sex"

RACE	SEX		
	Male	Female	Row marginals
White	f_{11} Frequency of joint observation of white males	f_{12} Frequency of joint observation of white females	$f_{1.} = f_{11} + f_{12}$
Nonwhite	f_{21} Frequency of joint observation of nonwhite males	f_{22} Frequency of joint observation of nonwhite females	$f_{2.} = f_{21} + f_{22}$
Column			Total
marginals	$f_{.1} = f_{11} + f_{21}$	$f_{.2} = f_{12} + f_{22}$	$N = f_{.1} + f_{.2}$ $N = f_{1.} + f_{2.}$

Table 11.2   Cross-tabulation of the Variable "Race" versus the Variable "Sex" for the United States in 1820.*

RACE	SEX		
	Male	Female	Row marginals
White	3,998 (41.5%)	3,869 (40.1%)	7,867 (81.6%)
Nonwhite	899 (9.3%)	873 (9.1%)	1,772 (18.4%)
Column marginals	4,897 (50.8%)	4,742 (49.2%)	Total 9,639 (100%)

* Frequencies are in thousands of persons.

(*Source: Historical Statistics of the United States, Colonial Times to 1957*, Bureau of the Census.)

percentages in the cells of the table adds up to the frequency and percentage in the row marginal (e.g., $3,998 + 3,869 = 7,867$ and $899 + 873 = 1,772$). Both the sum of the row marginals and the sum of the column marginals equal the same value. The sum of frequencies equals the total number of observations and the sum of percentages equals 100 percent.

There is a standard use of subscripts corresponding to the rows and columns of a table. Let f_{ij} refer to the frequency with which the joint occurrence of the ith value of the row variable and the jth value of the column variable is observed in a sample of observations. The first subscript associated with f always refers to the row of a table. The second subscript associated with f always refers to the column of a table. In the interest of simplicity in this volume i will always refer to the row and be the first subscript, and j will always refer to the column and be the second subscript. As an illustration, in Table 11.2, $f_{11} = 3,998$, $f_{12} = 3,869$, $f_{21} = 899$, and $f_{22} = 873$.

In the process of social research, we are usually interested in determining the extent to which the percentages in a cross-tabulation of data obtained from a sample of respondents correspond to the true percentages (parameter values) in the population from which the sample of respondents came or to the percentages predicted from a theory. Thus, the hypothesis-testing procedure involving a cross-tabulation of two or more variables compares the observed data such as those in Table 11.2 and the expected data deduced from a theory or population. How does one find the expected data?

The expected data represent the deduced percentages or frequencies for a cross-tabulation, which the theorist in fact wishes to reject. For example, if the theorist is proposing that there were more males among the white population than among the black population in the United States in 1820, then, one way to support such a proposition is to provide evidence to show that the null hypothesis that there were just as many males among the black population as among the white population should be rejected. In the testing, then, the procedure is to reject a null hypothesis so that a proposed (theoretical) hypothesis may receive greater credibility.

The expected frequencies and percentages deduced from the null hypothesis (for example, that there were just as many males among the black population as among the white population) are then compared with the observed frequencies and percentages. If the discrepancies between the expected and observed frequencies and percentages are substantial, then one claims that the theoretical hypothesis proposed (that there were more males among the white population than among the black population) gains credibility. On the other hand, if the discrepancies between the expected and observed frequencies and percentages are small, then one admits that there is little or no evidence to support such a theoretical hypothesis and the null hypothesis (that there were just as many males among the black population as among the white population) cannot be rejected.

The task at hand, then, is that a theoretical hypothesis proposed by the theorist is to be tested by a comparison between (1) the observed data in a cross-tabulation, and (2) the deduced data from a null hypothesis. The theoretical hypothesis tested in a cross-tabulation format is called *a contingency hypothesis which specifies the likelihood of occurrence of one category of a variable, given the occurrence of one category of another variable.* For example, one contingency hypothesis may be that given the one value of race, white, we would predict more males as compared with the other value of race, black.

For contingency hypotheses, this comparison of observed and deduced data conditions is accomplished through the use of the chi-square statistic (χ^2). The *chi-square statistic* (χ^2) is a probability measure of the significance of the lack of fit between deduced data and observed data. The use of the chi-square statistic assumes that the observed cases in the sample have been randomly selected from the population of cases.

While the common practice in social research seems to imply that a null hypothesis indicates *no* relationship between variables under study, there are in fact three possible types of null hypotheses which can help test a contingency hypothesis. The decision as to which null hypothesis to use depends on the amount of knowledge about the population and the theory available to the theorist. The three types of null hypotheses are: (1) that the probability or likelihood of a joint occurrence is the same for all cells in a cross-tabulation, (2) that the probability or likelihood of a joint occurrence in a cell is proportionate to the frequencies or percentages of the marginals of the two values of the variables defining that particular cell, and (3) that the probability or likelihood of a joint occurrence in a cell is set a priori by the theorist. Let us elaborate the three types of null hypotheses with the sample data in Table 11.2.

The first type of null hypotheses, independence (equal-probability) of all joint occurrences would suggest that there should be equal numbers of cases appearing in each and every cell in the cross-tabulation. Thus, the frequencies of white-male, white-female, nonwhite-male, and nonwhite-female should all be approximately the same. This null hypothesis is used when the theorist has no knowledge whatsoever about the frequencies or percentages of race and sex in the population and no prior theory would lead to one to suspect any different patterns. Rejection of this null hypothesis lends credibility to the contingency hypothesis that not all joint occurrences in a cross-tabulation are equally likely.

The second type of null hypothesis, probability of each joint occurrence proportionate to the marginals, would suggest that the frequency or percentage of cases in each cell depends on the frequencies or percentages of the values of the variables involved in the identification of the cell. In other words, there is no interaction between the two variables. For example, to predict the frequency or percentage of white-male cases, one can take into account the frequencies or percentages of whites and males relative to the total number of cases. Thus, the fact that 82 percent of the cases were white (the first row marginal) and 51 percent male (the first column marginal) should allow one to predict that the percentage of white-male cases should be some average of the two marginal percentages. This null hypothesis should be formulated when the theorist has the knowledge about the frequencies or percentages of the values for each and every variable involved in the cross-tabulation. Because of the knowledge about the marginals, predictions tend to improve (especially when the distributions of the marginals deviate from the 50–50 split as was the case with the race variable where there were 82 percent whites and 18 percent nonwhites). Rejection of this null hypothesis lends credibility to the contingency hypothesis that there is some interaction between the variables.

The third type of null hypothesis, a priori probability of a joint occurrence, is set when the theorist, informed either by previous research or theory, makes a precise prediction of what a frequency or percentage should be for a given cell. This null hypothesis is made when the theorist has knowledge not only about the marginals but about previous research and theory and, therefore, is also the most precise. Rejection of this null hypothesis improves further the predicted probability of a joint occurrence, as the range of such possible probabilities is now narrowed.

The exercise to be followed will describe the testing of a contingency hypothesis with the use of each of the three types of null hypothesis.

OBJECTIVES

1   To introduce the idea of cross-tabulation as discussed above.
2   To familiarize you with the use of the chi-square statistic for assessing the adequacy of a contingency (theoretical) hypothesis proposed.

3 To emphasize that the assessment of a theoretical hypothesis will vary depending on what deduced data from a null hypothesis are compared with observed data. In other words, a single theoretical hypothesis can be assessed as poor by one theorist and assessed as adequate by another theorist if each theorist bases his or her assessment on different deduced data from different null hypotheses.

ASSIGNMENT

Using the example of observed frequencies of cross-tabulations given out at the beginning of the lab session and the predicted percentages given with each table on the forms at the end of the chapter, for each of the three assigned cross-tabulations:

1 Compute expected frequencies F_{ij} for each of the three types of null hypotheses using equations (11.2), (11.3), and (11.4).

2 Compute the chi-square statistic for each of the three types of null hypotheses using equation (11.1).

3 Compute the degrees of freedom associated with each of the three types of null hypotheses conditions using equations (11.5) and (11.6).

4 Decide (using the chi-square values in Table A.3), if the observed data are significantly different from each of the deduced data, i.e., decide if the observed frequencies are significantly different from the expected frequencies of a null hypothesis (use the .05 level of significance).

5 Based on your analysis, decide which of the three deduced empirical conditions is the most accurate description of the observed empirical conditions and justify your decision.

You will hand in the four assignment sheets at the end of the chapter.

THE LAB SESSION

The lab session will be spent completing as much of the assignment as possible given the time restrictions. The forthcoming discussion, to guide you through the lab session, is broken into sections corresponding to the five aspects of the assignment given above: (1) computing expected frequencies, (2) computing the chi-square statistic, (3) computing degrees of freedom, (4) decisions regarding the significance of the chi-square statistic, and (5) evaluation of the three types of hypotheses. Naturally, the whole assignment cannot be completed in the lab session. However, the more prepared you are for the lab, the more of the assignment you will be able to complete during the lab session. Three cross-tabulations are due as an assignment. The first one is based on the data given previously in Table 11.2. These data will be analyzed during the lab session. The other two cross-tabulations are based on the class data.

The Example of Observed Frequencies

At the end of this chapter are three assignment sheets corresponding to the three assigned cross-tabulations. Take out the first of these assignment sheets (both pages) and copy the cross-tabulation of the observed frequencies given in Table 11.2 into the table at the top of sheet no. 1. Your lab instructor will give you the observed frequencies for the tables on assignment sheets no. 2 and no. 3. Be careful to put the observed frequencies in the correct positions in the tables.

In order to check that you have copied the data correctly and that the lab instructor has not made a mistake, compute row and column marginals. Now add up the row marginals to see if they sum to N. Similarly add up the column marginals to see if they sum to N. This is a quick method of checking the accuracy of the frequencies presented in a cross-tabulation.

Computing Expected Frequencies for Each of the Three Types of Null Hypotheses

Let the symbol N refer to the total number of observations which constitute a sample of elements drawn randomly from a population. From the introduction, F_{ij} refers to the expected frequency in the cell where the ith row intersects with the jth column in a table. In other words, F_{ij} is the expected frequency deduced from a particular null hypothesis as the joint occurrence of the ith value of the row variable with the jth value of the column variable. A theorist never actually deduces a particular frequency of observations in a cell. Rather, a proportion of the total observations is deduced as expected to occur in a particular cell of a table. Let the symbol P_{ij} refer to the expected proportion of all the observations which will have the joint occurrence of the ith value of the row variable and the jth value of the column variable. The expected frequency F_{ij} can then be found as the product of the expected proportion and the number of observations in the sample of elements. For example, imagine that an individual proposes that there should be an equal number of males and females in the population. This means that 50 percent of the population should be male, and 50 percent of the population should be female. P_{male} then equals .50, and P_{female} then equals .50. If 50 persons are sampled from the population, we should observe 25 males and 25 females, since .50 times 50 equals 25. In general, expected frequencies are found from expected proportions:

$$F_{ij} = P_{ij}(N)$$

Expected Frequencies for the Null Hypothesis of the Independence of Joint Occurrences   The hypothesis of the independence of joint occurrences says that each and every combination of the possible values of both variables in a cross-tabulation has an equal chance of occurring. This is the same as saying that there are no relationships among any of the values in the cross-tabulation. This hypothesis, therefore, must be rejected if there is any pattern in the observation of values of the two variables.

Since the joint occurrence of each combination of values is independent of the other joint occurrences and therefore equally probable, each cell should have the same frequency as every other cell. The expected proportion of observations in any one cell will equal 1 over the number of possible cells. Let I refer to the number of possible values the row variable can assume, and let J refer to the number of possible values the column variable can assume. Then the expected frequencies under this hypothesis (using the above relation between expected proportion and expected frequency), can be found with equation (11.1):

$$F_{ij} = P_{ij}(N)$$

$$= \frac{1}{(I)(J)} N \tag{11.1}$$

For example, consider your list of expected frequencies on sheet no. 1, the F_{ij}. From looking at Table 11.1, we can see that I equals 2 (white, nonwhite) and J equals 2 (male, female). Thus, the proportion for every cell equals .25 ($\frac{1}{2} \cdot 2$). Since the total number of observations (given in thousands) is 9,639, the F_{ij} can be computed from equation (11.1). Make this computation and write the expected frequencies on the first table on sheet no. 1.

Expected Frequencies for the Null Hypothesis of No Interaction Between the two Variables   This hypothesis says that there is no relationship between the two variables. The computation of expected proportions for this hypothesis is more complicated than for the previous hypothesis. However, expected frequencies are still computed as the product of expected proportion and N.

It was pointed out in connection with Tables 11.1 and 11.2 that the sum of the row frequencies equals the marginal frequency for the row, and the same applies to the column frequencies summing to the marginal frequency for the column. In the common notation for marginal frequencies one of the subscripts of f_{ij} is replaced with a dot corresponding to the summed frequencies. For example, the sum of frequencies in row 1 is indicated by $f_{1.}$ which shows that f_{11} and f_{12} have been added together. The symbol $f_{1.}$ then refers to the marginal frequency for row 1. Column marginal frequencies are referred to in the same fashion. For example, in Table 11.1, the symbol $f_{.1}$ refers to the sum of f_{11} and f_{21} and therefore equals the column marginal frequency for column 1.

If the null hypothesis of no interaction between the two variables is accurate, then it can be deduced that the expected proportion of all observations which should appear in cell i,j will equal the product of the proportion of N which had value i on the row variable and the proportion of N which had value j on the column variable. If the above notation for marginal frequencies is used, P_{ij} for this hypothesis can be computed:

$$P_{ij} = \left(\frac{f_{i.}}{N}\right)\left(\frac{f_{.j}}{N}\right)$$

so that the expected frequencies under this hypothesis can be computed from equation (11.2) :[1]

$$F_{ij} = P_{ij}(N)$$

$$= \left[\frac{f_{i.}}{N}\right]\left[\frac{f_{.j}}{N}\right](N) \tag{11.2}$$

For example, consider the list of expected frequencies in the second table on sheet no. 1. The row marginals and column marginals for the data are given in Table 11.2. As an example computation, F_{11} will be computed. First, the row marginal for row 1 is 7,867. $f_{1.} = 7,867$. Second, the column marginal for column 1 is 4,897. $f_{.1} = 4,897$. N equals 9,639 (where frequencies are in thousands). With these three numbers the expected frequency for cell 1,1 can be computed from equation (11.2):

$$F_{11} = P_{11}(N)$$

$$= \frac{(7,867)}{9,639}\frac{(4,897)}{9,639}(9,639) = 3996.8$$

Now make the same calculation for the other three expected frequencies, F_{12}, F_{21}, and F_{22}.

Expected Frequencies for the Null Hypothesis of A Priori Predicted Probability of Joint Occurrence   In some cases of social research, the theorist will deduce exact probabilities for the observation of a joint occurrence. When he or she can do this for all the joint occurrences in a cross-tabulation, then the expected proportions, the P_{ij}, are given by the deduction, and expected frequencies can be computed very easily. The hypothesis of predicted probability of joint occurrence says that the observed frequencies are completely predictable from the theoretical structure and a knowledge of the number of cases in the sample.

If the P_{ij} are given by deduction, then the computation of expected frequencies is simply the product of P_{ij} and the number of observations N. This is given in equation (11.3):

$$F_{ij} = P_{ij}(N) \tag{11.3}$$

For example, imagine that a theoretical structure proposes that there was no change in the racial and sexual composition of the United States from 1820

---

[1] This equation is frequently presented in a simplified form which eliminates the two redundant N's so that equation (11.2) becomes:

$$F_{ij} = \frac{(f_{i.})\ (f_{.j})}{(N)}$$

The original form of equation (11.2) has been retained in order to emphasize the fact that a theorist deduces expected proportions from which expected frequencies are computed based on the number of observations in a sample. In actual practice there is no need for a shorthand computing formula, since the values of chi-square will be computed by a computer.

to 1900. The observed data for 1820 are given in Table 11.2. The proportions observed in each cell i,j in the year 1900 are given in the third table of sheet no. 1 under the column P_{ij}. For example, since P_{11} equals .45, we know that 45 percent of the population of the United States in 1900 was white and male. Using equation (11.3), the expected frequency F_{11} which we should observe in 1820 if there was no change in the racial and sexual composition from 1820 to 1900 can be computed:

$$F_{11} = P_{11}(N)$$

$$= .45(9,639) = 4337.6$$

In a similar fashion, compute the other expected frequencies for the third table of sheet no. 1, F_{12}, F_{21}, and F_{22}.

Computing the Value of Chi-Square

The chi-square statistic is computed in the same fashion for all three null hypotheses being considered in this lab session. The formula for the chi-square statistic is given in equation (11.4):

$$\chi^2 = \sum \left[\frac{\text{observed frequency in cell } i,j - \text{expected frequency in cell } i,j}{\text{expected frequency in cell } i,j} \right]$$

$$= \sum \left[\frac{(f_{ij} - F_{ij})^2}{F_{ij}} \right] \tag{11.4}$$

where f_{ij} = observed frequency in cell i,j
F_{ij} = expected frequency in cell i,j

$\sum$ indicates that the quantity $(f_{ij} - F_{ij})^2/F_{ij}$ should be summed over all cells in a cross-tabulation.

There are five steps in computing the value of chi square for a given hypothesis. The columns on the sheets for the assignment have been labeled and numbered according to their step in computation.

1   For each cell i,j, compute the expected frequency F_{ij}.
2   For each cell i,j, subtract the expected frequency from the observed frequency, $f_{ij} - F_{ij}$.
3   For each cell i,j, square the difference between the observed and the expected frequency, $(f_{ij} - F_{ij})^2$.
4   For each cell i,j, divide the squared difference from step 3 by the expected frequency, $(f_{ij} - F_{ij})^2/F_{ij}$.
5   Finally, sum the values computed in step 4 across all cells in the cross-tabulation. In reference to the forms for the assignment this means adding up the values in the fourth column of each table. The sum of the values computed in step 4 equals the chi-square statistic.

For the null hypothesis of the independence of joint occurrence on sheet no. 1 the above computations have already been finished. Check through the computations to verify that each of the above steps has been done as you understand it.

Now compute chi-square values for the other two contingency hypotheses on sheet no. 1. You have already completed step 1, since the expected frequencies for each hypothesis have been computed.

Computing the Degrees of Freedom Associated with Each Hypothesis

The magnitude of the value of the chi-square statistic tells the theorist how different the observed frequencies are from the expected frequencies. Just as there are observed and expected frequencies, there are observed and expected chi-square values associated with a proposed hypothesis. The chi-square value computed by equation (11.4) is the observed value of chi square. In order to determine the expected value of the chi-square statistic for a null hypothesis, the theorist needs to know the number of degrees of freedom associated with the hypothesis.

The degrees of freedom associated with a null hypothesis equals the number of cell frequencies which must be known in order to predict the remaining cell frequencies. In general terms, the degrees of freedom associated with a hypothesis equals the number of cells with observed data (empirical conditions) which must be known about the hypothesis before the remaining cells with observed data (empirical conditions) associated with the hypothesis can be predicted.

Degrees of freedom: The number of empirical conditions which must be known about a hypothesis before the remaining empirical conditions associated with the hypothesis can be predicted.

This concept of degrees of freedom is an important point which will come up frequently in the remainder of the volume as well as throughout your career if you go into any area dealing with research.

For example, the hypothesis of the independence of joint occurrences says that each combination of values of the two variables has an equal probability of occurring. Thus, since the sum of the cell frequencies must equal the total number of observations, the number of cell frequencies which must be known before all cell frequencies are known equals the total number of cells in the cross-tabulation minus 1. This is so because each cell can have any frequency except that, when all but one cell have a known frequency, the last cell in the table must equal N minus the sum of all the other cell frequencies. Therefore, for the hypothesis of the independence of joint occurrences, the degrees of freedom can be computed by equation (11.5):

$$df = IJ - 1 \qquad\qquad (11.5)$$

As given earlier, I refers to the number of values of the row variable, and J refers to the number of values of the column variable in the cross-tabulation.

Equation (11.5) also computes the degrees of freedom for the null hypothesis of a priori predicted probability of joint occurrences, since this third hypothesis to be considered in the lab session places the same number of restrictions on the cell frequencies as does the first hypothesis.

Since you know that I equals 2 for the example data in Table 11.2, and J equals 2 for the example data, compute the degrees of freedom associated with (1) the null hypothesis of the independence of joint occurrences and (2) the null hypothesis of a priori predicted probability of joint occurrences using equation (11.5). Write the appropriate number of degrees of freedom in the first and last tables of sheet no. 1.

The computation of degrees of freedom for the hypothesis of no interaction between the two variables follows the same logic as above but uses a different formula. This second null hypothesis to be considered in the lab session restricts only the marginal frequencies of a cross-tabulation. Thus, the sum of the row marginal frequencies must equal N, so that the degrees of freedom for the row marginals equals $I - 1$. Similarly, the sum of the column marginal frequencies must equal N, so that the degrees of freedom for the column marginals equals $J - 1$. Therefore the degrees of freedom for the cross-tabulation of the row and column variable will equal the product of the degrees of freedom for row and column marginals as given in equation (11.6):

$$df = (I - 1)(J - 1) \tag{11.6}$$

Now compute the degrees of freedom associated with the null hypothesis of no interaction between the two variables "race" and "sex" in the sample data and write the number in the appropriate place in the second table on sheet no. 1.

Deciding Whether or Not the Expected Frequencies Are Significantly Different from the Observed Frequencies

In order to decide whether or not the observed value of chi-square computed in equation (11.4) is actually significant, it must be compared to an expected value of chi-square given the number of degrees of freedom associated with the hypothesis being evaluated. In general, the larger the number of degrees of freedom associated with a hypothesis, the larger the expected value of chi-square (in other words, the larger the allowable difference will be between the observed and the expected cell frequencies). If the observed value of chi-square is larger than the expected value of chi-square, then the hypothesis is rejected as inadequate. If the observed value of chi-square is smaller than the expected value of chi-square, then the hypothesis being evaluated does not contradict and is compatible with the observed data.

In order to select the expected value of chi-square, a theorist must have two pieces of information. First, he or she must select a level of significance at which the proposed hypothesis will be tested. In the present discussion the level has been arbitrarily set at .05. This means that, in 5 percent of the observations of many samples of data, we would expect to observe no difference between the observed and expected frequencies under the null hypothesis being tested. Second, the theorist must know the degrees of freedom associated with the hypothesis. These were computed in the previous section.

If you turn to the table of chi-square values in the back of the volume (Table A.3), you will see that the table columns have levels of significance printed above them. Select the column with .05 above it, since we are considering only this level of significance for the present. At the extreme left of the table are given the degrees of freedom. Each row of expected values of chi-square is associated with a specific number of degrees of freedom. In order to select the expected value of chi-square associated with a hypothesis, locate the row corresponding to the degrees of freedom for the hypothesis and find the value given in the .05 column. For example, for the null hypothesis of the independence of joint occurrences being evaluated in reference to the observed frequencies given in Table 11.2, the degrees of freedom was 3. The expected value of chi-square for the hypothesis is therefore 7.82.

Now find the expected value of chi-square for the other two hypotheses and write the value in the appropriate places on sheet no. 1.

Compare the observed value of chi-square to the expected value of chi square. If the observed value is larger than the expected value, then the null hypothesis is rejected. The null hypothesis of the independence of joint occurrences is rejected for the 1820 data, since the observed chi-square equals 3,857.6 and the expected chi-square equals only 7.8. Therefore, a "yes" is written into the space asking if the null hypothesis is rejected. Now compare the observed and expected chi-square values for the other two null hypotheses and write a "yes" or a "no" in the space asking if the hypothesis should be rejected.

Evaluating Alternative Null Hypotheses and Interpretation

Take out assignment sheet no. 4 which appears at the end of this chapter. This assignment sheet is concerned with interpreting your previous work in the lab. At the beginning of the sheet are questions relevant to the example data.

First, if the null hypothesis of the independence of joint occurrences is rejected, then the theorist knows that there are some interactions among the values of the two variables. Otherwise the joint occurrences of the values would be independent. For the population data on the United States in 1820 we know that the hypothesis of the independence of joint occurrences is rejected, so the answer to the first question is "yes." You know it is "yes" because the null hypothesis was rejected.

Second, if the hypothesis of no interaction between the two variables is rejected, then the theorist knows that there is some form of relationship between the two variables. Use your comparison of the observed and expected chi-square values for the example data to answer question 2 on sheet no. 4. The third question refers to the hypothesis of predicted probabilities. Answer question 3 on sheet no. 4 just by following the same logic you used for question 2.

Last, the null hypothesis which is the most accurate description of the observed frequencies will be the hypothesis which has the smallest difference between the observed value of chi square and the expected value of chi square. Look at the three tables on sheet no. 1 and compare the differences between observed and expected chi square for each table. Write in the null hypothesis which has the smallest difference between observed and expected chi square as the answer to question 4 on sheet no. 4.

The four questions concerning the other two cross-tabulations will be answered in the same manner.

Assignment Sheet No. 1a

CONDUCTING SOCIAL RESEARCH

Chapter 11   Cross-tabulation of Two Variables in Contingency Hypothesis

Cross-tabulation of Race Versus Sex in United States in 1820

RACE   SEX

	Male	Female	$f_{i.}$
White			7,867
Nonwhite			1,772
$f_{.j}$	4,897	4,742	Total 9,639

(*Source: Historical Statistics of the United States, Colonial Times to 1957*, Bureau of the Census.)

FOR THE NULL HYPOTHESIS OF THE INDEPENDENCE OF JOINT OCCURRENCES:

CELLS	P_{ij}	F_{ij}	$f_{ij} - F_{ij}$	$(f_{ij} - F_{ij})^2$	$(f_{ij} - F_{ij})^2/F_{ij}$
	STEP 1		STEP 2	STEP 3	STEP 4
1,1	.25		−1588.2	2522379.2	1046.7
1,2	.25		−1459.2	2129264.6	883.6
2,1	.25		1510.8	2282516.6	947.2
2,2	.25		1536.8	2361754.2	980.1

$$\text{STEP } 5 = \text{observed chi-square} \quad \underline{3857.6}$$

Degrees of freedom _____   Expected chi-square $\underline{7.8}$

Hypothesis rejected? $\underline{\text{YES}}$

Assignment Sheet No. 1b

FOR THE NULL HYPOTHESIS OF NO INTERACTION BETWEEN THE TWO VARIABLES IN THE CROSS-TABULATION:

CELL	P_{ij}	F_{ij}	$f_{ij} - F_{ij}$	$(f_{ij} - F_{ij})^2$	$(f_{ij} - F_{ij})^2/F_{ij}$
		STEP 1	STEP 2	STEP 3	STEP 4
1,1	.41	3996.8			
1,2					
2,1					
2,2					

$$\text{STEP } 5 = \text{observed chi-square} \quad \text{_____}$$

Degrees of freedom _____   Expected chi-square   _____

Hypothesis rejected?   _____

FOR THE NULL HYPOTHESIS OF A PRIORI PREDICTED PROBABILITIES OF JOINT OCCURRENCES:

CELL	$P_{ij}*$	F_{ij}	$f_{ij} - F_{ij}$	$(f_{ij} - F_{ij})^2$	$(f_{ij} - F_{ij})^2/F_{ij}$
		STEP 1	STEP 2	STEP 3	STEP 4
1,1	.45	4337.6			
1,2	.43				
2,1	.06				
2,2	.06				

$$\text{STEP } 5 = \text{observed chi-square} \quad \text{_____}$$

Degrees of freedom _____   Expected chi-square   _____

Hypothesis rejected?   _____

* The predicted probabilities, i.e., the expected proportions P_{ij}, are based on data for the year 1900 *Historical Statistics of the United States, Colonial Times to 1957*, Bureau of the Census.

Assignment Sheet No. 2*a*

CONDUCTING SOCIAL RESEARCH

Chapter 11   Cross-tabulation of Two Variables in Contingency Hypotheses

Cross-tabulation of Race versus Sex for Class Data

RACE   SEX

	Male	Female	$f_i.$
White			
Nonwhite			
$f._j$			Total

FOR THE NULL HYPOTHESIS OF THE INDEPENDENCE OF JOINT OCCURRENCES:

CELL	P_{ij}	F_{ij}	$f_{ij} - F_{ij}$	$(f_{ij} - F_{ij})^2$	$(f_{ij} - F_{ij})^2/F_{ij}$
		STEP 1	STEP 2	STEP 3	STEP 4
1,1					
1,2					
2,1					
2,2					

STEP 5 = observed chi-square _____

Degrees of freedom _____   Expected chi-square _____

Hypothesis rejected? _____

Assignment Sheet No. 2*b*

FOR THE NULL HYPOTHESIS OF NO INTERACTION BETWEEN THE TWO VARIABLES IN THE CROSS-TABULATION:

CELL	P_{ij}	F_{ij}	$f_{ij} - F_{ij}$	$(f_{ij} - F_{ij})^2$	$(f_{ij} - F_{ij})^2/F_{ij}$
		STEP 1	STEP 2	STEP 3	STEP 4
1,1					
1,2					
2,1					
2,2					

STEP 5 = observed chi-square _____

Degrees of freedom _____   Expected chi-square _____

Hypothesis rejected? _____

FOR THE NULL HYPOTHESIS OF A PRIORI PREDICTED PROBABILITIES OF JOINT OCCURRENCES:

CELL	$P_{ij}*$	F_{ij}	$f_{ij} - F_{ij}$	$(f_{ij} - F_{ij})^2$	$(f_{ij} - F_{ij})^2/F_{ij}$
		STEP 1	STEP 2	STEP 3	STEP 4
1,1	.43				
1,2	.45				
2,1	.06				
2,2	.07				

STEP 5 = observed chi-square _____

Degrees of freedom _____   Expected chi-square _____

Hypothesis rejected? _____

* These predicted probabilities, i.e., expected proportions, are taken from *The Statistical Abstract of the United States for 1970*, Bureau of the Census. If your school recruits students from all races and sexes according to their distribution in the United States, and if social research appeals to all sexes and races similarly, this hypothesis should not be rejected.

Assignment Sheet No. 3a

CONDUCTING SOCIAL RESEARCH

Chapter 11   Cross-tabulation of Two Variables in Contingency Hypotheses

Cross-tabulation of Student Status versus Attitude toward School

ATTITUDE
TOWARD
SCHOOL   STUDENT STATUS

	Freshman/Sophomore	Junior/Senior	$f_i.$
Good			
Indifferent			
Bad			
$f._j$			Total

FOR THE NULL HYPOTHESIS OF THE INDEPENDENCE OF JOINT OCCURRENCES:

CELL	P_{ij}	F_{ij} STEP 1	$f_{ij} - F_{ij}$ STEP 2	$(f_{ij} - F_{ij})^2$ STEP 3	$(f_{ij} - F_{ij})^2/F_{ij}$ STEP 4
1,1					
1,2					
2,1					
2,2					
3,1					
3,2					

STEP 5 = observed chi-square _____

Degrees of freedom _____   Expected chi-square _____

Hypothesis rejected? _____

Assignment Sheet No. 3*b*

FOR THE NULL HYPOTHESIS OF NO INTERACTION BETWEEN THE TWO VARIABLES IN THE CROSS-TABULATION:

CELL	P_{ij}	F_{ij} STEP 1	$f_{ij} - F_{ij}$ STEP 2	$(f_{ij} - F_{ij})^2$ STEP 3	$(f_{ij} - F_{ij})^2/F_{ij}$ STEP 4
1,1					
1,2					
2,1					
2,2					
3,1					
3,2					

STEP 5 = observed chi-square _____

Degrees of freedom _____   Expected chi-square _____

Hypothesis rejected? _____

FOR THE NULL HYPOTHESIS OF A PRIORI PREDICTED PROBABILITIES OF JOINT OCCURRENCES:

CELL	$P_{ij}*$	F_{ij}	$f_{ij} - F_{ij}$	$(f_{ij} - F_{ij})^2$	$(f_{ij} - F_{ij})^2/F_{ij}$
		STEP 1	STEP 2	STEP 3	STEP 4
1,1	.00				
1,2	.25				
2,1	.25				
2,2	.25				
3,1	.25				
3,2	.00				

STEP 5 = observed chi-square _____

Degrees of freedom _____   Expected chi-square _____

Hypothesis rejected? _____

* These predicted probabilities, i.e., expected proportions, are deduced from the proposition that 50 percent of the class is upper class and 50 percent is lower class and that upper-class members tend toward favorable attitudes while lower-class members tend toward unfavorable attitudes toward their school.

Assignment Sheet No. 4a

CONCERNING THE POPULATION DATA ON RACE AND SEX FOR THE UNITED STATES IN 1820:

1. Are there unequal probabilities of joint occurrences among the values of the two variables? Yes____-____ No_____
   How do you know?_____
2. Is there some relation between the two variables the two distributions of values?
   Yes_____ No_____
   How do you know?_____
3. Is the distribution of joint occurrences the same in 1820 as it is to be in 1900?
   Yes_____ No_____
   How do you know?_____
4. Which of the three null hypotheses is the most likely description of the observed frequencies?_____

CONCERNING THE CLASS DATA ON RACE AND SEX:

1. Are there unequal probabilities of joint occurrences among the values of the two variables? Yes_____ No_____
   How do you know?_____

2. Is there some relation between the two variables (the two distributions of values)?
   Yes_____ No_____
   How do you know?_____
3. Is the distribution of joint occurrences in your class the same as it was in the United States in 1970? Yes_____ No_____
   How do you know?_____
4. Which of the three null hypotheses is the most likely description of the observed frequencies for your class?_____

Assignment Sheet No. 4*b*

CONCERNING THE CLASS DATA ON STUDENT STATUS AND ATTITUDE TOWARD SCHOOL:

1. Are there unequal probabilities of joint occurrences among the values of the two variables? Yes_____ No_____
   How do you know?_____
2. Is there some relation between the two variables (the two distributions of values)?
   Yes_____ No_____
   How do you know?_____
3. Is the distribution of joint occurrences the same as would be expected if the predicted probabilities were correct? Yes_____ No_____
   How do you know?_____
4. Which of the three null hypotheses is the most likely description of the observed frequencies for your class?_____

Simple Analysis of Variance in Contingency Hypotheses

INTRODUCTION

In the previous chapter, the dependent variable as well as the independent variable are measured at the nominal level, such as sex, race, etc. The cross-tabulation is the appropriate way to present the data, and the chi-square (χ^2) test is used. When a contingency hypothesis involves a dependent variable, Y, which is measured at the interval or ratio level of measurement, a more precise testing of the hypothesis becomes possible. Such a hypothesis can be tested with the simple analysis of variance.[1] For example, if the independent variable is sex and the dependent variable is "years of education completed by respondent," then the contingency hypothesis may state that "males tend to complete different levels of education than do females." Since the dependent variable, years of education,

---

[1] The analysis of variance as it is to be discussed here refers to one-way ANOVA and when there are only two groups distinguished by the independent variable, X, the method reduces to a t-test for difference of means. This caution is provided so that the reader knows where he stands when confronting a more general discussion of the flexible methods of studying behavior based on ANOVA. An excellent, readable introduction to ANOVA which is generalized to more complicated forms is given in G. V. Glass and Julian C. Stanley, *Statistical Methods in Education and Psychology* (Prentice-Hall, Englewood Cliffs, N.J., 1970, Chaps. 15–18).

is measured at the interval level, the simple analysis of variance provides the investigator with a method of testing whether the differences between two or more groups of respondents distinguishable in term of the independent variable (sex) are significantly greater than zero on some dependent variable (years of education in this case).

The example contingency hypothesis to be considered in this chapter concerns the rates of homicide occurring in the United States. One explanation for differing rates of homicide in separate states is the predominant culture in each state. It is argued, states in regions which have developed cultures emphasizing violence and aggression are likely to have higher rates of homicide than states in regions which have developed cultures emphasizing other norms. In the United States there are three broad regional areas: the North, the South, and the West. The proposition to be considered is, "The rate of homicide in a state is a function of the norms emphasized by the predominant regional culture in the state." From this proposition it is to be expected that states in different regions should tend to have different homicide rates. Notice that the proposition as given does not allow the deduction of *specific* differences in the homicide rates in different cultures—it only allows the deduction that there are differences in the homicide rates in states with different regional cultures.

As an operationalization of the concept of regional culture, the division of the states into northern states, southern states and western states by the Bureau of the Census is accurate and easily available. As an operationalization of the concept of rates of homicide in states, the FBI murder and nonnegligent man-

Table 12.1   Rate of Murder and Nonnegligent Manslaughter per 100,000 Inhabitants in the Fifty States in the Geographic Regions of the North, West, and South

North		South		West	
3.2	6.0	6.9	15.4	7.3	6.8
5.3	11.0	12.7	11.3	8.3	5.5
3.7	7.5	18.5	10.4	3.8	4.2
1.7	2.8	12.5	13.2	2.5	
1.3	1.7	12.8	7.0	13.5	
1.7	4.0	6.8	12.3	11.1	
6.5	2.4	9.6		2.9	
11.0	8.3	6.1		4.1	
6.0	2.9	14.1		9.5	
8.8	1.3	9.8		8.8	
	1.2				

Source: U.S. Department of Justice, *Uniform Crime Reports*, U.S. Government Printing Office, 1972, table 3.

slaughter rates reported to local police are available annually for each state. Table 12.1 presents the state rates for murder and nonnegligent manslaughter in 1972 for the three regions. By inspection you can see that the states in the South have higher homicide rates than the states in the North or the West. However, you do not know whether or not the differences you believe to be there are significantly different from zero. Can the observed differences be explained by random chance? It is at this point that simple ANOVA becomes useful.

The state homicide rates can be referenced as the dependent variable Y, and the independent variable X distinguishes three groups of states: (1) those in the North, (2) those in the South, and (3) those in the West. Let Y_{ij} refer to the rate of homicide in the ith state in the jth region. For example, Y_{11} is the rate of homicide in the first state in the first region (North), Y_{23} is the rate of homicide in the second state in the third region (West), Y_{12} is the rate of homicide in the first state in the second region (South), etc. From Table 12.1, $Y_{11} = 3.2$, $Y_{23} = 8.3$, and $Y_{12} = 6.9$.

In Chapter 8 the arithmetic mean of a variable was introduced. In this chapter, two different arithmetic means are used, so that some additional notation needs to be introduced. In Chapter 8 a bar was placed over the letter of a variable to denote the mean of the variable, e.g., $\bar{Y}$. This notation is standard, but in ANOVA there are two means: $\bar{Y}_{..}$, the mean of all values of Y_{ij}, and $\bar{Y}_{.j}$ the mean of the values of Y_{ij} only in the jth group. In the above notation, a dot is used to indicate what values have been averaged to form the arithmetic mean. The two dots in the mean of all values $Y_{..}$ show that all the values of Y_{ij} in each of the j groups (or regions here) have been combined in the arithmetic mean so that:

$$\bar{Y}_{..} = \frac{\sum_{j=1}^{N} Y_{ij}}{N}$$

or

$$\bar{Y}_{..} = \frac{\sum_{j=1}^{J} \sum_{i=1}^{n_j} Y_{ij}}{N} \tag{12.1}$$

where n_j = number of observations in the jth group (which in the present example is the number of states in the jth region)

J = number of groups (which in the present example is the number of regions)

$\bar{Y}_{..}$ is usually described as the *grand mean*. The single dot in the mean of values within a single group $\bar{Y}_{.j}$ shows that only the values in the jth group (region) have been combined in the arithmetic mean so that:

$$\bar{Y}_{.j} = \frac{\sum_{i=1}^{n_j} Y_{ij}}{n_j} \tag{12.2}$$

which is usually described as the *group mean* of the jth group. Notice that the grand mean is the average of all the group means:

$$\bar{Y}_{..} = \frac{\sum_{j=1}^{J} \sum_{i=1}^{n_j} Y_{ij}}{N} = \frac{\sum_{j=1}^{J} \bar{Y}_{.j}}{J}$$

Simple ANOVA views the substantive problem of multiple group differences from the assumption that the J samples of observations are randomly selected from populations in which observations are distributed in a normal distribution (bell-shaped, with the center of the distribution equal to the group mean) with equal variances for each group.[2] From this assumption, each observed homicide rate Y_{ij} can be decomposed into three parts:

$$Y_{ij} = \mu + \alpha_j + \epsilon_{ij} \tag{12.3a}$$

where μ = population grand mean of the homicide rates and is estimated as $\bar{Y}_{..}$ [equation (12.1)]

α_j = population difference between the grand mean and the group mean and is estimated as $\bar{Y}_{.j} - \bar{Y}_{..}$, so that α_j equals the part of Y_{ij} due to state i being in region j

ϵ_{ij} = population residual part of Y_{ij} which is unexplained by state i being in region j and is estimated as $Y_{ij} - \bar{Y}_{.j}$

---

[2] A common problem in social research is the failure of the observations to meet all the assumptions of a statistical model, so that it is highly desirable to know how the statistical model behaves when the assumptions are not met. In the ANOVA model, the estimates and inferences from the model are not greatly altered if (1) the distributions of values within each group are not normal, or (2) the variances of the groups are not equal—as long as the numbers of observations in each group are equal (i.e., as long as the n_j for each group j are equal). If there are different numbers of observations in the groups *and* there are different variances in the observations in the groups, then ANOVA will tend to overemphasize the significance of the differences between groups if groups with larger variances have fewer observations, and will tend to underemphasize the significance of differences between groups if groups with larger variances have larger numbers of observations. If the observations within each group have not been sampled randomly such that there are correlations or interactions between separate observations in separate groups, then ANOVA as presented here is inappropriate and some method of comparison which takes these correlations, interactions, or both into account should be employed. These conclusions are drawn from the discussion in G. V. Glass and Julian C. Stanley, *Statistical Methods in Education and Psychology* (Prentice-Hall, Englewood Cliffs, N.J., 1970, pp. 368–374). Additional references are given there.

The above equation is stated in terms of unobservable population parameters. Estimates of the population parameters computed from observed data are indicated by placing a "hat," "^", over the symbol representing the parameter. The observed homicide rates can also be stated in terms of the estimates of μ, the α_j, and the ϵ_{ij} which are computed from observed data such as that in Table 12.1:

$$Y_{ij} = \hat{\mu} + \hat{\alpha}_j + \hat{\epsilon}_{ij}$$
$$= \bar{Y}_{..} + (\bar{Y}_{.j} - \bar{Y}_{..}) + (Y_{ij} - \bar{Y}_{.j}) \tag{12.3b}$$

In Chapter 9, the concept of variability or variance in a distribution of observed scores was introduced as a measure of the degree to which scores were different from one another. The higher the variance in a variable, the larger the differences among the observed values of the variable. What ANOVA does is to determine the extent to which differences among the observed values of a variable are due to the separation of distinct groups by variable X as opposed to random chance. It makes this comparison by forming a ratio of the variance in the Y_{ij} which can be stated in terms of the α_j over the variance of the Y_{ij} which is left unexplained, the ϵ_{ij}. The significance of the difference among the groups is a function of the magnitude of this ratio—the larger the ratio, then the larger the differences among the groups.

Just as in Chapter 9, these variances consist of sums of squared deviations around mean values divided by the degrees of freedom associated with the sum of squared deviations. The total sum of squared deviations of the Y_{ij} around the grand mean (the variance of the values of the Y variable as computed from Chapter 9) will be equal to two independent sums of squared deviations: (1) SS_b—the Sum of Squared deviations between groups and (2) SS_w—the Sum of Squared deviations within groups. In other words:

$$\text{Total sum of squared deviations around the grand mean} = SS_b + SS_w$$

where SS_b = deviations of the Y_{ij} from the grand mean. It represents the portion of the variability of the dependent variable, Y, which can be explained in terms of the X variable which distinguishes the J groups of observations.

SS_w = deviations of the Y_{ij} which cannot be explained by the X variable.

SS_w equals the sum of squared residual scores and is calculated:

$$SS_w = \sum_{}^{N} (\hat{\epsilon}_{ij})^2$$

which from equation (12.3b) equals:

$$SS_w = \sum_{j=1}^{J} \sum_{i=1}^{n_j} (Y_{ij} - \bar{Y}_{.j})^2 \tag{12.4}$$

SS_b equals the sum of squared deviations of group means from the grand mean, the j, for each observation and is calculated:

$$SS_b = \sum_{j=1}^{J} \sum_{i=1}^{n_j} (\hat{\alpha}_j)^2 = \sum_{j=1}^{J} nj(\hat{\alpha}_j)^2$$

which from equation (12.3b) equals:

$$SS_b = \sum_{j=1}^{J} n_j (\bar{Y}_{.j} - \bar{Y}_{..})^2 \tag{12.5}$$

There are computational formulas for SS_b and SS_w for the reader who does not have access to a computer. The formulas in equations (12.4) and (12.5) are the more important ones to remember, since they express the conceptual basis of ANOVA. The computational formula for SS_w is:

$$SS_w = \sum_{}^{N} (Y_{ij}{}^2) - \sum_{j=1}^{J} \frac{\left[\sum_{i=1}^{n_j} (Y_{ij}) \right]^2}{n_j}$$

and the computational formula for SS_b is:

$$SS_b = \sum_{j=1}^{J} \frac{\left[\sum_{i=1}^{n_j} (Y_{ij}) \right]^2}{n_j} - \frac{\left[\sum_{}^{N} (Y_{ij}) \right]^2}{N}$$

The variability or dispersion of the group means equals SS_b divided by the degrees of freedom associated with SS_b which equals the number of groups minus 1 degree of freedom, $J - 1$. This quantity of dispersion is called the Mean Squares between groups, MS_b. MS_b is computed:

$$MS_b = \frac{SS_b}{J - 1} \tag{12.6}$$

The variability or dispersion of the residual scores equals SS_w divided by the associated degrees of freedom which equals the number of observations minus the number of groups, $N - J$. This quantity of dispersion is called the Mean Squares within groups, MS_w, and is computed:

$$MS_w = \frac{SS_w}{N - J} \tag{12.7}$$

When there are no population differences in variable Y across the groups distinguished by variable X, then both MS_b and MS_w are expected to equal the random variance in the observed data. Thus, when there are no population differences in Y across the groups, the ratio of MS_b to MS_w is expected to equal 1.0. As the differences among the groups become increasingly large relative to the random variance in the observed data, the ratio of MS_b to MS_w becomes larger. This ratio is distributed as an F distribution with $J - 1$ and $N - J$ degrees of freedom when there are no population differences in variable Y across the groups:

$$F = \frac{MS_b}{MS_w} \tag{12.8}$$

In order to test the significance of the differences in variable Y across the groups distinguished by variable X, the computed value of F from equation (12.8) is compared to the expected value of F with $J - 1$ and $N - J$ degrees of freedom at some level of confidence such as the .05 level or higher. If the observed value of F is larger than the expected value at the chosen level of confidence, then the differences among the groups are significant, and the researcher can continue with his analysis in order to determine why the groups are different and what the consequences of the differences are.

OBJECTIVES

The objectives of this lab session are related to the use of simple ANOVA to explore contingency hypotheses of multiple group differences. There are two main objectives:

1   To introduce the idea of explaining the variation in one variable as a function of the distinctions made by another variable (variable Y explained by variable X)

2   To familiarize you with the use of the F statistic as a means of comparing the adequacy of a proposed explanation of variation in an observed variable with the adequacy of random chance

ASSIGNMENT

You will perform the same operations on the example observed data given out during class that is performed during the lab session. For each of the ANOVA problems assigned, complete the forms attached at the end of the chapter, which means:

1   Compute the grand mean and each of the J group means using equations (12.1) and (12.2).

2   Compute the estimated residual scores using equation (12.3).

3   Compute SS_w using equation (12.4).

4   Compute SS_b using equation (12.5).

5   Compute MS_b and MS_w using equations (12.6) and (12.7).

6   Compute the observed value of F using equation (12.8) and compare it to the expected value of F with $J - 1$ and $N - J$ degrees of freedom in order to determine the significance of the group differences on variable Y.

7   Based on your analysis, decide whether further analysis is justified and explain your decision.

THE LAB SESSION

After completing the example ANOVA problem concerning the regional differences in homicide rates, the remainder of the lab session can be spent working on the assignment. It is assumed that you are familiar with the material in the introduction, so that the lab session time can be spent on interpreting ANOVA procedures rather than on introducing them. The forthcoming discussion is divided according to the above seven aspects of the assignment.

The Example Data

At the end of the chapter are three assignment sheets with forms for completing the ANOVA. The first assignment sheet contains the data you have been given in Table 12.1. On the second and third assignment sheets write down the data your lab instructor has sampled from the entire set of class data in an independent, random sample. Write the data in the columns labeled Y_{ij}.

Take out assignment sheet no. 1. During the lab session you will fill in the blanks on assignment sheet no. 1. Doing this will enable you to complete the other two assignment sheets.

Computing the Grand Mean and Group Means

The group means, the $\bar{Y}_{.j}$, have already been computed for the first and last groups on assignment sheet no. 1. Using equation (12.2) compute the group mean for the second group of states. Once you have $\bar{Y}_{.2}$, you can compute the grand mean, the $\bar{Y}_{..}$, since you already have $\bar{Y}_{.1}$ and $\bar{Y}_{.3}$. Enter $\bar{Y}_{.2}$ on the sheet.

Computing Estimates of the Residual Scores

Since you now have $\bar{Y}_{.2}$, compute the residual scores for the second group of states using equation (12.3b). Write your estimates of ϵ_{ij} is the column labeled $\hat{\epsilon}_{ij}$ on the assignment sheet. Since the $\hat{\epsilon}_{ij}$ for the first and third groups have already been computed for you, you now have all the information you need to compute SS_w and SS_b.

Computing the Sum of Squared Deviations within Groups—SS_w

Using the three columns of estimates of the residual scores, compute SS_w using equation (12.4). Write the estimate you compute on the assignment sheet in the appropriate space.

Computing the Sum of Squared Deviations between Groups—SS_b

Using the three estimates of the group means, the $Y_{.j}$ given on assignment sheet no. 1, compute SS_b using equation (12.5). Notice that equation (12.5) is the sum of the squared estimates of α_j for the observations, not the sum of the squared group means for the observations. Write your estimate of SS_b on the assignment sheet in the appropriate space.

Computing the Mean Squares

Write the appropriate degrees of freedom on the assignment sheet for SS_b and SS_w. Using these degrees of freedom, compute the mean sum of squared deviations between groups MS_b using equation (12.6), and compute the mean sum of squared deviations within groups MS_w using equation (12.7). Write your estimates in the appropriate spaces on assignment sheet no. 1.

Computing the Observed Value of F and Locating the Expected Value of F

Using equation (12.8), compute the value of the ratio of MS_b to MS_w and enter your estimate in the appropriate space on the assignment sheet. This ratio is the observed value of F for the proposition as it has been operationalized here.

In order to determine the significance of the observed differences among the regions, the observed value of F has to be compared to the value of F which would be expected if the differences among the states in the three regions were due entirely to random change. As in the last chapter, the 5 percent level of confidence has been selected as an arbitrary point at which the significance of the differences between groups will be accepted. If you turn to the back of the volume, you will find a table of values of F for different degrees of freedom at the 5 percent level of confidence (Table A.5). The number of degrees of freedom across the top of the table refer to the degrees of freedom in SS_b, $J - 1$. The degrees of freedom down the side of the table refer to the degrees of freedom in SS_w, $N - J$. Find the expected value of F when the degrees of freedom is 2 and 47, as they are here, and write that number in the appropriate space on the assignment sheet.

If the observed value of F is larger than the expected value of F, then there are significant differences in the homicide rates in the states in the three regions. If the observed value of F is smaller than the expected value of F, then the observed differences between the regions in Table 12.1 can be attributed to random chance. Compare the observed value of F with the expected value of F on the assignment sheet and write in your decision on whether the differences between regions are significant.

Using ANOVA to Aid Further Analysis

Since the differences among the states in different regions are so highly significant, it makes sense to continue the analysis of homicide rates in order to determine what aspects of regional culture are responsible for the observed differences. There is no "best" manner in which to proceed; however, a useful beginning point is to determine which groups—regions—are the most different from the average groups. Which groups have the highest values of the Y variable? Which groups have the lowest values of the Y variable? Once you have found these two extreme groups, try to think of other characteristics of these two extreme groups which also tend to separate them. For example, in the homicide data analyzed during the lab session, the states in the southern region have the highest levels of homicide, and the states in the northern region have the lowest levels of homicide. What characteristics of a regional culture also tend to separate these two regions into opposite extremes?[3] When you justify your decision to do further research (or not to continue), indicate how you would go about this further research. You may need more than the available space on the assignment sheet.

Assignment Sheet No. 1

CONDUCTING SOCIAL RESEARCH

Chapter 12   Simple ANOVA in Contingency Hypotheses

Rates on Murder and Nonnegligent Manslaughter from Table 12.1

NORTH		SOUTH		WEST	
Y_{ij}	$\hat{\epsilon}_{ij}$	Y_{ij}	$\hat{\epsilon}_{ij}$	Y_{ij}	$\hat{\epsilon}_{ij}$
3.2	−1.48	6.9	_____	7.3	0.51
5.3	0.62	12.7	_____	8.3	1.51
3.7	−0.98	18.5	_____	3.8	−2.99
1.7	−2.98	12.5	_____	2.5	−4.29
1.3	−3.38	12.8	_____	13.5	6.71
1.7	−2.98	16.8	_____	11.1	4.31
6.5	1.82	9.6	_____	2.9	−3.89
11.0	6.32	6.1	_____	4.1	−2.69
6.0	1.32	14.1	_____	9.5	2.71
8.8	4.12	9.8	_____	8.8	2.01
6.0	1.32	15.4	_____	6.8	0.01
11.0	6.32	11.3	_____	5.5	−1.29
7.5	2.82	10.4	_____	4.2	−2.59
2.8	−1.88	13.2	_____		
1.7	−2.98	7.0	_____		
4.0	−0.68	12.3	_____		
2.4	−2.28				
8.3	3.62				
2.9	−1.78				
1.3	−3.38				
1.2	−3.48				

	NORTH	SOUTH	WEST
$n_j =$	21	16	13
$\bar{Y}_{.j}$	4.68		6.79
SS_b	_____	$df_b = (J - 1) =$ _____	$MS_b =$ _____
SS_w	_____	$df_w = (N - J) =$ _____	$MS_w =$ _____

[3] Readers interested in this problem of high homicide rates are referred to R. D. Gastil, "Homicide and a Regional Culture of Violence," *American Sociological Review*, **36**: 412–427, 1971, as an initial reading.

Observed value of F = _____

Expected value of F at the 5 percent level of confidence = _____

Are there significant differences among the groups?_____

Would you do further research? Why and how?_____

_____

_____

Assignment Sheet No. 2

CONDUCTING SOCIAL RESEARCH

Chapter 12   Simple ANOVA in Contingency Hypotheses

Father's Income Differences across Father's Political Party

REPUBLICAN		DEMOCRAT		OTHER	
Y_{ij}	$\hat{\epsilon}_{ij}$	Y_{ij}	$\hat{\epsilon}_{ij}$	Y_{ij}	$\hat{\epsilon}_{ij}$

n_j = _____

$\bar{Y}_{.j}$ = _____

SS_b = _____ df_b = _____ MS_b = _____

SS_w = _____ df_w = _____ MS_w = _____

Observed value of F = _____

Expected value of F at the 5 percent level of confidence = _____

Are there significant differences among the groups?_____

Would you do further research? Why and how?_____

_____

_____

_____

Assignment Sheet No. 3

CONDUCTING SOCIAL RESEARCH

Chapter 12   Simple ANOVA in Contingency Hypotheses

Father's Income Differences across Student Educational Goals

BACHELOR		GRADUATE DEGREE		OTHER	
Y_{ij}	$\hat{\epsilon}_{ij}$	Y_{ij}	$\hat{\epsilon}_{ij}$	Y_{ij}	$\hat{\epsilon}_{ij}$

$n_j =$ _____

$\bar{Y}_{.j} =$ _____

$SS_b =$ _____ $df_b =$ _____ $MS_b =$ _____

$SS_w =$ _____ $df_w =$ _____ $MS_w =$ _____

Observed value of $F =$ _____

Expected value of F at the 5 percent level of confidence = _____

Are there significant differences among the groups?_____

Would you do further research? Why and how?_____

_____

_____

_____

Simple Regression Analysis in Associative and Functional Hypotheses

INTRODUCTION

There are some theoretical structures in the social sciences which have been stated in such a fashion that associative and functional hypotheses can be deduced from them.[1] For example, within the American social system, "Individuals who complete high levels of educational attainment usually reach high levels of occupational achievement," "Individuals who are rewarded for performing certain behaviors will tend to repeat those behaviors," "Individuals who do not identify themselves with any groups of persons have a higher tendency to commit suicide," etc. In each of these statements, the variables can be measured at the interval level. For each of these hypotheses, an investigator can specify variation in one variable in terms of a different variable. Simple regression analysis provides the investigator with a method of testing whether the relationship between the two variables measured at the interval or ratio level is significantly different from some expected relationship. In this chapter, only linear relationships between variables are considered, although regression methods can

---

[1] For detailed discussion of the contingency, associative and functional hypotheses, see Nan Lin, *Foundations of Social Research*, McGraw-Hill, New York, 1976, Chaps. 3, 6, and 16.

be extended to deal with nonlinear relations. As a first step in analyzing a social phenomenon, however, the linear relation is a useful first hypothesis, since it is simple to conceptualize and it will ignore minor errors in the observed data which result from an investigator not being certain of what he is searching for as the "optimal" explanation of a phenomenon.

The example hypotheses to be considered in this chapter concern the increasing involvement of the federal government in the affairs of persons in the United States from 1900 to 1972. Emile Durkheim, a French sociologist who completed his best known work around the turn of the century, specified the proposition that, as the jobs individuals hold in society require increasingly specialized knowledge, as happens with increasing technology, then persons become more dependent on one another in order to survive; the government of the society, which is intended to enforce moral order within the society, is forced to become more involved in the affairs of persons in the society in order to ensure that some persons do not take advantage of others as a result of the increasing interdependence among persons (under the current social norms).[2] Since the United States has been characterized since 1900 by increasing industrialization and specialization of knowledge required for jobs, government should be assuming increasing involvement in the affairs of persons in the United States if the specified proposition is correct. As an operationalization of the involvement of the government in the affairs of persons, the average percentage of the front page of *The New York Times* which concerns government activities has been measured for every four years beginning with the four-year interval 1897–1900. Table 13.1 presents the percentages for each four-year interval from 1897–1900 to 1968–1972. Next to each percentage in Table 13.1 is the last year in the time interval during which the percentage was observed. By inspection, you can see that an increasing percentage of the front page of *The New York Times* has been devoted to discussing the activities of the government. Simple regression analysis becomes useful when the investigator wishes to explore or test the significance of the prediction of differences in one variable from differences in another variable. In this chapter, the example hypothesis concerns predicting changes in attention to government activities from differences in the time period. How well can differences in time predict changes in the attention given to governments? Can the observed increases in attention paid to governments be explained by random chance?

In the last chapter, differences in a variable Y were attributed to the distinctions among groups of observations using a variable X plus a residual part of Y which was unexplained by variable X. In the simple regression model, the same approach is used to explain differences in variable Y from variable X,

---

[2] Durkheim's discussion is far more complicated than this sentence can convey. For a well-organized introduction to Durkheim's thoughts on the role of government in an increasingly specialized society, see A. Giddens, *Emile Durkheim: Selected Writings*, Cambridge University Press, Cambridge, 1972, pp. 1–20 discussion. Giddens provides relevant citations to Durkheim's translated and original discussion.

Table 13.1   Average Percentage of the Front Page of *The New York Times* Devoted to Government Activities by Four-Year Intervals from 1897–1900 to 1969–1972

Last year in time interval		Percentage of front page	
X_i	$X_i - \bar{X}$	Y_i	$Y_i - \bar{Y}$
1900	−36	45%	−23.21
1904	−32	50%	−18.21
1908	−28	39%	−29.21
1912	−24	60%	−8.21
1916	−20	48%	−20.21
1920	−16	79%	10.79
1924	−12	71%	2.79
1928	−8	65%	−3.21
1932	−4	69%	.79
1936	0	64%	−4.21
1940	4	81%	12.79
1944	8	86%	17.79
1948	12	87%	18.79
1952	16	73%	4.79
1956	20	78%	9.79
1960	24	65%	−3.21
1964	28	81%	12.79
1968	32	73%	4.79
1972	36	82%	13.79

Source: R. S. Burt, "Corporate Society: A Time Series Analysis of Network Structure," Corporate Actor Project Report, National Opinion Research Center, University of Chicago, 1975, Chapter 5 and Appendix D.

except that groups are both distinguished by variable X *and* ordered on a continuum by variable X. In other words, instead of variable X being measured at the nominal level of measurement, as in the last chapter, the simple regression model assumes that X is measured at the interval or ratio level of measurement. In this chapter, the Y variable (the dependent variable) consists of the observed changes in the attention given to governments, and the X variable (the independent variable) consists of the changes in time as shown in Table 13.1. What the simple regression model does is to assess the ability of the deviations of the X_i around their arithmetic mean to predict the deviations of the Y_i around their arithmetic mean using a straight line. Consider the graph in Figure 13.1 which presents the data from Table 13.1.

Each observed percentage in Figure 13.1 can be decomposed into three parts: (1) the arithmetic mean of the Y_i, (2) the deviations of the Y_i from their arithmetic means which can be predicted from the X_i, and (3) a residual score which equals the deviations of the Y_i from their arithmetic mean which cannot be predicted from the X_i. These three parts can be added together, and their

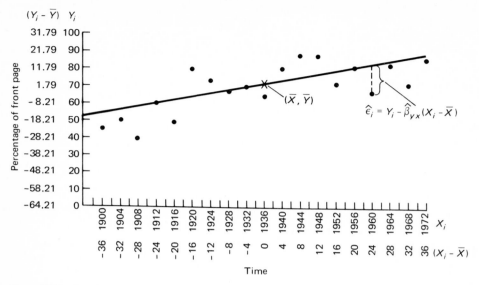

Figure 13-1   Average percentage of the front page of *The New York Times* devoted to government activities by four-year intervals from 1897–1900 to 1969–1972.

sum equals the observed percentage Y_i for each time period. Each observed percentage Y_i can be decomposed as shown below[3];

$$Y_i = \mu + \beta_{yx}(X_i - \bar{X}) + \epsilon_i \qquad (13.1)$$

where μ = population mean of the Y variable

β_{yx} = population slope of the regression line predicting $Y_i - \bar{Y}$ from $X_i - \bar{X}$. It is called the regression coefficient of Y on X and interpreted as the predicted deviation of Y_i from $\bar{Y}$ which is associated with the change $(X_i - \bar{X})$

ϵ_i = population residual score, $Y_i - \bar{Y}$, which is unpredictable from the regression line

The above equation is stated in terms of population parameters. Estimates of the population parameters computed from observed data are indicated by placing a "hat", "^", over the symbol representing the parameter. The Y_i are assumed to be measured at the interval or ratio level of measurement and to be sampled in an independent, random fashion from a population of Y_i which are normally distributed around their associated X_i with a constant variance [compare with

[3] Notice the similarity of the simple regression model given in equation (13.1) to the simple ANOVA model given in equation (12.3a) in the last chapter. Imagine that the groups in the simple ANOVA model could be ordered along a continuum of values determined by variable X. What the regression model seeks to do is draw a straight line through the group means $\bar{Y}_{.j}$ for each of the J unique values of X. That line is the *regression line* in Figure 13.1, and the slope of that line is the *regression coefficient* β_{yx} in equation (13.1).

the assumptions of ANOVA associated with equation $(13.3a)$].[4] By making these assumptions, an investigator is able to estimate the population parameters using samples of observations drawn from the population of Y_i and make inferences about the true values of the population parameters from his estimates.

The population mean of the Y_i's is estimated in the same manner given in Chapters 8 and 12:

$$\hat{\mu} = \frac{\sum_{i=1}^{N} Y_i}{N} \tag{13.2}$$

where N equals the number of observations.

The regression coefficient is estimated such that the sum of the squared residual scores, the $\hat{\epsilon}_{ij}$, will be as small as possible. In this sense, the regression line is the "best-fitting" straight line which can be drawn through the observed Y_i as a function of $X_i - \bar{X}$. This criterion for estimating the regression coefficient is called *least-squares estimation*, since it seeks to minimize the sum of squared residuals. The regression coefficient is estimated:[5]

$$\hat{\beta}_{yx} = \frac{\sum_{i=1}^{N} (X_i - \bar{X})(Y_i - \bar{Y})}{\sum_{i=1}^{N} (X_i - \bar{X})^2} \tag{13.3}$$

[4] As with the ANOVA model, since there are many sets of data which do not meet all the assumptions of the regression model, it is highly desirable to know when the regression model will lead to erroneous conclusions if the data do not meet its assumptions. It is beyond the scope of the present discussion to give an adequate treatment of either the assumptions of regression analysis or the ability of the regression analysis model to lead to correct conclusions concerning the relation between X and Y, despite the failure of the data to meet its assumptions. As a general rule, the regression model is sensitive to the same assumptions as the ANOVA model, which were presented in the last chapter in footnote 2. Readers interested in further discussion can turn to G. V. Glass and J. C. Stanley, *Statistical Methods in Education and Psychology*, Prentice-Hall, Englewood Cliffs, 1970, pp. 368–374, or G. W. Bohrnstedt and T. M. Carter, "Robustness in Regression Analysis," pp. 118–146 in *Sociological Methodology*, 1971, edited by H. L. Costner.

[5] As in the previous treatment of ANOVA, since computers are available at most institutions, the text has presented only the computationally long formula for computing the regression coefficient which more clearly shows the conceptual basis for the regression coefficient, rather than the short-cut computational formula which obscures the meaning of the regression coefficient. For readers who do not have access to a computer, however, β_{yx} can be estimated with fewer tedious computations by the formula below rather than by equation (13.3):

$$\hat{\beta}_{yx} = \frac{\sum_{i=1}^{N} X_i Y_i - \left(\sum_{i=1}^{N} X_i\right)\left(\sum_{i=1}^{N} Y_i\right)}{\sum_{i=1}^{N} X_i^2 - \left(\sum_{i=1}^{N} X_i\right)^2}$$

Using the estimate of the regression coefficient, the deviations of the Y_i around their arithmetic mean can be predicted from the deviations of the X_i around their arithmetic mean. The estimated value of Y_i based on the hypothesis of variable Y being linearly predictable from variable X can then be computed:

$$\hat{Y}_i = \mu + \beta_{yx}(X_i - \bar{X})$$

which in terms of the estimates given above equals:

$$\hat{Y}_i = \hat{\mu} + \hat{\beta}_{yx}(X_i - \bar{X}) \tag{13.4}$$
$$= \bar{Y} + \hat{\beta}_{yx}(X_i - \bar{X})$$

When the estimated values of Y_i are graphed over the values of X_i, they will fall on a straight line. This straight line is the regression line of variable Y on variable X and is presented in Figure 13.1. This straight line will be the only line that minimizes the sum of the squared residual scores of the Y_i when predicted from the X_i.

The residual score associated with Y_i is estimated as the difference between the observed value of Y_i and the estimated value of Y_i, using equation (13.4):

$$\hat{\epsilon}_i = Y_i - \hat{Y}_i \tag{13.5}$$
$$= Y_i - [\bar{Y} + \hat{\beta}_{yx}(X_i - \bar{X})]$$

The Relationship between the Estimated Regression Coefficient $\hat{\beta}_{yx}$, the Estimated Correlation Coefficient r_{xy}, and the Estimated Covariance Coefficient s_{xy}

Let the estimated variance of a variable X be referenced with the symbol s_x^2 so the standard deviation of the variable equals s_x. Multiply equation (13.3), the equation for estimating the regression coefficient, by 1 in the form of $[1/(N-1)]/[1/(N-1)]$:

$$\hat{\beta}_{yx}[1] = \frac{\dfrac{1}{(N-1)}\left[\sum_{i=1}^{N}(X_i - \bar{X})(Y_i - \bar{Y})\right]}{\dfrac{1}{(N-1)}\left[\sum_{i=1}^{N}(X_i - \bar{X})^2\right]} = \frac{s_{xy}}{s_x^2} \tag{13.6}$$

Multiply each side of equation (13.6) by s_x:

$$\hat{\beta}_{yx}(s_x) = \frac{s_{xy}}{s_x^2}(s_x) = \frac{s_{xy}}{s_x}$$

and then divide each side by s_y, the standard deviation of the Y variable:

$$\hat{\beta}_{yx}\frac{s_x}{s_y} = \frac{s_{xy}}{s_x s_y} = r_{xy} \tag{13.7}$$

In summary, once you have computed the estimated regression coefficient you can compute the estimated covariance from equation (13.6):

$$s_{xy} = \hat{\beta}_{yx}(s_x^2)$$

and the estimated correlation coefficient from equation (13.7):

$$r_{xy} = \hat{\beta}_{yx}\frac{s_x}{s_y}$$

As can be seen from equation (13.6), the covariance coefficient between two variables is a measure of the degree to which high positive deviations from the arithmetic mean of one variable occur simultaneously with high positive deviations from the arithmetic mean of the other variable. The covariance between two variables will be a maximum when $X_i - \bar{X}$ equals $Y_i - \bar{Y}$ for every observation i. In this sense, the covariance between two variables is a measure of the association between the two variables. The correlation coefficient is identical to the covariance coefficient, except that it equals only values from -1 to $+1$. The correlation coefficient is useful when the investigator does not have much confidence in the meaning of the absolute values of one or both of the variables X and Y and only wishes to obtain a general measure of the degree of association between the variables. Both the covariance coefficient and the correlation coefficient are frequently used in social research, because they are symmetric rather than asymmetric like the regression coefficient (in other words, $r_{xy} = r_{yx}$ and $s_{xy} = s_{yx}$, but β_{yx} equals β_{xy} only when the variance of the X variable equals the variance of the Y variable), and because they provide a starting point for many advanced statistical procedures in the social sciences such as multiple regression, path analysis, factor analysis, and canonical correlation.

Assessing the Adequacy of a Deduced Associative of Functional Hypothesis

A deduced associative hypothesis between variables X and Y only states that there is some nonzero relation between the variables, while a functional hypothesis between X and Y actually states the form of the relation. An associative hypothesis will therefore be assessed in terms of whether or not the relationship between X and Y is significantly different from zero. A functional hypothesis will be assessed in terms of whether or not the estimated relationship is significantly different from the deduced relationship.

In the case of simple regression analysis there are two procedures for assessing the adequacy of the deduced hypothesis: (1) Assess the significance of the ability of the X variable to predict differences in the Y variable, and (2) assess the difference of the estimated coefficient from a particular value of the coefficient. The first procedure is usually used only to test associative hypotheses, while the second procedure can be used to test either associative or functional hypotheses. Both procedures are presented here, because the first procedure will be useful in considering hypotheses involving many X variables which predict one Y variable.

Assessing the Significance of the Ability of the X Variable to Predict Differences in the Y Variable   Just as in the simple ANOVA model presented in the last chapter, the regression analysis model assesses the significance of the prediction of the Y variable by the X variable. It constructs a ratio of the variance of the Y_i which can be stated in terms of the X variable (the variance of the estimated Y_i) to the variance of the Y_i which cannot be stated in terms of the X variable (the variance of the $\hat{\epsilon}_i$). The larger this ratio, the more adequate the prediction of the Y variable from the X variable.

SS_p, the portion of the differences in the Y_i which is predictable from the X variable, equals the Sum of the Squared deviations of the predicted values of the Y_i from their arithmetic mean $\hat{\bar{Y}}$. SS_r, the portion of the differences in the Y_i which is unpredictable from the X variable, equals the Sum of the Squared deviations of the residual values of the Y_i. But, since the mean of the residual values is zero, SS_r equals the sum of the squared residual values. SS_r plus SS_p equals the total sum of the squared deviations of the Y_i from their arithmetic mean SS_t:

$$SS_{total} = SS_{predicted} + SS_{residual}$$

which can be stated in terms of equations (13.4) and (13.5):

$$\sum_{i=1}^{N} (Y_i - \bar{Y})^2 = \sum_{i=1}^{N} (\hat{Y}_i - \hat{\bar{Y}})^2 + \sum_{i=1}^{N} (\hat{\epsilon}_i - \hat{\bar{\epsilon}})^2$$

so that:

$$SS_p = \sum_{i=1}^{N} (\hat{Y}_i - \hat{\bar{Y}})^2 = \sum_{i=1}^{N} (\hat{Y}_i - \bar{Y})^2$$

$$= \sum_{i=1}^{N} [\hat{\beta}_{yx}(X_i - \bar{X})]^2 \tag{13.8}$$

and $$SS_r = \sum_{i=1}^{N} (\hat{\epsilon}_i - \hat{\bar{\epsilon}})^2 = \sum_{i=1}^{N} \hat{\epsilon}_i^2$$

$$= \sum_{i=1}^{N} (Y_i - \hat{Y}_i)^2 \tag{13.9}$$

The variability of the predicted values of the Y_i will equal SS_p divided by the degrees of freedom in the prediction of Y from X. In the case of the simple regression model, it is equal to 1 when there is only one X variable. Therefore, the Mean Squares of prediction in the simple regression model equals SS_p:

$$MS_p = \frac{SS_p}{df_p} = \frac{SS_p}{1} = SS_p \tag{13.10}$$

The variability of the residual scores will equal SS_r divided by the remaining degrees of freedom in the total sum of squared deviations of Y_i around $\bar{Y}$ after prediction, which equals N minus 1 degree of freedom for $\bar{Y}$ and another degree of freedom for the prediction—$N - 2$—for the simple regression model. The Mean Squares of residual scores is therefore computed:

$$MS_r = \frac{SS_r}{N - 2} \tag{13.11}$$

for the simple regression model.

Just as in the ANOVA model, when the Y variable is completely unpredictable from the X variable, then MS_p will be equal to MS_r, so that the ratio of MS_p to MS_r will equal 1. This ratio is distributed as an F distribution with 1 and $N - 2$ degrees of freedom when the population differences in the Y_i cannot be predicted from the differences in the X_i:

$$F = \frac{MS_p}{MS_r} \tag{13.12}$$

The same procedures given in Chapter 12 for testing the significance of the observed value of F are used here to test the significance of the ability of the differences in the Y_i to be predicted from the differences in the X_i.

Assessing the Significance of the Difference between an Estimated Regression Coefficient $\hat{\beta}_{yx}$ and a Hypothesized Regression Coefficient β_{yx}   There are research situations in which sufficient previous research has accumulated to allow the investigator to hypothesize that a Y variable is a particular function of the X variable. Alternatively, an investigator may have specified a theoretical structure with sufficient precision to allow a specific value of the regression coefficient β_{yx} to be deduced. In either of the previous two research situations, the estimated regression coefficient should not be tested for the significance of its difference from zero, but rather should be tested for the significance of its difference from the hypothesized or deduced regression coefficient $\beta_{yx}{}^0$.

Using equation (13.11) to compute the mean squares of residual scores, the observed value of t given in equation (13.13) will be distributed as a t distribution with $N - 2$ degrees of freedom when there is no difference between the estimated and the hypothesized regression coefficients:[6]

$$t = \sqrt{\frac{(\hat{\beta}_{yx} - \beta_{yx}{}^0)^2 \sum_{i=1}^{N} (X_i - \bar{X})^2}{MS_r}} \tag{13.13}$$

Since the estimated regression coefficient can be larger or smaller than the hypothesized regression coefficient, a two-tailed significance test should be used, which means that after the observed value of t is computed from equation

[6] Notice that associative hypotheses can also be tested using the t statistic in equation (13.13) by setting $\beta_{yx}{}^0$ equal to zero.

(13.13) it should be compared to the expected value of t at the 2.5 percent level of confidence in order to guarantee the insignificance of the difference $\hat{\beta}_{yx} - \beta_{yx}^0$ at the 5 percent level of confidence.[7] If the absolute value of the observed value of t is larger than the expected value of t, then the estimated regression coefficient is significantly different from the hypothesized regression coefficient.

OBJECTIVES

There are three main objectives of this lab session involving the use of simple regression analysis to analyze associative and functional hypotheses:

1 To introduce the idea of stating a variable Y as a linear function of another variable X
2 To introduce the interpretative relations among correlation, covariance, and regression coefficients
3 To familiarize you with the use of F and t statistics as a means of assessing the adequacy of associative and functional hypotheses.

ASSIGNMENT

As in the last two lab sessions, you will perform the same operations on the example data given out during class that are performed on the observed data analyzed during the lab session. This means that, for the assigned regression problems, you will:

1 Compute deviation scores for the X variable $(X_i - \bar{X})$, for the Y variable $(Y_i - \bar{Y})$, and for the cross-product $[(X_i - \bar{X})(Y_i - \bar{Y})]$.
2 Compute the regression coefficient of Y on X, the correlation coefficient between Y and X, and the covariance coefficient between Y and X.
3 Compute the predicted and residual scores of Y_i.
4 Plot the graph of Y_i against X_i and $\hat{Y}_i$ against X_i as was done in Figure 13.1.
5 Compute the observed value of F.
6 Compare the observed value of F to the expected value of F in order to determine the adequacy of the associative hypothesis that Y can be predicted from X.
7 Compute the observed value of t.
8 Compare the observed value of t to the expected values of t for the two functional hypotheses: (1) Y cannot be predicted from X at all; and (2) Y can be perfectly predicted from X.

[7] For discussions comparing one-tailed and two-tailed significance tests, the reader is referred to G. V. Glass and J. C. Stanley, *Statistical Methods in Education and Psychology* Prentice-Hall, Englewood Cliffs, 1970, pp. 288–289; H. M. Blalock, *Social Statistics*, McGraw-Hill Book Company, New York, 1972, pp. 159–165; N. Lin, *Foundations of Social Research*, McGraw-Hill Book Company, New York, 1976, Chapter 7.

THE LAB SESSION

As with the previous two lab sessions, this lab session will be spent performing the above eight operations on the example data given in Table 13.1. In order to complete the lab session, it will be necessary for you to be familiar with the contents of the introductory section on simple regression analysis. The forthcoming discussion is divided according to the above seven aspects of the assignment.

The Example Data

At the end of the chapter are two assignment sheets, one to be completed during the lab session and one to be completed on your own. The first assignment sheet has listed the observed X_i and Y_i, the deviation scores $X_i - \bar{X}$ and $Y_i - \bar{Y}$, and most of the cross-product of the deviations scores $(X_i - \bar{X})(Y_i - \bar{Y})$. On the second assignment sheet, write the observed data your instructor has sampled from the class data. Write the Y_i in the column labeled Y_i and the predictor variable values in the column labeled X_i.

Computing Deviation Scores and Cross-products of Deviation Scores

You have been given the deviation scores for the lab session data, since the computation of these scores is a simple matter of computing the arithmetic mean of a variable and then subtracting the arithmetic mean from each observed score to find the deviation score $Y_i - \bar{Y}$. Just to make sure you understand the idea of a deviation score, you may wish to check your procedure by computing some of the Y_i given on assignment sheet no. 1. If you make a mistake while computing the deviation scores on your assignment, all the rest of the assignment will be wrong, since it is based on the deviation scores. It is therefore important that you are careful at this stage.

Once you have the deviation scores written down on the assignment sheet, multiply corresponding deviation scores for the ith observation together in order to compute the cross-product of the deviation scores $(X_i - \bar{X})(Y_i - \bar{Y})$. Complete the blank spaces on assignment sheet no. 1 now.

Computing the Regression Coefficient, Correlation Coefficient, and Covariance Coefficient

At the bottom of the columns of deviation scores and cross-products of deviation scores are spaces for the sum-of-squared-deviation scores and the sum-of-the-cross-products-of-deviation scores. Now compute these elements and write your computations into the three spaces. Once you have these three estimates, you can compute the regression coefficient using equation (13.3).

Now use equation (13.6) to compute the covariance coefficient, and use equation (13.7) to compute the correlation coefficient.

At this point stop your work and check your estimates against the correct values which your instructor has. If you have made a mistake somewhere up to this point, it is desirable to find out before computing predicted values of the Y_i and the residual scores.

Computing Predicted and Residual Scores for the Y_i

Now that you have computed the regression coefficient of Y on X and have made sure that your estimate is correct, you can compute predicted scores of the Y_i and residual scores of the Y_i using equations (13.4) and (13.5), respectively. Write your estimates of the predicted scores in the column labeled $\hat{Y}_i$ on the assignment sheet. Write your estimates of the residual scores in the column labeled $\hat{\epsilon}_i$ on the assignment sheet.

Plotting Observed and Predicted Values of the Y_i Against the X_i

It is frequently useful to graph the data for which you have computed a regression coefficient or correlation in order to obtain a better idea of where you are finding the best and worst prediction of the Y variable using the X variable. If the simple regression model you have specified is correct, then the observed Y_i should be randomly distributed around the regression line which goes through each of the predicted values of the Y_i. On the graph attached to assignment sheet no. 1, plot the Y_i and $\hat{Y}_i$ against the X_i and connect the predicted scores with a straight line. This straight line is the regression line of Y on X and equals the distribution of the Y_i over the range of values of the X variable under the assumption that only the X variable influences the observed values of the Y_i. When completed, your graph should be identical to the graph given in Figure 13.1. The vertical distance from each of the observed Y_i to the regression line equals the error of prediction as indicated in Figure 13.1.

Computing the Observed Value of F

Compute SS_p and SS_r from equations (13.8) and (13.9), respectively, and write your estimates into the spaces on assignment sheet no. 1 underneath the columns of predicted and residual scores, respectively. MS_p equals SS_p, as demonstrated in equation (13.10). Compute MS_r using equation (13.11) and write your estimate in the space on the assignment sheet. Now that you have MS_p and MS_r, you can compute the observed value of F by using equation (13.12). Write your estimate on the assignment sheet.

Determining the Adequacy of the Associative Hypothesis That Y Can be Predicted from X

Just as you did in the last chapter, turn to Table A.5 to find the expected value of F with 1 and with $N - 2$ degrees of freedom. Write the expected value of F on the assignment sheet. Compare the observed to the expected value and write your answer to the question concerning the adequacy of the associative hypothesis on the assignment sheet. Simply write "yes" or "no" as an answer to whether the associative hypothesis is rejected.

Computing the Observed Values of t

The t statistic can be used to test both associative and functional hypotheses. In order to test the adequacy of the associative hypothesis that Y can be predicted from X, compute the value of the t statistic given in equation (13.13) by setting $\beta_{yx}{}^0$ equal to zero and taking the other components of the equation from your assignment sheet (you should have estimates on your assignment sheet for the regression coefficient, MS_r, and the sum of squared deviations of the X_i around their arithmetic mean). Write your estimate of the observed value of t for the associative hypothesis of $\beta_{yx}{}^0 = 0.0$ in the space on the assignment sheet.

In order to compute the observed value of t for the functional hypothesis that Y can be completely, i.e., perfectly, predicted by X in the population, the hypothesized value of β_{yx} has to be computed. If you reread the first pages of this chapter, you will see that the original hypothesis about government involvement in the affairs of persons should increase with increasing differentiation of jobs, i.e., with increasing specialization of jobs. If it is assumed that technology has increased as a linear function of time, then it makes sense to say that attention given to government activities should increase as a linear function of time also. Therefore, the relation between X and Y as given here should be a perfect linear relation, so that the correlation between X and Y equals $+1$ (remembering that the correlation varies only between -1 and $+1$, so that a correlation of $+1$ reflects the highest positive linear relationship possible between two variables). Since you have computed estimates of the sum of squared deviations of the Y_i and the X_i from their respective arithmetic means, you can use equation (13.7) to compute the hypothesized value of the regression coefficient if the correlation coefficient in the population is $+1$:

$$\beta_{yx} = r_{yx} \frac{s_y}{s_x}$$

$$= (1) \frac{s_y}{s_x}$$

$$= \frac{s_y}{s_x}$$

Using the above equation, compute the hypothesized value of the regression coefficient and then compute the t statistic using your computed value of the hypothesized regression coefficient in equation (13.13). Write the observed value of t for the functional hypothesis of a perfect prediction of Y by X in the space on the assignment sheet.

Determining the Adequacy of the Associative and Functional Hypotheses Relating Y to X Using the t Statistic

Turn to the back of the text to Table A.4 and find the expected value of the t statistic with $N - 2$ degrees of freedom, under the assumption of no difference between the observed and the hypothesized regression coefficient. Write the expected value of t on the assignment sheet.

First, for the associative hypothesis that Y can be predicted from X, compare the observed value of t to the expected value of t. If the absolute value of the observed value of t is larger than the expected value of t, then there is a significant difference between the two regression coefficients, which means that the observed regression coefficient is significantly greater than zero and the associative hypothesis is not rejected. Write your answer to the question concerning rejection of the associative hypothesis using the t statistic next to your answer to the same question using the F statistic. Are your answers different for the two statistics? They should not be different.

For the functional hypothesis that Y can be perfectly predicted as a linear function of X, again compare the observed value of t to the expected value of t. If the absolute value of the observed value of t is larger than the expected value of t, then there is a significant difference between the estimated and hypothesized regression coefficients, which means that the functional hypothesis is rejected. Write your conclusion in the appropriate space on the assignment sheet.

This completes the example data. If you have any time left in the lab session, you can spend it on the data assigned as homework.

Assignment Sheet No. 1a

CONDUCTING SOCIAL RESEARCH

Chapter 13   Simple Regression Analysis in Associative and Functional Hypotheses

Attention to Government (Y_i) over Time (X_i) from Table 13.1

X_i	$X_i - \bar{X}$	$(X_i - \bar{X})(Y_i - \bar{Y})$	$Y_i - \bar{Y}$	Y_i	$\hat{Y}_i$	$\hat{\epsilon}_i$
1900	-36	835.56	-23.21	45	_____	_____
1904	-32	582.72	-18.21	50	_____	_____
1908	-28	817.88	-29.21	39	_____	_____
1912	-24	197.04	-8.21	60	_____	_____
1916	-20	404.20	-20.21	48	_____	_____
1920	-16	-172.78	10.79	79	_____	_____
1924	-12	-33.48	2.79	71	_____	_____
1928	-8	25.68	-3.21	65	_____	_____
1932	-4	-3.16	.79	69	_____	_____
1936	0	0.00	-4.21	64	_____	_____
1940	4	51.16	12.79	81	_____	_____

X_i	$X_i - \bar{X}$	$(X_i - \bar{X})(Y_i - \bar{Y})$	$Y_i - \bar{Y}$	Y_i	$\hat{Y}_i$	$\hat{\epsilon}_i$
1944	8	142.32	17.79	86	_____	_____
1948	12	_____	18.79	87	_____	_____
1952	16	_____	4.79	73	_____	_____
1956	20	_____	9.79	78	_____	_____
1960	24	_____	−3.21	65	_____	_____
1964	28	_____	12.79	81	_____	_____
1968	32	_____	4.79	73	_____	_____
1972	36	_____	13.79	82	_____	_____

$$\overline{\sum^{N} (X_i - \bar{X})^2} \quad \overline{\sum^{N} (X_i - \bar{X})(Y_i - Y)} \quad \overline{\sum^{N} (Y_i - \bar{Y})^2} \quad \overline{\begin{array}{c} SS_p = \\ \sum^{N} (\hat{Y}_i - \bar{Y})^2 \end{array}} \quad \overline{SS_r = \sum^{N} \hat{\epsilon}_i^2}$$

$\hat{\beta}_{yx} =$ _____ $MS_r =$ _____   Observed value of $F =$ _____

$s_{xy} =$ _____   Observed value of T when $\beta_{yx}{}^0 = 0 =$ _____

$r_{xy} =$ _____   Observed value of t when $\beta_{yx}{}^0$ is perfect = _____

Expected value of F at the 5 percent level of confidence = _____

Expected value of t at the 2.5 percent level of confidence = _____

Can the associative hypothesis of Y can be predicted from X rejected?

For the F statistic?_____   For the t statistic?_____

Can Y be perfectly predicted from X?_____

Assignment Sheet No. 1*b*

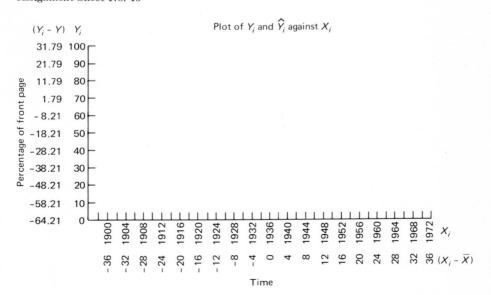

Plot of Y_i and $\hat{Y}_i$ against X_i

Assignment Sheet 2a

CONDUCTING SOCIAL RESEARCH

Chapter 13   Simple Regression Analysis in Associative and Functional Hypotheses

Number of Siblings (Y_i) Being Predicted from Father's Income (X_i)

X_i	$(X_i - \bar{X})$	$(X_i - \bar{X})(Y_i - \bar{Y})$	$(Y_i - \bar{Y})$	Y_i	$\hat{Y}_i$	$\hat{\epsilon}_i$
___	___	___	___	___	___	___
___	___	___	___	___	___	___
___	___	___	___	___	___	___
___	___	___	___	___	___	___
___	___	___	___	___	___	___
___	___	___	___	___	___	___
___	___	___	___	___	___	___
___	___	___	___	___	___	___
___	___	___	___	___	___	___
___	___	___	___	___	___	___
___	___	___	___	___	___	___
___	___	___	___	___	___	___

$$\sum_{}^{N} (X_i - \bar{X})^2 \quad \sum_{}^{N} (X_i - \bar{X}) \times (Y_i - \bar{Y}) \quad \sum_{}^{N} (Y_i - \bar{Y})^2 \quad SS_p = \quad SS_r =$$

$$\sum_{}^{N} (\hat{Y}_i - \bar{Y})^2 \quad \sum_{}^{N} \hat{\epsilon}_i^2$$

$\hat{\beta}_{yx} = $ _____ $MS_r = $ _____   Observed value of $F = $ _____

$s_{xy} = $ _____   Observed value of t when $\beta_{yx}^0 = 0 = $ _____

$r_{xy} = $ _____   Observed value of t when β_{yx}^0 perfect $= $ _____

Expected value of F at the 5 percent level of confidence $= $ _____

Expected value of t at the 2.5 percent level of confidence $= $ _____

Can the associative hypothesis of Y can be predicted from X rejected?

For the F statistic?_____   For the t statistic?_____

Can Y be perfectly predicted from X?_____

Plot of $\hat{Y}_i$ and Y_i against X_i

Number of Siblings — Y_i

X_i — Father's income

Attention to Government (Y_i) over Time (X_i) from Table 13.1

Cross-tabulation of More Than Two Variables in Contingency Hypotheses

INTRODUCTION

The previous three chapters extended the discussion of variables one at a time to a discussion of the relationship between variables two at a time. Chapter 11 used cross-tabulation to analyze the joint occurrences of values of two variables. Chapter 12 used simple ANOVA to analyze differences in a continuous variable Y in terms of multiple groups distinguished by a variable X measured at the nominal level of measurement. Chapter 13 used simple regression analysis to analyze the differences in a continuous variable Y in terms of their predictability from a variable X measured at the interval or ratio level of measurement.

In this chapter, the scope of analysis will be extended once again. Instead of analyzing variables two at a time, the focus of attention is now on more than two variables. Just as it was inappropriate to analyze variables only one at a time as if they were independent of their surrounding conditions, it is also inappropriate to analyze the relationship between pairs of variables as if the relationship were unaffected by the surrounding conditions.

This chapter is concerned with the problem of introducing a third variable into a previously observed relationship between two variables analyzed in a cross-tabulation. Although the examples consider only three variables at a time, the idea of controlling for the influence of a variable on an observed relationship extends to research situations of more than three variables with no methodological changes from the forthcoming discussion. Since the present discussion relies on the contents of Chapter 11, you are advised to review Chapter 11 before beginning the lab session outlined in this chapter.[1]

Controlling for Confounding Influences on the Observed Relationship Between Two Variables X and Y

Imagine a situation in which you have observed the cross-tabulation of two variables X and Y and have performed the types of analyses discussed in Chapter 11 for contingency hypotheses. Just when you are feeling quite pleased with yourself for a job well done, someone comes along and tells you that your analysis has been short-sighted because the relationship between X and Y is influenced by a third variable T which you have failed to consider. In order to support your analysis, you have to control the influence of the variable T on your observed relation between X and Y and demonstrate that T does not affect your analysis. The research problem then becomes, "How do you control the influence of T on the relationship between X and Y?" In other words, "How can I remove the influence of T from the observed relation between X and Y?"

The influence of T (or any group of variables T_1, T_2, etc.) is removed from the relationship between X and Y in a manner identical to that used in simple ANOVA to analyze the differences of a variable Y in terms of a variable X. In ANOVA, several groups of observations were separated in terms of a variable X. For example, if X is "sex," then two groups can be easily distinguished: "male" and "female." The values of Y for observations within each of the groups distinguished by X are then compared to see if the observations in one group tend to have different Y values than the observations in other groups. Removing the influence of a variable T from a relationship between X and Y is an identical process when groups are distinguished by the variable T and for each group of observations the investigator analyzes the relation between X and Y to see if the relation is different for the observations in one group from the relation between X and Y for observations in other groups. If there are differences in the cross-tabulations for the groups distinguishable in terms of T, then it has been demonstrated that T influences the relation between X and Y. If there are no significant differences between the cross-tabulations of X and Y across the groups distinguished by T, then it has been demonstrated that T does not influence the observed relation between X and Y. An example will give empirical meaning to the above statements.

---

[1] Two excellent volumes are available to the introductory reader which discuss relationships involving more than two variables in terms of cross-tabulations: J. A. Davis, *Elementary Survey Analysis*, Prentice-Hall, Englewood Cliffs, 1971, and M. Rosenberg, *The Logic of Survey Analysis*, Free Press, New York, 1968. This chapter is only a brief introduction to the ideas explored by these two authors.

Table 14.1   Qualitative Cross-tabulation of Father's and Son's
Occupational Classification for the Population of the United
States during the 1960s

Father's Occupational Classification	Son's Occupational Classification		
	White collar	Blue collar	
White collar	High %	Low %	100%
Blue collar	Low %	High %	100%

Table 14.1 presents the joint occurrences generally observed during the 1960–1970 decade between the occupation of a father in the United States and the occupation of his son or sons. The general conclusion to be drawn from the cross-tabulation in Table 14.1 is that most sons of persons with white-collar occupations end up with white-collar occupations, and that most sons of persons with blue-collar occupations end up with blue-collar occupations.[2] Using the methods introduced in Chapter 11, an investigator could test the fit of the contingency hypothesis of high proportions of sons having the same occupational classification as their fathers.

If the investigator is interested in the possibility of discrimination in the mobility of males in the United States, however, the cross-tabulation in Table 14.1 is inadequate, since it combines all races into a single population. In order to test the adequacy of the contingency hypothesis that the mobility of sons from their fathers' occupational classification is different for different races, the investigator could make two cross-tabulations—one cross-tabulation for whites and one cross-tabulation for nonwhites. By cross-tabulating father's occupation and son's occupation for each racial group, the investigator has controlled the effects of race on mobility, since all observations within each group have the same race. The influence of a variable T is completely removed from the relationship between X and Y when the XY relationship is analyzed only on groups of observations having identical values of T. The investigator then analyzes the XY relationship as it exists for each different value of T.

Controlling for T: The removal of the influence of a variable (or set of variables) "*T*" on observations by analyzing sets of observations which have identical values of T.

The investigator can then test the adequacy of the contingency hypothesis of no difference between the cross-tabulation for whites and the cross-tabulation for nonwhites. If the two cross-tabulations are different, then the investigator has demonstrated that race has a significant influence on the mobility of sons

[2] Readers interested in exact numerical estimates of the cells in Tables 14.1 and 14.2 are referred to O. D. Duncan, "Patterns of Occupational Mobility Among Negro Men," *Demography*, **5**: 11–22, 1968.

from their fathers' occupational classification. If the two cross-tabulations are different, then the investigator can explore the reasons why the cross-tabulations are different for different races, or the particular joint occurrences which differ the most between the two cross-tabulations. This process of exploring the conditions which affect a cross-tabulation is described as an *elaboration* of the cross-tabulation.

Elaboration: The analysis of observed relations between variables by controlling for the influence of additional variables on the relations. By knowing how an observed relationship between two variables is affected by additional variables, the investigator develops a deeper understanding of the original observed relationship.

The use of additional variables in the analysis of observed relations between pairs of variables is not just an exploratory device. The value of a specified theoretical structure in the elaboration of an observed relationship lies in the fact that the theoretical structure tells the investigator what variables should have an effect on the observed relationship. For example, if a specified theoretical structure suggests the diagram below, then the observed relationship

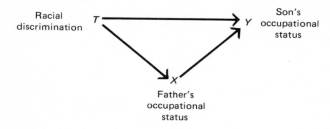

between father's occupational status and son's occupational status should be greatly changed when the investigator controls for the influence of race on the relationship. If there is no change in the observed relationship between X and Y when T is controlled, then the specified theoretical structure is inadequate for the data being considered.

Table 14.2 presents the changes which occur in the cross-tabulation given in Table 14.1 when the variable of race is controlled. Notice that the cross-tabulation of X and Y is the same for the racial group "white" as it was in the general population. There appears to be a great deal of discrimination in the mobility of nonwhite sons from their fathers' occupational classification, however, since nonwhite sons tend to end up in blue-collar jobs whether their fathers had white-collar jobs or blue-collar jobs. This is an example of how an observed cross-tabulation can change when an investigator controlls the influence of a third variable T on the original relationship. By comparing the tables in Table 14.2 with the original cross-tabulation in Table 14.1, you can see that an explanation of social mobility in the United States during the 1960s is incomplete without an explicit discussion of the effects of racial discrimination on the mobility process.

Table 14.2   The Qualitative Cross-tabulation in Table 14.1 after Controlling for the Influence of Race on the Observed Cross-tabulation.

Father's Occupational Classification	RACE Whites Son's Occupational Classification			Nonwhites Son's Occupational Classification		
	White collar	Blue collar		White collar	Blue collar	
White collar	High %	Low %	100%	Low %	High %	100%
Blue collar	Low %	High %	100%	Low %	High %	100%

The example social phenomenon to be considered in this lab session is the influence of reference groups on the expectations of persons. The example data are those gathered by Stouffer and his associates during World War II from American soldiers. The general procedure to be followed in the lab session and then in your assignments has three steps and uses the techniques in Chapter 11:

1   Cross-tabulate an original relationship between two variables X and Y.
2   Test the contingency hypothesis of no change in the original relationship when a third variable is controlled.
3   Test the contingency hypothesis of a significant relationship between X and Y being reduced to no relationship after a third variable is controlled.

If the contingency hypothesis of no change in the original relationship between X and Y after controlling for T is adequate, then T has no influence on the original relation between X and Y. If the above hypothesis is rejected, on the other hand, then T does have some influence on the relationship between X and Y. If the contingency hypothesis of a relationship between X and Y is reduced to no relationship after controlling for T is shown to be adequate, the investigator can say that any relation between X and Y in the original cross-tabulation of X and Y can be explained in terms of the variable T.

OBJECTIVES

The objectives for this lab session are an extension of the objectives of the previous lab session on cross-tabulation. They are:

1   To extend the idea of cross-tabulation between two variables to the cross-tabulation of multiple variables.
2   To familiarize you with the use of chi-square for assessing the adequacy of a multiple-variable explanation from which contingency hypotheses have been deduced.

3   To emphasize the difference between a test that the original relation between X and Y has been affected by T (some changes in the relation between X and Y) from a test that the original relation between X and Y is due to T (no relation between X and Y when T is controlled).

4   To familiarize you with the idea of controlling the influence of a variable T on an observed relationship by studying the relationship within each group of observations distinguished by T.

ASSIGNMENT

The lab session will perform the three steps of analysis given in the section, "Introduction" on the example data gathered during World War II using the statistical methods introduced in Chapter 11. Your assignment will be to perform the same steps of analysis on the two example cross-tabulations taken from the class data. You will hand in the three assignment sheets at the end of the chapter.

THE LAB SESSION

The Example Data

At the end of the chapter are three assignment sheets. The first assignment sheet already has cell frequencies on it and will be the example data for the lab session. Your lab instructor will now give you the cell frequencies for the other assignment sheets based on the class data.

As mentioned in the lab session in Chapter 11, in order to check that you have copied the data correctly and that the lab instructor has not made a mistake, compute row and column marginals. Now add up the row marginals and see if they equal N. Also, add up the column marginals and see if they equal N. If the sum of either marginal frequencies does not add up to N, then you have made a mistake in the cell frequencies or the marginal frequencies and should check your work before beginning the homework assignment.

Cross-tabulate an Original Relationship between X and Y

Assignment sheet no. 1 presents the example data to be analyzed during the lab session. For this first section, consider the original cross-tabulation between "education" and "evaluation of army promotion opportunities." The column variable, "education," has two different values, "less than high school" and "high school graduate or more." The row variable, "evaluation of army promotion opportunities," also has two different values, "very good chance of promotion" and "other responses."

The example data on assignment sheet no. 1 were used by Stouffer and his colleagues (and later sociologists) to demonstrate that humans are satisfied when they feel they are doing as well as the persons with whom they compare themselves. Two persons who compare themselves to different types of other persons, i.e., to different reference groups, can evaluate the same objective empirical situation very differently. People who compare themselves to other persons who are doing very well in life are not satisfied unless they are doing as well as their reference persons. In contrast, people who compare themselves to reference persons who are not doing very well in life will usually be more satisfied with their own achievements, since they do not expect as much out of life. Now consider the example data in the original cross-tabulation of "educational achievement" (variable X) and "evaluation of army promotion opportunities" (variable Y) given at the top of the first page of assignment sheet no. 1.[3]

The data in the cross-tabulations on assignment sheet no. 1 were gathered from American soldiers during World War II. Let us relate the Stouffer data to the above discussion regarding reference groups. In order to do this, let us assume that one of the embodiments of the achievement value in the United States is in the expectation that persons with high educational attainment will receive job promotions providing greater responsibility, prestige, and income at a faster rate than is the case for persons with little education. Then it should generally be the case that army personnel who had completed high levels of education would compare their achievements (promotions) in the army with persons of similarly high education and therefore expect faster promotions. It should also be the case that army personnel with little education would compare themselves with persons with similarly little education. They would expect promotions at a slower rate than those provided for highly educated army personnel. If the particular embodiment of the achievement value stated above is generally held by army personnel possessing either high or low levels of educational attainment, then, under the condition that both educational groups were given the same promotion opportunities, it may be expected that personnel with high education would be more frustrated with the promotion opportunities than the personnel with low education would be. Therefore, variable X (educational achievement) and variable Y (evaluation of promotion opportunities) should not be independent. Using the methods discussed in Chapter 11, the contingency hypothesis of the independence of X and Y can be assessed. If it can be rejected, then X and Y are related in some untested manner.

Recall the notation used in Chapter 11 for the analysis of contingency hypotheses using chi-square; N refers to the total number of observations in a sample; f_{ij} is the observed frequency of the joint occurrence of the ith value of the row variable and the jth value of the column variable; F_{ij} is the expected frequency for the i,j joint occurrence; P_{ij} is the proportion of observations which have the i,j joint occurrence; $f_{i.}$ is the row marginal frequency for the ith row of a cross-tabulation ($f_{i.} = f_{i1} + f_{i2} + \cdots + f_{iJ}$, where J equals the number of different values the column variable can equal); and $f_{.j}$ is the column marginal

---

[3] Readers interested in a general discussion of reference groups and their influence on human behavior are referred to R. K. Merton, *Social Theory and Social Structure*, Free Press, New York, 1968, Chapters 10 and 11.

frequency for the jth column in a cross-tabulation $(f._j = f_{1j} + f_{2j} + \cdots + f_{Ij},$ where I equals the number of different values the row variable can equal). For example, in the two-by-two cross-tabulation of X and Y on assignment sheet no. 1, $f_{11} = 366$, $P_{11} = .180$, $f_{1.} = 573$, and $f._2 = 1,017$.

If the null hypothesis of variable X and variable Y being independent is adequate for the example data, then the expected proportion of the N observations which should appear in the i,j cell of a cross-tabulation will equal the product of the proportion of the N observations which are in the $f_{i.}$ marginal frequency and the proportion of the N observations which are in the $f._j$ marginal frequency:

$$P_{ij} = \frac{(f_{i.}/N)}{(f._j/N)} \tag{14.1}$$

so that the expected frequencies for the null hypothesis of independence of the distributions of X and Y can be computed as [cf. equation 11.2]:

$$F_{ij} = P_{ij}(N) \tag{14.2}$$

Using equations (14.1) and (14.2) compute the expected proportions and expected frequencies for the null hypothesis that X and Y are independent, and write your results in the appropriate columns on the second page of assignment sheet no. 1. Also, write the observed frequencies on the assignment sheet, the f_{ij}.

Now that you have estimates of the f_{ij} and F_{ij}, you can compute the chi-square goodness-of-fit statistic as given in equation (14.3) and reproduced here for convenience:

$$\chi^2 = \sum \frac{(f_{ij} - F_{ij})^2}{F_{ij}} \tag{14.3}$$

where the summation sign $\sum$ indicates that the quantity $(f_{ij} - F_{ij})^2/F_{ij}$ should be added over all cells in the cross-tabulation. The chi-square statistic will be distributed as a chi-square distribution with

Degrees of freedom $= (I - 1)(J - 1) \tag{14.4}$

when the null hypothesis that X and Y are independent fits the data exactly (i.e., the f_{ij} and the F_{ij} are identical).

Using equations (14.3) and (14.4), complete the table on the second page of assignment sheet no. 1 (except the original P^*_{ij} column), and write in the degrees of freedom and observed chi-square. In Table A.3 find the expected chi square at the 5 percent level of confidence with degrees of freedom equal to $(I - 1)(J - 1)$, and write the value on the assignment sheet. If the observed chi square is larger than the expected chi-square, then the contingency hypothesis that X and Y are independent is rejected and there is a significant relation between X and Y. Write your decision on the rejection of the null hypothesis on the assignment sheet.

As can be seen from the large value of the observed chi-square in relation to the expected value at the 5 percent level of confidence, army personnel do evaluate promotion opportunities according to the types of reference persons with whom they compare themselves. The original cross-tabulation between X and Y on assignment sheet no. 1 assumes that all army personnel are exposed to the same promotion opportunities. After seeing that the idea of reference groups influencing evaluations is supported in a two-variable cross-tabulation, a subsequent question asks whether the idea is supported when army personnel are exposed to different rates of promotion opportunities. Is the influence of variable X on variable Y maintained for personnel who have high promotion opportunities as well as for personnel who have low promotion opportunities? In other words, does education influence evaluation of promotion opportunities when we control for an additional variable T of objective rates of promotion? One way to test this question is to separate personnel who are in the military police from personnel who are in the air corps. The military police have very low rates of promotion—most of the personnel are enlisted men. In contrast, the air corps has very high rates of promotion—most of the personnel are officers, and promotions are given out frequently. As can be seen from assignment sheet no. 1, two cross-tabulations have been separated from the one cross-tabulation at the top of page 1. At the bottom of page 1, there is a cross-tabulation of X and Y for personnel in the military police (one value of the T variable), and there is a cross-tabulation of X and Y for personnel in the air corps (the other value of the T variable). Are the two cross-tabulations the same as the original cross-tabulation?

In order to test the null hypothesis that there is no change in the relation between X and Y when T is controlled, the investigator needs to know the proportions of the total number of observations which occurred in each cell of the original cross-tabulation of X and Y before controlling for T. On the second page of assignment sheet no. 1, there is a column of spaces labeled original P_{ij}^*. The asterisk is used here to distinguish the original proportions in the cross-tabulation of X and Y, the P_{ij}^*, from the expected proportions deduced as a null hypothesis, the P_{ij}. The P_{ij}^* can be computed from the observed frequencies in the cross-tabulation at the top of page 1 of assignment sheet no. 1:

$$P_{ij}^* = \frac{f_{ij}}{N} \tag{14.5}$$

Compute the original proportions using equation (14.5) and write your results on the second page of the assignment sheet in the upper table labeled Original P_{ij}^*. Notice that P_{11}^* has been written in for you so you can be sure you are computing correctly.

Test the Null Hypothesis of No Change in the Original Relationship When the Third Variable is Controlled

When a third variable is introduced into a cross-tabulation, the notation for a two-variable cross-tabulation has to be expanded. Let K refer to the number of different values of the third variable, the T variable. Instead of each cell being referenced with the two subscripts i and j, each cell in a three-variable cross-tabulation has three subscripts, k, i, and j. The joint occurrences in a three-variable cross-tabulation are between the kth value of the variable T, the ith value of the row variable, and the jth value of the column variable. For example, consider the three-variable cross-tabulation at the bottom of assignment sheet no. 1: $f_{111} = 329$, $f_{211} = 37$, $f_{122} = 548$, and $f_{222} = 262$. The total number of observations in each group of observations distinguished by the T variable can be referenced by the dot notation: $f_{1..}$ for the first value of the T variable (military police) which indicates that the frequencies of joint occurrences involving the first value of the T variable have been summed, and $f_{2..}$ for the second value of the T variable (air corps) which indicates that the frequencies of joint occurrences involving the second value of the T variable have been summed. Similarly the marginal frequencies for the cross-tabulations of X and Y at each level of the T variable have a different notation; $f_{ki.}$ refers to the row marginal frequency for the ith value of the row variable at the kth value of the T variable $(f_{ki.} = f_{ki1} + f_{ki2} + \cdots + f_{kiJ})$, and $f_{k.j}$ refers to the column marginal frequency for the jth value of the column variable at the kth value of the T variable $(f_{k.j} = f_{k.1} + f_{k.2} + \cdots + f_{kIj})$.

If the null hypothesis of no change in the relation between X and Y after controlling for T is adequate for the example data, then we will expect to observe the same proportions of joint occurrences in each cell of the X–Y cross-tabulation for each level of T observed in the original cross-tabulation of X and Y. The expected proportions are therefore the original proportions, the P^*_{ij}. Turn to the second page of assignment sheet no. 1. Copy the P^*_{ij} from the upper table into the blank spaces in the column labeled P^*_{ij} in the lower table for each level of T. P^*_{11} has been written in already as a guide for you. Also copy the observed frequencies onto the table in the column labeled f_{kij}.

The expected frequencies in each X–Y cross-tabulation for each value of T can now be computed from the proportions P^*_{ij} and the total number of observations at each value of T:

$$F_{kij} = P^*_{ij} \, (f_{k..}) \tag{14.6}$$

Using equation (14.6) compute the expected frequencies for the two X–Y cross-tabulations when k equals 1 and when k equals 2, and write your computations on the assignment sheet in the column labeled F_{kij}.

Now that you have the observed and expected frequencies, you can compute chi-square statistics. Complete the table on the second page of the assignment sheet for the $(f_{kij} - F_{kij})^2$ and the $(f_{kij} - F_{kij})^2/F_{kij}$ columns when k equals 1 and k equals 2, and write your computations on the assignment sheet.

There are two perspectives from which the null hypothesis of no change in the XY cross-tabulation after controlling for T can be tested: (1) within each group of observations having the same value of T, or (2) for all the K values of the variable T.

Testing within a Group of Observations with Identical Values of the Variable T
This perspective asks whether the hypothesis being tested is adequate for a specific value k of the variable T. The chi-square statistic is computed as:

$$\chi_k^2 = \sum \frac{(f_{kij} - F_{kij})^2}{F_{kij}} \tag{14.7}$$

where the summation sign refers to all values $(f_{kij} - F_{kij})^2/F_{kij}$ where the kth value of the T variable is a constant. For example, the chi-square value for $k = 1$ in the example assignment equals the sum of the four fractions:

$$\chi_1^2 = \frac{(f_{111} - F_{111})^2}{F_{111}} + \frac{(f_{112} - F_{112})^2}{F_{112}} + \frac{(f_{121} - F_{121})^2}{F_{121}} + \frac{(f_{122} - F_{122})^2}{F_{122}}$$

The statistic in equation (14.7) will be distributed as a chi-square distribution with

$$\text{Degrees of freedom} = IJ - 1 \tag{14.8}$$

when there are no differences between the observed and the expected frequencies for the kth value of the variable T [see the discussion in Chapter 11 associated with equation (11.5) for an explanation of equation (14.8)]. Now compute the observed value of chi square for each value of the T variable, compute the degrees of freedom, and look up the expected value of chi square with $IJ - 1$ degrees of freedom at the 5 percent level of confidence in Table A.3. Write your computations on the assignment sheet. If the observed chi-square associated with a particular value of the variable T is greater than the expected chi-square, then the hypothesis is rejected for that value of T. Is the null hypothesis of no change after controlling for T adequate for the personnel in the Military Police ($k = 1$)? Is it adequate for the personnel in the Air Corps ($k = 2$)? Write your answers on the assignment sheet.

Testing across All Values of the Variable T   It is frequently convenient to have a single chi-square value which is a summary measure of the lack of fit of the null hypothesis across all values of the variable T. That way the investigator can say that the variable T has no effect on the XY relationship if the null hypothesis of no change after controlling for T is rejected. Let χ_t^2 refer to the observed value of chi-square for the cross-tabulations of all values of the variable T. Under the assumption that the observations for each value of the T variable have been randomly sampled from separate populations corresponding to each value of T, the total chi-square equals the sum of the observed values of chi-square for each of the K values of T:

$$\chi_t^2 = \chi_1^2 + \chi_2^2 + \cdots + \chi_k^2 \tag{14.9}$$

where each χ_k^2 is computed from equation (14.7). χ_t^2 will be distributed as a chi-square distribution with

$$\text{Degrees of freedom} = K(IJ - 1) \tag{14.10}$$

when the null hypothesis of no change in the X–Y cross-tabulation after controlling for T is adequate across the separate levels of K. It should be emphasized that even if none of the X–Y cross-tabulations for each of the K values of T was able to reject the null hypothesis of no change, it is possible for the general test of adequacy across all levels of T to reject the null hypothesis of no change by pooling all the differences between the observed and expected frequencies across all values of T.[4] Using equations (14.9) and (14.10), compute the chi-square across all values of the T variable, the degrees of freedom associated with the chi-square, and look up the expected value of chi-square at the 5 percent level of confidence with $K(IJ - 1)$ degrees of freedom. Write your results in the appropriate blanks on the assignment sheet.

In summary, the null hypothesis of no change in the relationship between variable X and variable Y after controlling for variable T is rejected for each value of T and across all values of T. Therefore, the variable T has a significant influence on the relationship between X and Y. The issue to be analyzed now concerns whether or not the variable T completely accounts for the relationship between X and Y. Can the original relationship between X and Y, which was significant, be explained in terms of the variable T?

Test the Null Hypothesis of a Relationship between X and Y Reduced to No Relationship after the Third Variable Is Controlled

Once it has been demonstrated that a third variable T has a significant influence on the relationship between X and Y, it is meaningful to ask if T completely accounts for the original relationship between X and Y. In other words, after controlling for variable T, does the original XY relationship disappear? The null hypothesis to be tested here is that of independence of the distribution of the values of X and Y after controlling for T. If this hypothesis of independence cannot be rejected for the XY cross-tabulation at each value of the T variable or across all values of T, then the investigator has demonstrated that the original relation between X and Y is not completely explainable in terms of the variable T.

Turn to the third page of assignment sheet no. 1 and fill in the observed frequencies in the column labeled f_{kij}.

Just as for the two-by-two cross-tabulation of X and Y, the expected proportions of observations to be in the k,i,j cell of the three-variable cross-tabu-

---

[4] Another point to be emphasized, which is too complicated for the present discussion, concerns the interaction of the XY cross-tabulation with particular levels of the control variable T. An interaction between the XY cross-tabulation and the kth value of T exists when the XY cross-tabulation among observations with $T = k$ is significantly different from the XY cross-tabulation for other values of T. In order to apply the summary chi-square statistic with complete accuracy, it is assumed that the XY cross-tabulation for each value of the control variable T is roughly the same. For further discussion of the problem of interaction in contingency problems see H. M. Blalock, *Social Statistics*, McGraw-Hill Book Company, New York, 1972, pp. 303–311.

lation will equal the product of the ith row marginal frequency at the kth value of T and the jth column marginal frequency at the kth value of T if the null hypothesis of X and Y being independent is adequate:

$$P_{kij} = \frac{(f_{ki.}/f_{k..})}{(f_{k.j}/f_{k..})}$$
(14.11)

so that the expected frequencies for the null hypothesis of the independence of X and Y can be computed as [cf. equation (14.2)]:

$$F_{kij} = P_{kij}(f_{k..})$$
(14.12)

Using equations (14.11) and (14.12), compute the expected proportions and expected frequencies for the null hypothesis of X and Y being independent, and write your results on the assignment sheet in the columns labeled P_{kij} and F_{kij}, respectively. P_{111}, P_{211}, F_{111}, and F_{211} have already been written in for you, so you can check your computations to see if you are using the right procedure.

Now that you have observed and expected frequencies, you can compute chi-square statistics to test the hypothesis being analyzed. Complete the table on the third page of assignment sheet no. 1 for the two columns labeled $(f_{kij} - F_{kij})^2$ and $(f_{kij} - F_{kij})^2/F_{kij}$ for k equals 1 and k equals 2.

The same two perspectives used to test the null hypothesis of no change in the XY relationship after controlling for T can be used to test the null hypothesis of independence of X and Y after controlling for T.

Testing within a Group of Observations with Identical Values of the Variable T
Are X and Y independent for a specific value of the variable T? The chi-square statistic for this question is computed using the equation given previously in equation (14.7). χ_k^2 is distributed as a chi-square distribution with

$$\text{Degrees of freedom} = (I - 1)(J - 1)$$
(14.13)

where X and Y are independent for observations where the variable T equals k.

Compute the observed chi-square for $k = 1$ and $k = 2$ using equation (14.7), and the degrees of freedom using equation (14.13); look up the expected value of chi-square at the 5 percent level of confidence with $(I - 1)(J - 1)$ degrees of freedom in Table A.3. Write your results on the third page of the assignment sheet in the appropriate spaces. Is the observed chi-square greater than the expected chi-square for $k = 1$ or $k = 2$? Write your decisions on rejecting the null hypothesis of X and Y being independent for $k = 1$ and $k = 2$ on the assignment sheet.

Testing across All Values of the Variable T   The same procedures given before for testing across all values of the control variable T apply here. The summary chi-square statistic is computed by adding together the observed values of chi-square for each level of T, as described by equation (14.9). The degrees of freedom associated with the summary chi-square statistic again equals the number of different values of the control variable times the degrees of freedom for each chi-square value for a single value of T:

$$\text{Degrees of freedom} = K(I - 1)\,(J - 1) \qquad\qquad (14.14)$$

Using equations (14.9) and (14.14), compute the observed value of chi-square for the hypothesis across all values of the control variable, the degrees of freedom, and the expected value of chi-square at the 5 percent level of confidence with $K(I - 1)\,(J - 1)$ degrees of freedom. Write your results on the assignment sheet in the appropriate space on the third page. Can the null hypothesis of X and Y being independent be rejected at the 5 percent level of confidence across both levels of T? Write your answer on the assignment sheet after you have compared the observed and expected values of chi-square.

CONCLUSIONS

As a final part of the assignment, you are asked to interpret the relationship between the X and Y variables as it is affected by the control variable T. In general, T has a significant influence on the relationship between X and Y for the example data, although there is still a significant relationship between X and Y after controlling for T. This general conclusion should be elaborated on by considering the influence of each value of T on the relationship between X and Y. T certainly cannot be ignored in the present example.

Assignment Sheet No. 1

CONDUCTING SOCIAL RESEARCH

Chapter 14   Cross-tabulation of More than Two Variables in Contingency Hypotheses

X variable—Education
Y variable—Evaluation of Army Promotion Opportunities
T variable—Army Unit of Service

EVALUATION OF ARMY PROMOTION OPPORTUNITIES	EDUCATION ACHIEVEMENT		
	Less Than High School (1)	High School Or More (2)	$f_{i.}$
A Very Good Chance for for Promotion (1)	366 (287)	207 (286)	573
Other Evaluation (2)	655 (734)	810 (731)	1,465
$f_{.j}$	1,021	1,017	2,038 Total

ARMY UNIT OF SERVICE

MILITARY POLICE (1)	AIR CORPS (2)

	Education Achievement					Education Achievement		
Evaluation	< High school	≥ High school	$f_{1i.}$	Evaluation		< High school	≥ High school	$f_{2i.}$
Good	329	164	493	Good		37	43	80
Other	543	548	1091	Other		112	262	374
$f_{1.j}$	872	712	1584	$f_{2.j}$		149	305	454
			$f_{1..}$					$f_{2..}$

(*Source*: Stouffer, S. A., E. A. Suchman, L. C. DeVinney, S. A. Star and R. M. Williams, *The American Soldier: Adjustment during Army Life*, Princeton University Press, Princeton, N.J., 1949, p. 252, chart 9.)

FOR THE NULL HYPOTHESIS OF INDEPENDENCE OF X AND Y IN ORIGINAL CROSS-TABULATION

Original P^*_{ij}	CELL	P_{ij}	EXPECTED f_{ij}	F_{ij}	$(f_{ij} - F_{ij})^2$	$(f_{ij} - F_{ij})^2/F_{ij}$
.180	1,1	.141	366	287.1		
	1,2					
	2,1					
	2,2					

Observed chi-square _____

Degrees of freedom _____   Expected chi-square _____

Hypothesis rejected? _____

FOR THE NULL HYPOTHESIS OF NO CHANGE IN RELATION BETWEEN X AND Y AFTER CONTROLLING FOR ADDITIONAL VARIABLE T

CELL	P_{ij}^{*}	f_{kij}	F_{kij}	$(f_{kij} - F_{kij})^2$	$(f_{kij} - F_{kij})^2/F_{kij}$
1,1,1	.180	329	285.1		
1,1,2					
1,2,1					
1,2,2					

Observed chi-square for $k = 1$ _____

CELL	P_{ij}^{*}	f_{kij}	F_{kij}	$(f_{kij} - F_{kij})^2$	$(f_{kij} - F_{kij})^2/F_{kij}$
2,1,1	.180	37	81.7		
2,1,2					
2,2,1					
2,2,2					

Observed chi-square for $k = 2$ _____

Expected chi-square at 5 percent level of confidence for values of T _____

Degrees of freedom for values of T _____

Hypothesis rejected for $k = 1$? _____

Hypothesis rejected for $k = 2$? _____

Expected chi-square at 5 percent level of confidence for all k values _____

Degrees of freedom for all k values _____

Hypothesis rejected for all k values? _____

FOR THE NULL HYPOTHESIS OF INDEPENDENCE OF X AND Y AFTER CONTROLLING FOR ADDITIONAL VARIABLE T

CELL	P_{ij}	f_{kij}	F_{kij}	$(f_{kij} - F_{kij})^2$	$(f_{kij} - F_{kij})^2/F_{kij}$
1,1,1	.171	329	271.4		
1,1,2					
1,2,1					
1,2,2					

Observed chi-square for $k = 1$ _____

CELL	P_{ij}	f_{kij}	F_{kij}		
2,1,1	.058	37	26.3		
2,1,2					
2,2,1					
2,2,2					

Observed chi-square for $k = 2$ _____

Expected chi-square at 5 percent level of confidence for values of T _____

Degrees of freedom for values of T _____

Hypothesis rejected for $k = 1$? _____

Hypothesis rejected for $k = 2$? _____

Expected chi-square at 5 percent level of confidence for all k values _____

Degrees of freedom for all k values _____

Hypothesis rejected for all k values? _____

In as concise a manner as you can, describe the influence of the variable T on the original cross-tabulation of variable X with variable Y. _____

_____

_____

_____

_____

Would an investigator be wrong to ignore T in his or her analysis of the relationship between X and Y? Explain your decision. _____

_____

_____

_____

Assignment Sheet No. 2

CONDUCTING SOCIAL RESEARCH

Chapter 14   Cross-tabulation of More than Two Variables in Contingency Hypotheses

X variable—Father's Income Level
Y variable—Student Educational Goal
T variable—Sex

FATHER'S
INCOME   EDUCATIONAL GOAL

	B.A. or less (1)	More than B.A. (2)	$f_i.$
Below Mean (1)			
Above Mean (2)			
$f._j$			Total

SEX
MALES (1)   FEMALES (2)

Educational Goal   Educational Goal

Father's Income	B.A. or Less	More Than B.A.	$f_{1i.}$
Below Mean			
Above Mean			
$f_{1.j}$			$f_{1..}$

Father's Income	B.A. or Less	More Than B.A.	$f_{2i.}$
Below Mean			
Above Mean			
$f_{2.j}$			$f_{2..}$

FOR THE NULL HYPOTHESIS OF INDEPENDENCE OF X AND Y IN ORIGINAL CROSS-TABULATION

Original P^*_{ij}	CELL	EXPECTED P_{ij}	f_{ij}	F_{ij}	$(f_{ij} - F_{ij})^2$	$(f_{ij} - F_{ij})^2/F_{ij}$
	1,1					
	1,2					
	2,1					
	2,2					

Observed chi-square _____

Degrees of freedom _____   Expected chi-square _____

Hypothesis rejected? _____

FOR THE NULL HYPOTHESIS OF NO CHANGE IN RELATION BETWEEN X AND Y AFTER CONTROLLING FOR ADDITIONAL VARIABLE T

CELL	P^*_{ij}	f_{kij}	F_{kij}	$(f_{kij} - F_{kij})^2$	$(f_{kij} - F_{kij})^2/F_{kij}$
1,1,1					
1,1,2					
1,2,1					
1,2,2					

Observed chi-square for $k = 1$ _____

2,1,1					
2,1,2					
2,2,1					
2,2,2					

Observed chi-square for $k = 2$ _____

Expected chi-square at 5 percent level of confidence for values of T _____

Degrees of freedom for values of T _____

Hypothesis rejected for $k = 1$? _____

Hypothesis rejected for $k = 2$? _____

Expected chi-square at 5 percent level of confidence for all k values _____

Degrees of freedom for all k values _____

Hypothesis rejected for all k values? _____

FOR THE NULL HYPOTHESIS OF INDEPENDENCE OF X AND Y AFTER CONTROLLING FOR ADDITIONAL VARIABLE T

CELL	P_{ij}	f_{kij}	F_{kij}	$(f_{kij} - F_{kij})^2$	$(f_{kij} - F_{kij})^2/F_{kij}$
1,1,1					
1,1,2					
1,2,1					
1,2,2					
2,1,1					
2,1,2					
2,2,1					
2,2,2					

Observed chi-square for $k = 1$ _____

Observed chi-square for $k = 2$ _____

Expected chi-square at 5 percent level of confidence for values of T _____

Degrees of freedom for values of T _____

Hypothesis rejected for $k = 1$? _____

Hypothesis rejected for $k = 2$? _____

Expected chi-square at 5 percent level of confidence for all k values _____

Degrees of freedom for all k values _____

Hypothesis rejected for all k values? _____

In as concise a manner as you can, describe the influence of the variable T on the original cross-tabulation of variable X with variable Y. _____

_____

_____

_____

Would an investigator be wrong to ignore T in his or her analysis of the relationship between X and Y? Explain your decision. _____

_____

_____

_____

Assignment Sheet No. 3

CONDUCTING SOCIAL RESEARCH

Chapter 14   Cross-tabulations of More than Two Variables in Contingency Hypotheses

X variable—Number of Siblings in Respondent's Home
Y variable—Number of Children Respondent Plans to Have
T variable—Educational Goal

NUMBER OF
SIBLINGS IN
RESPONDENT'S   NUMBER OF CHILDREN RESPONDENT
HOME   PLANS TO HAVE

	One or Two (1)	More Than Two (2)	$f_{i.}$
One or Two (1)			
More Than Two (2)			
$f_{.j}$			Total

EDUCATIONAL GOAL

B.A. or LESS (1)   MORE THAN B.A. (2)

Planned Children   Planned Children

Respondent's Siblings	One or Two	More Than Two	$f_{1i.}$		One or Two	More Than Two	$f_{2i.}$
One or Two				One or Two			
More Than Two				More Than Two			
$f_{1.j}$			$f_{1..}$	$f_{2.j}$			$f_{2..}$

FOR THE NULL HYPOTHESIS OF INDEPENDENCE OF X AND Y IN ORIGINAL
CROSS-TABULATION

Original P^*_{ij}	CELL	EXPECTED P_{ij}	f_{ij}	F_{ij}	$(f_{ij} - F_{ij})^2$	$(f_{ij} - F_{ij})^2/F_{ij}$
	1,1					
	1,2					
	2,1					
	2,2					

Degrees of freedom _____

Observed chi-square _____

Expected chi-square _____

Hypothesis rejected? _____

FOR THE NULL HYPOTHESIS OF NO CHANGE IN RELATION BETWEEN X
AND Y AFTER CONTROLLING FOR ADDITIONAL VARIABLE T

CELL	P^*_{ij}	f_{kij}	F_{kij}	$(f_{kij} - F_{kij})^2$	$(f_{kij} - F_{kij})^2/F_{kij}$
1,1,1					
1,1,2					
1,2,1					
1,2,2					
2,1,1					
2,1,2					
2,2,1					
2,2,2					

Observed chi-square for $k = 1$ _____

Observed chi-square for $k = 2$ _____

Expected chi-square at 5 percent level of confidence for values of T _____

Degrees of freedom for values of T _____

Hypothesis rejected for $k = 1$? _____

Hypothesis rejected for $k = 2$ _____

Expected chi-square at 5 percent level of confidence for all k values _____

Degrees of freedom for all k values _____

Hypothesis rejected for all k values? _____

FOR THE NULL HYPOTHESIS OF INDEPENDENCE OF X AND Y AFTER CONTROLLING FOR ADDITIONAL VARIABLE T

CELL	P_{ij}	f_{kij}	F_{kij}	$(f_{kij} - F_{kij})^2$	$(f_{kij} - F_{kij})^2/F_{kij}$
1,1,1					
1,1,2					
1,2,1					
1,2,2					

Observed chi-square for $k = 1$ _____

2,1,1					
2,1,2					
2,2,1					
2,2,2					

Observed chi-square for $k = 2$ _____

Expected chi-square at 5 percent level of confidence for values of T _____

Degrees of freedom for values of T _____

Hypothesis rejected for $k = 1$? _____

Hypothesis rejected for $k = 2$? _____

Expected chi-square at 5 percent level of confidence for all k values _____

Degrees of freedom for all k values _____

Hypothesis rejected for all k values? _____

In as concise a manner as you can, describe the influence of the variable T on the original cross-tabulation of variable X with variable Y._____

_____

_____

_____

_____

Would an investigator be wrong to ignore T in his or her analysis of the relationship between X and Y? Explain your decision._____

_____

_____

_____

Chapter 15

Presenting Research Ideas

Having learned the essential technical details of social research, you are now prepared to embark on a research adventure or to present the results of a research project undertaken. This chapter will introduce you to some mechanical procedures and issues involved in organizing and presenting research ideas.

There are many different occasions on which research ideas must be written down and presented. For example, a researcher has to write a research proposal in seeking financial support for a research project. A student may have to write a term paper reporting a project undertaken for a course or seminar. A professor may have to write an article to be submitted to a professional journal. Before one sits down to write one must consider several issues: (1) Who is the intended audience? (2) What is the purpose of the presentation? (3) How is it to be presented? (4) What writing style should be adopted?

OBJECTIVES

This chapter will introduce you to:

1 The considerations which must be made before research ideas can be presented
2 The organization and format of a presentation

ASSIGNMENT

The student is asked to write a research proposal on a topic of his or her choice. The student should first write a brief note preceding the proposal which specifies the considerations given to the selection of audience, the purpose of the study, and the medium to be used.

1 Read the introduction to this chapter.

2 Prepare in writing a brief note describing the research proposal you will construct. Include in this note the three items (audience, purpose, medium) mentioned above. Be prepared to make a five-minute oral presentation during the lab session.

The proposal itself should be no more than twelve pages, and should include:

1 A statement of the problem—the theoretical and methodological considerations which have been taken into account in the study. Because of the limitations of time and space, no literature review is necessary.

2 Research methodology. The following topics should be discussed in this section: (*a*) What concepts are involved? (*b*) How are the concepts to be operationalized into variables? (*c*) What items or questions will be used to measure the variables? (*d*) What is the population? (*e*) How will the sample be drawn from the population? (*f*) How will the data be collected? Observation, experiment, survey, or documentary analysis? A sample of items and questions to be used should be included (not necessarily a complete questionnaire, but the major items tapping the variables and instructions to interviewers or observers).

3 Proposed analyses of data: The student should give reasons why certain techniques of analysis are to be used. For example, it may be that the data are nominal, thus any relationships must be analyzed in a contingency table. On the other hand, if the independent variable is nominal and the dependent variable is interval, then ANOVA may be used. When all the variables are measured on the interval or ratio scale, regression and correlation techniques can be used. This section should also specify any additional variables which may affect the variables under consideration and therefore must be incorporated as control variables.

4 Anticipated and unanticipated results: The final section should discuss the potential contribution to theory or methods if the proposed relationships are verified. Attention should be given to the possibility that the results do not verify the anticipated relationships and how further analysis can be made in such case.

INTRODUCTION

The Audience

A presentation can be addressed to a wide variety of audiences, ranging from scientists engaged in basic research to the general public. In general, there are five groups of audiences: (1) scientists engaged in basic research, (2) scientists engaged in applied research, (3) practitioners and service agents, (4) policy makers, (5) sponsors of research, and (6) the general public.

Scientists engaged in basic research are interested in information which contributes to the body of scientific knowledge. They are familiar with the concepts, theories, and procedures of research. Therefore, they expect the report to be precise, accurate, and tightly structured. Scientists engaged in applied research, on the other hand, seek information which can be of use to their efforts in applying scientific methods and knowledge to the formulation of policies providing solutions to specific problems. They may not be as familiar with the concepts and theories as their colleagues engaged in basic research. The report they read must demonstrate the feasibility of the methods or knowledge in helping them to solve the problems at hand.

Practitioners and service agents utilize information in their work for their clients. They are interested in information which has clear procedural instructions, implementational instructions, or both, so that it can be incorporated in their practices and services. Librarians, teachers, physicians, social workers, and nurses are examples of this type of audience.

Policy makers are interested in information which suggests improvements in or alternatives to existing policies and administrations. They expect the report to be minimal in scientific and disciplinary jargon and maximal in providing information for solutions of problems.

Sponsors of research are interested in the technical details of the proposed study and in information which demonstrates that the study will proceed to and arrive at its findings as proposed.

A research report should focus on a specific audience as the target audience. Any wavering or uncertainty on the part of the researcher as to who the target audience is usually results in ineffective communication of the presentation.

The Purpose

The presentation is also influenced by the purpose the researcher has in mind in preparing it. A report can summarize and synthesize all the research activities in a given area—a state-of-the-art presentation. A report can describe a piece of information new to the existing body of knowledge. Or a report can be prepared to demonstrate the practical utility of the information to practitioners and to the public.

The Medium

The researcher has a choice of the form in which the presentation appears. The selection is determined by the target audience, the purpose of the presentation, and the scientific and practical usefulness of the information to be presented. The media generally available to a reporting researcher include: journal articles, in-house technical reports, monographs, chapters in a book or books, presentations at a meeting or conference, and news releases. Further, within each type of medium, different documents and forums are geared for a specific target audience. There is, however, a pattern of association between the media and the target audience. Scientists engaged in basic research tend to use journals and books as outlets for their work. Scientists in applied research tend to use technical reports and monographs. And scientists addressing themselves to the general public tend to use news releases or the mass media (magazines, television, etc.) available to the general public. The matching of a particular channel of communication, on the one hand, with the target audience and the purpose, on the other hand, determines to a large extent whether or not a presentation will receive attention. There is no particular restriction as to how many places a researcher can report, as long as the presentations are made one at a time and citations of earlier presentations are properly noted in subsequent presentations. It is often the case that a study generates a series of publications and presentations. In the case of research proposals, the rule usually is that multiple submissions are permissible as long as each considering sponsor is informed of the situation.

The Writing Style

Many writing styles have been used in research presentations, ranging from a straightforward style written in the first person ("I have discovered . . . .") to an impersonal style written in the third person ("It was discovered. . . ."). There is no consensus as to what style should be adopted. General usage favors the impersonal style. Moreover, there is a growing trend toward using the active ("The data suggest. . . .") rather than the passive ("It is suggested. . . .") voice. Also, there is a trend toward the use of simple rather than complex sentence structure. It is nevertheless up to individual researcher to choose the writing style with which he is the most comfortable and feels to be the most effective in communicating his ideas to the target audience.

When a presentation contains graphs and tables, the text should flow independently of the graphs and tables. In other words, while the graphs and tables clarify the discussion, the reader should be able to follow the discussion without having to read the graphs and tables if he so chooses. Thus, while the researcher may refer to the graphs and tables in the text, the gist of the information contained therein should appear and be explained in the text. If there is a choice, graphs and figures are preferred to tables, as the audience is more likely to grasp the main ideas or findings if they are presented with lines and circles rather than with numbers.

A researcher should consult two sources in formulating a specific writing style: (1) the conventions adopted by researchers who have used the same medium in the past, and (2) books on writing styles and scientific writing.[1]

The Content

The content of a presentation should in general be organized into five major sections: (1) statement of the problem, (2) study design and procedure, (3)

[1] William Strunk, Jr., and E. B. White, *The Elements of Style*, Macmillan, New York, 1962; S. F. Trelease, *How to Write Scientific and Technical Papers*, Cambridge, Mass.: MIT Press, 1969; F. Peter Woodford (ed.), *Scientific Writing for Graduate Students*, Rockefeller University Press, New York, 1968.

analysis and interpretation, (4) conclusions and discussion, and (5) bibliography. The format varies, depending to a large extent on the purpose of the presentation. The above format is most frequently used in reporting a completed study. A research proposal focuses more on the proposed theoretical and methodological considerations for the conduct of a study.

The statement of the problem includes a general introduction to the subject matter area, a review of points and issues in past studies and discussions, the specific topic to be studied, and the justification and importance of the selected topic for research. The review of theoretical (or methodological) issues in an area should be short, precise, and focused. The researcher then should pinpoint the critical issues and propositions with which his study is or will be concerned, present his position and argument on these issues, and elaborate potential contributions of the proposed effort to the theoretical (or methodological) advance in the subject matter area. At the same time the researcher should point out the limitations of his effort, so as not to mislead the readers into expectations of major "breakthrough" when no such results are forthcoming in the presentation.

The presentation proceeds to describe the study design and procedures. Starting from deductions of theoretical propositions and operationalization of concepts into variables, the presentation states any proposed hypotheses to be tested. Then, it presents the sampling procedure (including a general and historical, if appropriate, description of the population and events to be studied), the instrumentation and measurement process, the method of data collection, and the plans for the data analysis. Unless the data set is well known (e.g., the Census or NORC general social surveys), details of sampling (e.g., the type, the procedure, and possible errors), measurement (with actual or selected items and numbers used), data collection (training of collaborators such as interviewers, observers and confederates, instructions for collaborators and respondents), and plans for the data analysis (introduction and justification of analytical techniques to be used) must be provided.

The next section presents results of the data analysis and inferences from the results to the theoretical structure under consideration. This section should begin with a brief but sufficient description of the characteristics of the sampled respondents. If possible, the sampled characteristics should be compared with available information about the same characteristics of the population from which the sample was drawn, to demonstrate the extent of possible error in the sampling and measurement procedures. Findings should be presented in such a manner as to make it possible for a reader to derive or evaluate independently the final statistics from the basic data presented. For example, the means and standard deviations of variables should be presented when regression or correlation coefficients were computed, so that the reader can evaluate whether the distributions of the variables allow the use of regression techniques.

Finally, the report can elaborate the findings relative to the verification or modification of the theoretical structure initially considered. The researcher should also state the shortcomings and limitations of the study, so that interpretations and inferences of the findings will be made with caution. Further courses of research can be suggested.

The above outlined organization varies, of course, depending on the audience, the purpose, the medium, and the writing style. For example, in a book or dissertation, the detailed review of literature may be separated from the statement of the problem. Also, the final discussion section may lead to further analysis and interpretation of the reported data or other relevant data available to the researcher. However, a report must deal with all the issues outlined above, providing the audience with a comprehensive understanding and evaluation of the study.

THE LAB SESSION

This session will be devoted to oral presentations of the brief notes prepared by each student outlining the research proposal, including specification of the audience to which the proposal is addressed, the purpose of the study, and the medium to be used.

Following each presentation, other students and the instructor will comment on the proposal and suggest ways for improvement.

Appendixes

Table A-1   Random Numbers

10 09 73 25 33	76 52 01 35 86	34 67 35 48 76	80 95 90 91 17	39 29 27 49 45
37 54 20 48 05	64 89 47 42 96	24 80 52 40 37	20 63 61 04 02	00 82 29 16 65
08 42 26 89 53	19 64 50 93 03	23 20 90 25 60	15 95 33 47 64	35 08 03 36 06
99 01 90 25 29	09 37 67 07 15	38 31 13 11 65	88 67 67 43 97	04 43 62 76 59
12 80 79 99 70	80 15 73 61 47	64 03 23 66 53	98 95 11 68 77	12 17 17 68 33
66 06 57 47 17	34 07 27 68 50	36 69 73 61 70	65 81 33 98 85	11 19 92 91 70
31 06 01 08 05	45 57 18 24 06	35 30 34 26 14	86 79 90 74 39	23 40 30 97 32
85 26 97 76 02	02 05 16 56 92	68 66 57 48 18	73 05 38 52 47	18 62 38 85 79
63 57 33 21 35	05 32 54 70 48	90 55 35 75 48	28 46 82 87 09	83 49 12 56 24
73 79 64 57 53	03 52 96 47 78	35 80 83 42 82	60 93 52 03 44	35 27 38 84 35
98 52 01 77 67	14 90 56 86 07	22 10 94 05 58	60 97 09 34 33	50 50 07 39 98
11 80 50 54 31	39 80 82 77 32	50 72 56 82 48	29 40 52 42 01	52 77 56 78 51
83 45 29 96 34	06 28 89 80 83	13 74 67 00 78	18 47 54 06 10	68 71 17 78 17
88 68 54 02 00	86 50 75 84 01	36 76 66 79 51	90 36 47 64 93	29 60 91 10 62
99 59 46 73 48	87 51 76 49 69	91 82 60 89 28	93 78 56 13 68	23 47 83 41 13
65 48 11 76 74	17 46 85 09 50	58 04 77 69 74	73 03 95 71 86	40 21 81 65 44
80 12 43 56 35	17 72 70 80 15	45 31 82 23 74	21 11 57 82 53	14 38 55 37 63
74 35 09 98 17	77 40 27 72 14	43 23 60 02 10	45 52 16 42 37	96 28 60 26 55
69 91 62 68 03	66 25 22 91 48	36 93 68 72 03	76 62 11 39 90	94 40 05 64 18
09 89 32 05 05	14 22 56 85 14	46 42 75 67 88	96 29 77 88 22	54 38 21 45 98
91 49 91 45 23	68 47 92 76 86	46 16 28 35 54	94 75 08 99 23	37 08 92 00 48
80 33 69 45 98	26 94 03 68 58	70 29 73 41 35	53 14 03 33 40	42 05 08 23 41
44 10 48 19 49	85 15 74 79 54	32 97 92 65 75	57 60 04 08 81	22 22 20 64 13
12 55 07 37 42	11 10 00 20 40	12 86 07 46 97	96 64 48 94 39	28 70 72 58 15
63 60 64 93 29	16 50 53 44 84	40 21 95 25 63	43 65 17 70 82	07 20 73 17 90
61 19 69 04 46	26 45 74 77 74	51 92 43 37 29	65 39 45 95 93	42 58 26 05 27
15 47 44 52 66	95 27 07 99 53	59 36 78 38 48	82 39 61 01 18	33 21 15 94 66
94 55 72 85 73	67 89 75 43 87	54 62 24 44 31	91 19 04 25 92	92 92 74 59 73
42 48 11 62 13	97 34 40 87 21	16 86 84 87 67	03 07 11 20 59	25 70 14 66 70
23 52 37 83 17	73 20 88 98 37	68 93 59 14 16	26 25 22 96 63	05 52 28 25 62
04 49 35 24 94	75 24 63 38 24	45 86 25 10 25	61 96 27 93 35	65 33 71 24 72
00 54 99 76 54	64 05 18 81 59	96 11 96 38 96	54 69 28 23 91	23 28 72 95 29
35 96 31 53 07	26 89 80 93 54	33 35 13 54 62	77 97 45 00 24	90 10 33 93 33
59 80 80 83 91	45 42 72 68 42	83 60 94 97 00	13 02 12 48 92	78 56 52 01 06
46 05 88 52 36	01 39 09 22 86	77 28 14 40 77	93 91 08 36 47	70 61 74 29 41
32 17 90 05 97	87 37 92 52 41	05 56 70 70 07	86 74 31 71 57	85 39 41 18 38
69 23 46 14 06	20 11 74 52 04	15 95 66 00 00	18 74 39 24 23	97 11 89 63 38
19 56 54 14 30	01 75 87 53 79	40 41 92 15 85	66 67 43 68 06	84 96 28 52 07
45 15 51 49 38	19 47 60 72 46	43 66 79 45 43	59 04 79 00 33	20 82 66 95 41
94 86 43 19 94	36 16 81 08 51	34 88 88 15 53	01 54 03 54 56	05 01 45 11 76

Source: The RAND Corporation, *A Million Random Digits*, Free Press, Glencoe, Ill., 1955, pp. 1–3, by permission of the publisher.

Table A-1 Random Numbers

98 08 62 48 26   45 24 02 84 04   44 99 90 88 96   39 09 47 34 07   35 44 13 18 80
33 18 51 62 32   41 94 15 09 49   89 43 54 85 81   88 69 54 19 94   37 54 87 30 43
80 95 10 04 06   96 38 27 07 74   20 15 12 33 87   25 01 62 52 98   94 62 46 11 71
79 75 24 91 40   71 96 12 82 96   69 86 10 25 91   74 85 22 05 39   00 38 75 95 79
18 63 33 25 37   98 14 50 65 71   31 01 02 46 74   05 45 56 14 27   77 93 89 19 36

74 02 94 39 02   77 55 73 22 70   97 79 01 71 19   52 52 75 80 21   80 81 45 17 48
54 17 84 56 11   80 99 33 71 43   05 33 51 29 69   56 12 71 92 55   36 04 09 03 24
11 66 44 98 83   52 07 98 48 27   59 38 17 15 39   09 97 33 34 40   88 46 12 33 56
48 32 47 79 28   31 24 96 47 10   02 29 53 68 70   32 30 75 75 46   15 02 00 99 94
69 07 49 41 38   87 63 79 19 76   35 58 40 44 01   10 51 82 16 15   01 84 87 69 38

09 18 82 00 97   32 82 53 95 27   04 22 08 63 04   83 38 98 73 74   64 27 85 80 44
90 04 58 54 97   51 98 15 06 54   94 93 88 19 97   91 87 07 61 50   68 47 66 46 59
73 18 95 02 07   47 67 72 52 69   62 29 06 44 64   27 12 46 70 18   41 36 18 27 60
75 76 87 64 90   20 97 18 17 49   90 42 91 22 72   95 37 50 58 71   93 82 34 31 78
54 01 64 40 56   66 28 13 10 03   00 68 22 73 98   20 71 45 32 95   07 70 61 78 13

08 35 86 99 10   78 54 24 27 85   13 66 15 88 73   04 61 89 75 53   31 22 30 84 20
28 30 60 32 64   81 33 31 05 91   40 51 00 78 93   32 60 46 04 75   94 11 90 18 40
53 84 08 62 33   81 59 41 36 28   51 21 59 02 90   28 46 66 87 95   77 76 22 07 91
91 75 75 37 41   61 61 36 22 69   50 26 39 02 12   55 78 17 65 14   83 48 34 70 55
89 41 59 26 94   00 39 75 83 91   12 60 71 76 46   48 94 97 23 06   94 54 13 74 08

77 51 30 38 20   86 83 42 99 01   68 41 48 27 74   51 90 81 39 80   72 89 35 55 07
19 50 23 71 74   69 97 92 02 88   55 21 02 97 73   74 28 77 52 51   65 34 46 74 15
21 81 85 93 13   93 27 88 17 57   05 68 67 31 56   07 08 28 50 46   31 85 33 84 52
51 47 46 64 99   68 10 72 36 21   94 04 99 13 45   42 83 60 91 91   08 00 74 54 49
99 55 96 83 31   62 53 52 41 70   69 77 71 28 30   74 81 97 81 42   43 86 07 28 34

33 71 34 80 07   93 58 47 28 69   51 92 66 47 21   58 30 32 98 22   93 17 49 39 72
85 27 48 68 93   11 30 32 92 70   28 83 43 41 37   73 51 59 04 00   71 14 84 36 43
84 13 38 96 40   44 03 55 21 66   73 85 27 00 91   61 22 26 05 61   62 32 71 84 23
56 73 21 62 34   17 39 59 61 31   10 12 39 16 22   85 49 65 75 60   81 60 41 88 80
65 13 85 68 06   87 64 88 52 61   34 31 36 58 61   45 87 52 10 69   85 64 44 72 77

38 00 10 21 76   81 71 91 17 11   71 60 29 29 37   74 21 96 40 49   65 58 44 96 98
37 40 29 63 97   01 30 47 75 86   56 27 11 00 86   47 32 46 26 05   40 03 03 74 38
97 12 54 03 48   87 08 33 14 17   21 81 53 92 50   75 23 76 20 47   15 50 12 95 78
21 82 64 11 34   47 14 33 40 72   64 63 88 59 02   49 13 90 64 41   03 85 65 45 52
73 13 54 27 42   95 71 90 90 35   85 79 47 42 96   08 78 98 81 56   64 69 11 92 02

07 63 87 79 29   03 06 11 80 72   96 20 74 41 56   23 82 19 95 38   04 71 36 69 94
60 52 88 34 41   07 95 41 98 14   59 17 52 06 95   05 53 35 21 39   61 21 20 64 55
83 59 63 56 55   06 95 89 29 83   05 12 80 97 19   77 43 35 37 83   92 30 15 04 98
10 85 06 27 46   99 59 91 05 07   13 49 90 63 19   53 07 57 18 39   06 41 01 93 62
39 82 09 89 52   43 62 26 31 47   64 42 18 08 14   43 80 00 93 51   31 02 47 31 67

Table A-1   Random Numbers

```
59 58 00 64 78    75 56 97 88 00    88 83 55 44 86    23 76 80 61 56    04 11 10 84 08
38 50 80 73 41    23 79 34 87 63    90 82 29 70 22    17 71 90 42 07    95 95 44 99 53
30 69 27 06 68    94 68 81 61 27    56 19 68 00 91    82 06 76 34 00    05 46 26 92 00
65 44 39 56 59    18 28 82 74 37    49 63 22 40 41    08 33 76 56 76    96 29 99 08 36
27 26 75 02 64    13 19 27 22 94    07 47 74 46 06    17 98 54 89 11    97 34 13 03 58

91 30 70 69 91    19 07 22 42 10    36 69 95 37 28    28 82 53 57 93    28 97 66 62 52
68 43 49 46 88    84 47 31 36 22    62 12 69 84 08    12 84 38 25 90    09 81 59 31 46
48 90 81 58 77    54 74 52 45 91    35 70 00 47 54    83 82 45 26 92    54 13 05 51 60
06 91 34 51 97    42 67 27 86 01    11 88 30 95 28    63 01 19 89 01    14 97 44 03 44
10 45 51 60 19    14 21 03 37 12    91 34 23 78 21    88 32 58 08 51    43 66 77 08 83

12 88 39 73 43    65 02 76 11 84    04 28 50 13 92    17 97 41 50 77    90 71 22 67 69
21 77 83 09 76    38 80 73 69 61    31 64 94 20 96    63 28 10 20 23    08 81 64 74 49
19 52 35 95 15    65 12 25 96 59    86 28 36 82 58    69 57 21 37 98    16 43 59 15 29
67 24 55 26 70    35 58 31 65 63    79 24 68 66 86    76 46 33 42 22    26 65 59 08 02
60 58 44 73 77    07 50 03 79 92    45 13 42 65 29    26 76 08 36 37    41 32 64 43 44

53 85 34 13 77    36 06 69 48 50    58 83 87 38 59    49 36 47 33 31    96 24 04 36 42
24 63 73 87 36    74 38 48 93 42    52 62 30 79 92    12 36 91 86 01    03 74 28 38 73
83 08 01 24 51    38 99 22 28 15    07 75 95 17 77    97 37 72 75 85    51 97 23 78 67
16 44 42 43 34    36 15 19 90 73    27 49 37 09 39    85 13 03 25 52    54 84 65 47 59
60 79 01 81 57    57 17 86 57 62    11 16 17 85 76    45 81 95 29 79    65 13 00 48 60

03 99 11 04 61    93 71 61 68 94    66 08 32 46 53    84 60 95 82 32    88 61 81 91 61
38 55 59 55 54    32 88 65 97 80    08 35 56 08 60    29 73 54 77 62    71 29 92 38 53
17 54 67 37 04    92 05 24 62 15    55 12 12 92 81    59 07 60 79 36    27 95 45 89 09
32 64 35 28 61    95 81 90 68 31    00 91 19 89 36    76 35 59 37 79    80 86 30 05 14
69 57 26 87 77    39 51 03 59 05    14 06 04 06 19    29 54 96 96 16    33 56 46 07 80

24 12 26 65 91    27 69 90 64 94    14 84 54 66 72    61 95 87 71 00    90 89 97 57 54
61 19 63 02 31    92 96 26 17 73    41 83 95 53 82    17 26 77 09 43    78 03 87 02 67
30 53 22 17 04    10 27 41 22 02    39 68 52 33 09    10 06 16 88 29    55 98 66 64 85
03 78 89 75 99    75 86 72 07 17    74 41 65 31 66    35 20 83 33 74    87 53 90 88 23
48 22 86 33 79    85 78 34 76 19    53 15 26 74 33    35 66 35 29 72    16 81 86 03 11

60 36 59 46 53    35 07 53 39 49    42 61 42 92 97    01 91 82 83 16    98 95 37 32 31
83 79 94 24 02    56 62 33 44 42    34 99 44 13 74    70 07 11 47 36    09 95 81 80 65
32 96 00 74 05    36 40 98 32 32    99 38 54 16 00    11 13 30 75 86    15 91 70 62 53
19 32 25 38 45    57 62 05 26 06    66 49 76 86 46    78 13 86 65 59    19 64 09 94 13
11 22 09 47 47    07 39 93 74 08    48 50 92 39 29    27 48 24 54 76    85 24 43 51 59

31 75 15 72 60    68 98 00 53 39    15 47 04 83 55    88 65 12 25 96    03 15 21 92 21
88 49 29 93 82    14 45 40 45 04    20 09 49 89 77    74 84 39 34 13    22 10 97 85 08
30 93 44 77 44    07 48 18 38 28    73 78 80 65 33    28 59 72 04 05    94 20 52 03 80
22 88 84 88 93    27 49 99 87 48    60 53 04 51 28    74 02 28 46 17    82 03 71 02 68
78 21 21 69 93    35 90 29 13 86    44 37 21 54 86    65 74 11 40 14    87 48 13 72 20
```

Table A-1   Random Numbers

```
41 84 98 45 47    46 85 05 23 26    34 67 75 83 00    74 91 06 43 45    19 32 58 15 49
46 35 23 30 49    69 24 89 34 60    45 30 50 75 21    61 31 83 18 55    14 41 37 09 51
11 08 79 62 94    14 01 33 17 92    59 74 76 72 77    76 50 33 45 13    39 66 37 75 44
52 70 10 83 37    56 30 38 73 15    16 52 06 96 76    11 65 49 98 93    02 18 16 81 61
57 27 53 68 98    81 30 44 85 85    68 65 22 73 76    92 85 25 58 66    88 44 80 35 84

20 85 77 31 56    70 28 42 43 26    79 37 59 52 20    01 15 96 32 67    10 62 24 83 91
15 63 38 49 24    90 41 59 36 14    33 52 12 66 65    55 82 34 76 41    86 22 53 17 04
92 69 44 82 97    39 90 40 21 15    59 58 94 90 67    66 82 14 15 75    49 76 70 40 37
77 61 31 90 19    88 15 20 00 80    20 55 49 14 09    96 27 74 82 57    50 81 69 76 16
38 68 83 24 86    45 13 46 35 45    59 40 47 20 59    43 94 75 16 80    43 85 25 96 93

25 16 30 18 89    70 01 41 50 21    41 29 06 73 12    71 85 71 59 57    68 97 11 14 03
65 25 10 76 29    37 23 93 32 95    05 87 00 11 19    92 78 42 63 40    18 47 76 56 22
36 81 54 36 25    18 63 73 75 09    82 44 49 90 05    04 92 17 37 01    14 70 79 39 97
64 39 71 16 92    05 32 78 21 62    20 24 78 17 59    45 19 72 53 32    83 74 52 25 67
04 51 52 56 24    95 09 66 79 46    48 46 08 55 58    15 19 11 87 82    16 93 03 33 61

83 76 16 08 73    43 25 38 41 45    60 83 32 59 83    01 29 14 13 49    20 36 80 71 26
14 38 70 63 45    80 85 40 92 79    43 52 90 63 18    38 38 47 47 61    41 19 63 74 80
51 32 19 22 46    80 08 87 70 74    88 72 25 67 36    66 16 44 94 31    66 91 93 16 78
72 47 20 00 08    80 89 01 80 02    94 81 33 19 00    54 15 58 34 36    35 35 25 41 31
05 46 65 53 06    93 12 81 84 64    74 45 79 05 61    72 84 81 18 34    79 98 26 84 16

39 52 87 24 84    82 47 42 55 93    48 54 53 52 47    18 61 91 36 74    18 61 11 92 41
81 61 61 87 11    53 34 24 42 76    75 12 21 17 24    74 62 77 37 07    58 31 91 59 97
07 58 61 61 20    82 64 12 28 20    92 90 41 31 41    32 39 21 97 63    61 19 96 79 40
90 76 70 42 35    13 57 41 72 00    69 90 26 37 42    78 46 42 25 01    18 62 79 08 72
40 18 82 81 93    29 59 38 86 27    94 97 21 15 98    62 09 53 67 87    00 44 15 89 97

34 41 48 21 57    86 88 75 50 87    19 15 20 00 23    12 30 28 07 83    32 62 46 86 91
63 43 97 53 63    44 98 91 68 22    36 02 40 09 67    76 37 84 16 05    65 96 17 34 88
67 04 90 90 70    93 39 94 55 47    94 45 87 42 84    05 04 14 98 07    20 28 83 40 60
79 49 50 41 46    52 16 29 02 86    54 15 83 42 43    46 97 83 54 82    59 36 29 59 38
91 70 43 05 52    04 73 72 10 31    75 05 19 30 29    47 66 56 43 82    99 78 29 34 78
```

Table A-2   Ordinates and Areas of the Standard Normal Curve

z	Area	Ordinate	z	Area	Ordinate	z	Area	Ordinate
.00	.0000	.3989	.50	.1915	.3521	1.00	.3413	.2420
.01	.0040	.3989	.51	.1950	.3503	1.01	.3438	.2396
.02	.0080	.3989	.52	.1985	.3485	1.02	.3461	.2371
.03	.0120	.3988	.53	.2019	.3467	1.03	.3485	.2347
.04	.0160	.3986	.54	.2054	.3448	1.04	.3508	.2323
.05	.0199	.3984	.55	.2088	.3429	1.05	.3531	.2299
.06	.0239	.3982	.56	.2123	.3410	1.06	.3554	.2275
.07	.0279	.3980	.57	.2157	.3391	1.07	.3577	.2251
.08	.0319	.3977	.58	.2190	.3372	1.08	.3599	.2227
.09	.0359	.3973	.59	.2224	.3352	1.09	.3621	.2203
.10	.0398	.3970	.60	.2257	.3332	1.10	.3643	.2179
.11	.0438	.3965	.61	.2291	.3312	1.11	.3665	.2155
.12	.0478	.3961	.62	.2324	.3292	1.12	.3686	.2131
.13	.0517	.3956	.63	.2357	.3271	1.13	.3708	.2107
.14	.0557	.3951	.64	.2389	.3251	1.14	.3729	.2083
.15	.0596	.3945	.65	.2422	.3230	1.15	.3749	.2059
.16	.0636	.3939	.66	.2454	.3209	1.16	.3770	.2036
.17	.0675	.3932	.67	.2486	.3187	1.17	.3790	.2012
.18	.0714	.3925	.68	.2517	.3166	1.18	.3810	.1989
.19	.0753	.3918	.69	.2549	.3144	1.19	.3830	.1965
.20	.0793	.3910	.70	.2580	.3123	1.20	.3849	.1942
.21	.0832	.3902	.71	.2611	.3101	1.21	.3869	.1919
.22	.0871	.3894	.72	.2642	.3079	1.22	.3888	.1895
.23	.0910	.3885	.73	.2673	.3056	1.23	.3907	.1872
.24	.0948	.3876	.74	.2703	.3034	1.24	.3925	.1849
.25	.0987	.3867	.75	.2734	.3011	1.25	.3944	.1826
.26	.1026	.3857	.76	.2764	.2989	1.26	.3962	.1804
.27	.1064	.3847	.77	.2794	.2966	1.27	.3980	.1781
.28	.1103	.3836	.78	.2823	.2943	1.28	.3997	.1758
.29	.1141	.3825	.79	.2852	.2920	1.29	.4015	.1736
.30	.1179	.3814	.80	.2881	.2897	1.30	.4032	.1714
.31	.1217	.3802	.81	.2910	.2874	1.31	.4049	.1691
.32	.1255	.3790	.82	.2939	.2850	1.32	.4066	.1669
.33	.1293	.3778	.83	.2967	.2827	1.33	.4082	.1647
.34	.1331	.3765	.84	.2995	.2803	1.34	.4099	.1626
.35	.1368	.3752	.85	.3023	.2780	1.35	.4115	.1604
.36	.1406	.3739	.86	.3051	.2756	1.36	.4131	.1582
.37	.1443	.3725	.87	.3078	.2732	1.37	.4147	.1561
.38	.1480	.3712	.88	.3106	.2709	1.38	.4162	.1539
.39	.1517	.3697	.89	.3133	.2685	1.39	.4177	.1518
.40	.1554	.3683	.90	.3159	.2661	1.40	.4192	.1497
.41	.1591	.3668	.91	.3186	.2637	1.41	.4207	.1476
.42	.1628	.3653	.92	.3212	.2613	1.42	.4222	.1456
.43	.1664	.3637	.93	.3238	.2589	1.43	.4236	.1435
.44	.1700	.3621	.94	.3264	.2565	1.44	.4251	.1415
.45	.1736	.3605	.95	.3289	.2541	1.45	.4265	.1394
.46	.1772	.3589	.96	.3315	.2516	1.46	.4279	.1374
.47	.1808	.3572	.97	.3340	.2492	1.47	.4292	.1354
.48	.1844	.3555	.98	.3365	.2468	1.48	.4306	.1334
.49	.1879	.3538	.99	.3389	.2444	1.49	.4319	.1315
.50	.1915	.3521	1.00	.3413	.2420	1.50	.4332	.1295

Source: This table is reproduced from J. E. Wert, *Educational Statistics*, by permission of McGraw-Hill Book Company, New York.

Table A-2   Ordinates and Areas of the Standard Normal Curve

z	Area	Ordinate	z	Area	Ordinate	z	Area	Ordinate
1.50	.4332	.1295	2.00	.4772	.0540	2.50	.4938	.0175
1.51	.4345	.1276	2.01	.4778	.0529	2.51	.4940	.0171
1.52	.4357	.1257	2.02	.4783	.0519	2.52	.4941	.0167
1.53	.4370	.1238	2.03	.4788	.0508	2.53	.4943	.0163
1.54	.4382	.1219	2.04	.4793	.0498	2.54	.4945	.0158
1.55	.4394	.1200	2.05	.4798	.0488	2.55	.4946	.0154
1.56	.4406	.1182	2.06	.4803	.0478	2.56	.4948	.0151
1.57	.4418	.1163	2.07	.4808	.0468	2.57	.4949	.0147
1.58	.4429	.1145	2.08	.4812	.0459	2.58	.4951	.0143
1.59	.4441	.1127	2.09	.4817	.0449	2.59	.4952	.0139
1.60	.4452	.1109	2.10	.4821	.0440	2.60	.4953	.0136
1.61	.4463	.1092	2.11	.4826	.0431	2.61	.4955	.0132
1.62	.4474	.1074	2.12	.4830	.0422	2.62	.4956	.0129
1.63	.4484	.1057	2.13	.4834	.0413	2.63	.4957	.0126
1.64	.4495	.1040	2.14	.4838	.0404	2.64	.4959	.0122
1.65	.4505	.1023	2.15	.4842	.0395	2.65	.4960	.0119
1.66	.4515	.1006	2.16	.4846	.0387	2.66	.4961	.0116
1.67	.4525	.0989	2.17	.4850	.0379	2.67	.4962	.0113
1.68	.4535	.0973	2.18	.4854	.0371	2.68	.4963	.0110
1.69	.4545	.0957	2.19	.4857	.0363	2.69	.4964	.0107
1.70	.4554	.0940	2.20	.4861	.0355	2.70	.4965	.0104
1.71	.4564	.0925	2.21	.4864	.0347	2.71	.4966	.0101
1.72	.4573	.0909	2.22	.4868	.0339	2.72	.4967	.0099
1.73	.4582	.0893	2.23	.4871	.0332	2.73	.4968	.0096
1.74	.4591	.0878	2.24	.4875	.0325	2.74	.4969	.0093
1.75	.4599	.0863	2.25	.4878	.0317	2.75	.4970	.0091
1.76	.4608	.0848	2.26	.4881	.0310	2.76	.4971	.0088
1.77	.4616	.0833	2.27	.4884	.0303	2.77	.4972	.0086
1.78	.4625	.0818	2.28	.4887	.0297	2.78	.4973	.0084
1.79	.4633	.0804	2.29	.4890	.0290	2.79	.4974	.0081
1.80	.4641	.0790	2.30	.4893	.0283	2.80	.4974	.0079
1.81	.4649	.0775	2.31	.4896	.0277	2.81	.4975	.0077
1.82	.4656	.0761	2.32	.4898	.0270	2.82	.4976	.0075
1.83	.4664	.0748	2.33	.4901	.0264	2.83	.4977	.0073
1.84	.4671	.0734	2.34	.4904	.0258	2.84	.4977	.0071
1.85	.4678	.0721	2.35	.4906	.0252	2.85	.4978	.0069
1.86	.4686	.0707	2.36	.4909	.0246	2.86	.4979	.0067
1.87	.4693	.0694	2.37	.4911	.0241	2.87	.4979	.0065
1.88	.4699	.0681	2.38	.4913	.0235	2.88	.4980	.0063
1.89	.4706	.0669	2.39	.4916	.0229	2.89	.4981	.0061
1.90	.4713	.0656	2.40	.4918	.0224	2.90	.4981	.0060
1.91	.4719	.0644	2.41	.4920	.0219	2.91	.4982	.0058
1.92	.4726	.0632	2.42	.4922	.0213	2.92	.4982	.0056
1.93	.4732	.0620	2.43	.4925	.0208	2.93	.4983	.0055
1.94	.4738	.0608	2.44	.4927	.0203	2.94	.4984	.0053
1.95	.4744	.0596	2.45	.4929	.0198	2.95	.4984	.0051
1.96	.4750	.0584	2.46	.4931	.0194	2.96	.4985	.0050
1.97	.4756	.0573	2.47	.4932	.0189	2.97	.4985	.0048
1.98	.4761	.0562	2.48	.4934	.0184	2.98	.4986	.0047
1.99	.4767	.0551	2.49	.4936	.0180	2.99	.4986	.0046
2.00	.4772	.0540	2.50	.4938	.0175	3.00	.4987	.0044

Table A-3   Percentile Values of the Chi-square Distribution

ν	$\chi^2_{.999}$	$\chi^2_{.995}$	$\chi^2_{.99}$	$\chi^2_{.98}$	$\chi^2_{.976}$	$\chi^2_{.95}$	$\chi^2_{.90}$	$\chi^2_{.75}$	$\chi^2_{.50}$	$\chi^2_{.25}$	$\chi^2_{.10}$	$\chi^2_{.05}$	$\chi^2_{.025}$	$\chi^2_{.02}$	$\chi^2_{.01}$	$\chi^2_{.005}$	ν
1	10.8	7.9	6.6	5.4	5.0	3.8	2.7	1.3	.46	.10	.02	—	—	—	—	—	1
2	13.8	10.6	9.2	7.8	7.4	6.0	4.6	2.8	1.4	.58	.21	.10	.05	.04	.02	.01	2
3	16.3	12.8	11.3	9.8	9.4	7.8	6.3	4.1	2.4	1.21	.58	.35	.22	.18	.11	.07	3
4	18.5	14.9	13.3	11.7	11.1	9.5	7.8	5.4	3.4	1.92	1.1	.71	.48	.43	.30	.21	4
5	20.5	16.7	15.1	13.4	12.8	11.1	9.2	6.6	4.4	2.7	1.6	1.1	.83	.75	.55	.41	5
6	22.5	18.5	16.8	15.0	14.4	12.6	10.6	7.8	5.4	3.5	2.2	1.6	1.2	1.13	.87	.68	6
7	24.3	20.3	18.5	16.6	16.0	14.1	12.0	9.0	6.4	4.3	2.8	2.2	1.7	1.56	1.24	.99	7
8	26.1	22.0	20.1	18.2	17.5	15.5	13.4	10.2	7.3	5.1	3.5	2.7	2.2	2.03	1.65	1.3	8
9	27.9	23.6	21.7	19.7	19.0	16.9	14.7	11.4	8.3	5.9	4.2	3.3	2.7	2.53	2.09	1.7	9
10	29.6	25.2	23.2	21.2	20.5	18.3	16.0	12.5	9.3	6.7	4.9	3.9	3.2	3.06	2.55	2.2	10
11	31.3	26.8	24.7	22.6	21.9	19.7	17.3	13.7	10.3	7.6	5.6	4.6	3.8	3.61	3.05	2.6	11
12	32.9	28.3	26.2	24.1	23.3	21.0	18.5	14.8	11.3	8.4	6.3	5.2	4.4	4.18	3.57	3.1	12
13	34.5	29.8	27.7	25.5	24.7	22.4	19.8	16.0	12.3	9.3	7.0	5.9	5.0	4.76	4.11	3.6	13
14	36.1	31.3	29.1	26.9	26.1	23.7	21.1	17.1	13.3	10.2	7.8	6.6	5.6	5.37	4.66	4.1	14
15	37.7	32.8	30.6	28.3	27.5	25.0	22.3	18.2	14.3	11.0	8.5	7.3	6.3	5.98	5.23	4.6	15
16	39.3	34.3	32.0	29.6	28.8	26.3	23.5	19.4	15.3	11.9	9.3	8.0	6.9	6.61	5.81	5.1	16
17	40.8	35.7	33.4	31.0	30.2	27.6	24.8	20.5	16.3	12.8	10.1	8.7	7.6	7.26	6.41	5.7	17
18	42.3	37.2	34.8	32.3	31.5	28.9	26.0	21.6	17.3	13.7	10.9	9.4	8.2	7.91	7.02	6.3	18
19	43.8	38.6	36.2	33.7	32.9	30.1	27.2	22.7	18.3	14.6	11.7	10.1	8.9	8.57	7.63	6.9	19
20	45.3	40.0	37.6	35.0	34.2	31.4	28.4	23.8	19.3	15.5	12.4	10.9	9.6	9.24	8.26	7.4	20
21	46.8	41.4	38.9	36.3	35.5	32.7	29.6	24.9	20.3	16.3	13.2	11.6	10.3	9.9	8.9	8.0	21
22	48.3	42.8	40.3	37.7	36.8	33.9	30.8	26.0	21.3	17.2	14.0	12.3	11.0	10.6	9.5	8.6	22
23	49.7	44.2	41.6	39.0	38.1	35.2	32.0	27.1	22.3	18.1	14.8	13.1	11.7	11.3	10.2	9.3	23
24	51.2	45.6	43.0	40.3	39.4	36.4	33.2	28.2	23.3	19.0	15.7	13.8	12.4	12.0	10.9	9.9	24
25	52.6	46.9	44.3	41.6	40.6	37.7	34.4	29.3	24.3	19.9	16.5	14.6	13.1	12.7	11.5	10.5	25
26	54.0	48.3	45.6	42.9	41.9	38.9	35.6	30.4	25.3	20.8	17.3	15.4	13.8	13.4	12.2	11.2	26
27	55.5	49.6	47.0	44.1	43.2	40.1	36.7	31.5	26.3	21.7	18.1	16.2	14.6	14.1	12.9	11.8	27
28	56.9	51.0	48.3	45.4	44.5	41.3	37.9	32.6	27.3	22.7	18.9	16.9	15.3	14.8	13.6	12.5	28
29	58.3	52.3	49.6	46.7	45.7	42.6	39.1	33.7	28.3	23.6	19.8	17.7	16.0	15.6	14.3	13.1	29
30	59.7	53.7	50.9	48.0	47.0	43.8	40.3	34.8	29.3	24.5	20.6	18.5	16.8	16.3	15.0	13.8	30
40	73.5	66.8	63.7	60.4	59.3	55.8	51.8	45.6	39.3	33.7	29.1	26.5	24.4	23.8	22.2	20.7	40
60	99.7	92.0	88.4	84.6	83.3	79.1	74.4	67.0	59.3	52.3	46.5	43.2	40.5	39.7	37.5	35.5	60
100	149.5	140.2	135.8	131.1	129.6	124.3	118.5	109.1	99.3	90.1	82.4	77.9	74.2	73.1	70.0	67.3	100

Source: Abridged from table in *Biometrika*, Vol. 32 (1941), and published by permission of the author, Catherine M. Thompson, and the editor of *Biometrika*. Columns $\chi^2_{.02}$, $\chi^2_{.98}$, and $\chi^2_{.999}$ are reprinted abridged from R. A. Fisher and F. Yates, *Statistical Tables for Biological, Agricultural, and Medical Research*, published by Oliver & Boyd Ltd., Edinburgh, 1963, by permission of the publishers.

Table A-4 Percentile Values of "Student's" Distribution

ν	$t_{.75}$	$t_{.80}$	$t_{.90}$	$t_{.95}$	$t_{.975}$	$t_{.99}$	$t_{.995}$	$t_{.9995}$	ν
1	1.00	1.38	3.08	6.31	12.71	31.82	63.66	636.62	1
2	.82	1.06	1.89	2.92	4.30	6.96	9.92	31.60	2
3	.76	.98	1.64	2.35	3.18	4.54	5.84	12.94	3
4	.74	.94	1.53	2.13	2.78	3.75	4.60	8.61	4
5	.73	.92	1.48	2.02	2.57	3.36	4.03	6.86	5
6	.72	.91	1.44	1.94	2.45	3.14	3.71	5.96	6
7	.71	.90	1.42	1.89	2.36	3.00	3.50	5.40	7
8	.71	.89	1.40	1.86	2.31	2.90	3.36	5.04	8
9	.70	.88	1.38	1.83	2.26	2.82	3.25	4.78	9
10	.70	.88	1.37	1.81	2.23	2.76	3.17	4.59	10
11	.70	.88	1.36	1.80	2.20	2.72	3.11	4.44	11
12	.70	.87	1.36	1.78	2.18	2.68	3.05	4.32	12
13	.69	.87	1.35	1.77	2.16	2.65	3.01	4.22	13
14	.69	.87	1.34	1.76	2.14	2.62	2.98	4.14	14
15	.69	.87	1.34	1.75	2.13	2.60	2.95	4.07	15
16	.69	.87	1.34	1.75	2.12	2.58	2.92	4.02	16
17	.69	.86	1.33	1.74	2.11	2.57	2.90	3.96	17
18	.69	.86	1.33	1.73	2.10	2.55	2.88	3.92	18
19	.69	.86	1.33	1.73	2.09	2.54	2.86	3.88	19
20	.69	.86	1.32	1.72	2.09	2.53	2.85	3.85	20
21	.69	.86	1.32	1.72	2.08	2.52	2.83	3.82	21
22	.69	.86	1.32	1.72	2.07	2.51	2.82	3.79	22
23	.69	.86	1.32	1.71	2.07	2.50	2.81	3.77	23
24	.68	.86	1.32	1.71	2.06	2.49	2.80	3.74	24
25	.68	.86	1.32	1.71	2.06	2.48	2.79	3.72	25
26	.68	.86	1.32	1.71	2.06	2.48	2.78	3.71	26
27	.68	.86	1.31	1.70	2.05	2.47	2.77	3.69	27
28	.68	.85	1.31	1.70	2.05	2.47	2.76	3.67	28
29	.68	.85	1.31	1.70	2.04	2.46	2.76	3.66	29
30	.68	.85	1.31	1.70	2.04	2.46	2.75	3.65	30
40	.68	.85	1.30	1.68	2.02	2.42	2.70	3.55	40
60	.68	.85	1.30	1.67	2.00	2.39	2.66	3.46	60
120	.68	.85	1.29	1.66	1.98	2.36	2.62	3.37	120
∞	.6745	.842	1.282	1.645	1.960	2.326	2.576	3.291	∞
	$-t_{.25}$	$-t_{.20}$	$-t_{.10}$	$-t_{.05}$	$-t_{.025}$	$-t_{.01}$	$-t_{.005}$	$-t_{.0005}$	

Source: Reprinted abridged from R. A. Fisher and F. Yates, *Statistical Tables for Biological, Agricultural, and Medical Research,* published by Oliver & Boyd Ltd., Edinburgh, 1963, by permission of the authors and publishers.

Table A-5 99th and 95 Percentile Values of the *F* Distribution

95th Percentile in Lightface Type; 99th Percentile in Boldface Type;
ν_1 = Degrees of Freedom for Numerator

ν_2	1	2	3	4	5	6	7	8	9	10	11	12
1	161	200	216	225	230	234	237	239	241	242	243	244
	4,052	**4,999**	**5,403**	**5,625**	**5,764**	**5,859**	**5,928**	**5,981**	**6,022**	**6,056**	**6,082**	**6,106**
2	18.51	19.00	19.16	19.25	19.30	19.33	19.36	19.37	19.38	19.39	19.40	19.41
	98.49	**99.01**	**99.17**	**99.25**	**99.30**	**99.33**	**99.34**	**99.36**	**99.38**	**99.40**	**99.41**	**99.42**
3	10.13	9.55	9.28	9.12	9.01	8.94	8.88	8.84	8.81	8.78	8.76	8.74
	34.12	**30.81**	**29.46**	**28.71**	**28.24**	**27.91**	**27.67**	**27.49**	**27.34**	**27.23**	**27.13**	**27.05**
4	7.71	6.94	6.59	6.39	6.26	6.16	6.09	6.04	6.00	5.96	5.93	5.91
	21.20	**18.00**	**16.69**	**15.98**	**15.52**	**15.21**	**14.98**	**14.80**	**14.66**	**14.54**	**14.45**	**14.37**
5	6.61	5.79	5.41	5.19	5.05	4.95	4.88	4.82	4.78	4.74	4.70	4.68
	16.26	**13.27**	**12.06**	**11.39**	**10.97**	**10.67**	**10.45**	**10.27**	**10.15**	**10.05**	**9.96**	**9.89**
6	5.99	5.14	4.76	4.53	4.39	4.28	4.21	4.15	4.10	4.06	4.03	4.00
	13.74	**10.92**	**9.78**	**9.15**	**8.75**	**8.47**	**8.26**	**8.10**	**7.98**	**7.87**	**7.79**	**7.72**
7	5.59	4.74	4.35	4.12	3.97	3.87	3.79	3.73	3.68	3.63	3.60	3.57
	12.25	**9.55**	**8.45**	**7.85**	**7.46**	**7.19**	**7.00**	**6.84**	**6.71**	**6.62**	**6.54**	**6.47**
8	5.32	4.46	4.07	3.84	3.69	3.58	3.50	3.44	3.39	3.34	3.31	3.28
	11.26	**8.65**	**7.59**	**7.01**	**6.63**	**6.37**	**6.19**	**6.03**	**5.91**	**5.82**	**5.74**	**5.67**
9	5.12	4.26	3.86	3.63	3.48	3.37	3.29	3.23	3.18	3.13	3.10	3.07
	10.56	**8.02**	**6.99**	**6.42**	**6.06**	**5.80**	**5.62**	**5.47**	**5.35**	**5.26**	**5.18**	**5.11**
10	4.96	4.10	3.71	3.48	3.33	3.22	3.14	3.07	3.02	2.97	2.94	2.91
	10.04	**7.56**	**6.55**	**5.99**	**5.64**	**5.39**	**5.21**	**5.06**	**4.95**	**4.85**	**4.78**	**4.71**
11	4.84	3.98	3.59	3.36	3.20	3.09	3.01	2.95	2.90	2.86	2.82	2.79
	9.65	**7.20**	**6.22**	**5.67**	**5.32**	**5.07**	**4.88**	**4.74**	**4.63**	**4.54**	**4.46**	**4.40**
12	4.75	3.88	3.49	3.26	3.11	3.00	2.92	2.85	2.80	2.76	2.72	2.69
	9.33	**6.93**	**5.95**	**5.41**	**5.06**	**4.82**	**4.65**	**4.50**	**4.39**	**4.30**	**4.22**	**4.16**
13	4.67	3.80	3.41	3.18	3.02	2.92	2.84	2.77	2.72	2.67	2.63	2.60
	9.07	**6.70**	**5.74**	**5.20**	**4.86**	**4.62**	**4.44**	**4.30**	**4.19**	**4.10**	**4.02**	**3.96**
14	4.60	3.74	3.34	3.11	2.96	2.85	2.77	2.70	2.65	2.60	2.56	2.53
	8.86	**6.51**	**5.56**	**5.03**	**4.69**	**4.46**	**4.28**	**4.14**	**4.03**	**3.94**	**3.86**	**3.80**
15	4.54	3.68	3.29	3.06	2.90	2.79	2.70	2.64	2.59	2.55	2.51	2.48
	8.68	**6.36**	**5.42**	**4.89**	**4.56**	**4.32**	**4.14**	**4.00**	**3.89**	**3.80**	**3.73**	**3.67**
16	4.49	3.63	3.24	3.01	2.85	2.74	2.66	2.59	2.54	2.49	2.45	2.42
	8.53	**6.23**	**5.29**	**4.77**	**4.44**	**4.20**	**4.03**	**3.89**	**3.78**	**3.69**	**3.61**	**3.55**
17	4.45	3.59	3.20	2.96	2.81	2.70	2.62	2.55	2.50	2.45	2.41	2.38
	8.40	**6.11**	**5.18**	**4.67**	**4.34**	**4.10**	**3.93**	**3.79**	**3.68**	**3.59**	**3.52**	**3.45**
18	4.41	3.55	3.16	2.93	2.77	2.66	2.58	2.51	2.46	2.41	2.37	2.34
	8.28	**6.01**	**5.09**	**4.58**	**4.25**	**4.01**	**3.85**	**3.71**	**3.60**	**3.51**	**3.44**	**3.37**
19	4.38	3.52	3.13	2.90	2.74	2.63	2.55	2.48	2.43	2.38	2.34	2.31
	8.18	**5.93**	**5.01**	**4.50**	**4.17**	**3.94**	**3.77**	**3.63**	**3.52**	**3.43**	**3.36**	**3.30**
20	4.35	3.49	3.10	2.87	2.71	2.60	2.52	2.45	2.40	2.35	2.31	2.28
	8.10	**5.85**	**4.94**	**4.43**	**4.10**	**3.87**	**3.71**	**3.56**	**3.45**	**3.37**	**3.30**	**3.23**
21	4.32	3.47	3.07	2.84	2.68	2.57	2.49	2.42	2.37	2.32	2.28	2.25
	8.02	**5.78**	**4.87**	**4.37**	**4.04**	**3.81**	**3.65**	**3.51**	**3.40**	**3.31**	**3.24**	**3.17**
22	4.30	3.44	3.05	2.82	2.66	2.55	2.47	2.40	2.35	2.30	2.26	2.23
	7.94	**5.72**	**4.82**	**4.31**	**3.99**	**3.76**	**3.59**	**3.45**	**3.35**	**3.26**	**3.18**	**3.12**
23	4.28	3.42	3.03	2.80	2.64	2.53	2.45	2.38	2.32	2.28	2.24	2.20
	7.88	**5.66**	**4.76**	**4.26**	**3.94**	**3.71**	**3.54**	**3.41**	**3.30**	**3.21**	**3.14**	**3.07**
24	4.26	3.40	3.01	2.78	2.62	2.51	2.43	2.36	2.30	2.26	2.22	2.18
	7.82	**5.61**	**4.72**	**4.22**	**3.90**	**3.67**	**3.50**	**3.36**	**3.25**	**3.17**	**3.09**	**3.03**
25	4.24	3.38	2.99	2.76	2.60	2.49	2.41	2.34	2.28	2.24	2.20	2.16
	7.77	**5.57**	**4.68**	**4.18**	**3.86**	**3.63**	**3.46**	**3.32**	**3.21**	**3.13**	**3.05**	**2.99**
26	4.22	3.37	2.98	2.74	2.59	2.47	2.39	2.32	2.27	2.22	2.18	2.15
	7.72	**5.53**	**4.64**	**4.14**	**3.82**	**3.59**	**3.42**	**3.29**	**3.17**	**3.09**	**3.02**	**2.96**

Left margin: ν_2 = degrees of freedom for denominator

Source: From *Statistical Methods*, 6th edition, by George W. Snedecor and William G. Cochran, © 1967, the Iowa State University Press, Ames, Iowa, by permission of the publishers.

Table A-5 99th and 95 Percentile Values of the *F* Distribution (Continued)

95th Percentile in Lightface Type; 99th Percentile in Boldface Type;
ν_1 = Degrees of Freedom for Numerator

14	16	20	24	30	40	50	75	100	200	500	∞	ν_2
245	246	248	249	250	251	252	253	253	254	254	254	1
6,142	**6,169**	**6,208**	**6,234**	**6,258**	**6,286**	**6,302**	**6,323**	**6,334**	**6,352**	**6,361**	**6,366**	
19.42	19.43	19.44	19.45	19.46	19.47	19.47	19.48	19.49	19.49	19.50	19.50	2
99.43	**99.44**	**99.45**	**99.46**	**99.47**	**99.48**	**99.48**	**99.49**	**99.49**	**99.49**	**99.50**	**99.50**	
8.71	8.69	8.66	8.64	8.62	8.60	8.58	8.57	8.56	8.54	8.54	8.53	3
26.92	**26.83**	**26.69**	**26.60**	**26.50**	**26.41**	**26.35**	**26.27**	**26.23**	**26.18**	**26.14**	**26.12**	
5.87	5.84	5.80	5.77	5.74	5.71	5.70	5.68	5.66	5.65	5.64	5.63	4
14.24	**14.15**	**14.02**	**13.93**	**13.83**	**13.74**	**13.69**	**13.61**	**13.57**	**13.52**	**13.48**	**13.46**	
4.64	4.60	4.56	4.53	4.50	4.46	4.44	4.42	4.40	4.38	4.37	4.36	5
9.77	**9.68**	**9.55**	**9.47**	**9.38**	**9.29**	**9.24**	**9.17**	**9.13**	**9.07**	**9.04**	**9.02**	
3.96	3.92	3.87	3.84	3.81	3.77	3.75	3.72	3.71	3.69	3.68	3.67	6
7.60	**7.52**	**7.39**	**7.31**	**7.23**	**7.14**	**7.09**	**7.02**	**6.99**	**6.94**	**6.90**	**6.88**	
3.52	3.49	3.44	3.41	3.38	3.34	3.32	3.29	3.28	3.25	3.24	3.23	7
6.35	**6.27**	**6.15**	**6.07**	**5.98**	**5.90**	**5.85**	**5.78**	**5.75**	**5.70**	**5.67**	**5.65**	
3.23	3.20	3.15	3.12	3.08	3.05	3.03	3.00	2.98	2.96	2.94	2.93	8
5.56	**5.48**	**5.36**	**5.28**	**5.20**	**5.11**	**5.06**	**5.00**	**4.96**	**4.91**	**4.88**	**4.86**	
3.02	2.98	2.93	2.90	2.86	2.82	2.80	2.77	2.76	2.73	2.72	2.71	9
5.00	**4.92**	**4.80**	**4.73**	**4.64**	**4.56**	**4.51**	**4.45**	**4.41**	**4.36**	**4.33**	**4.31**	
2.86	2.82	2.77	2.74	2.70	2.67	2.64	2.61	2.59	2.56	2.55	2.54	10
4.60	**4.52**	**4.41**	**4.33**	**4.25**	**4.17**	**4.12**	**4.05**	**4.01**	**3.96**	**3.93**	**3.91**	
2.74	2.70	2.65	2.61	2.57	2.53	2.50	2.47	2.45	2.42	2.41	2.40	11
4.29	**4.21**	**4.10**	**4.02**	**3.94**	**3.86**	**3.80**	**3.74**	**3.70**	**3.66**	**3.62**	**3.60**	
2.64	2.60	2.54	2.50	2.46	2.42	2.40	2.36	2.35	2.32	2.31	2.30	12
4.05	**3.98**	**3.86**	**3.78**	**3.70**	**3.61**	**3.56**	**3.49**	**3.46**	**3.41**	**3.38**	**3.36**	
2.55	2.51	2.46	2.42	2.38	2.34	2.32	2.28	2.26	2.24	2.22	2.21	13
3.85	**3.78**	**3.67**	**3.59**	**3.51**	**3.42**	**3.37**	**3.30**	**3.27**	**3.21**	**3.18**	**3.16**	
2.48	2.44	2.39	2.35	2.31	2.27	2.24	2.21	2.19	2.16	2.14	2.13	14
3.70	**3.62**	**3.51**	**3.43**	**3.34**	**3.26**	**3.21**	**3.14**	**3.11**	**3.06**	**3.02**	**3.00**	
2.43	2.39	2.33	2.29	2.25	2.21	2.18	2.15	2.12	2.10	2.08	2.07	15
3.56	**3.48**	**3.36**	**3.29**	**3.20**	**3.12**	**3.07**	**3.00**	**2.97**	**2.92**	**2.89**	**2.87**	
2.37	2.33	2.28	2.24	2.20	2.16	2.13	2.09	2.07	2.04	2.02	2.01	16
3.45	**3.37**	**3.25**	**3.18**	**3.10**	**3.01**	**2.96**	**2.89**	**2.86**	**2.80**	**2.77**	**2.75**	
2.33	2.29	2.23	2.19	2.15	2.11	2.08	2.04	2.02	1.99	1.97	1.96	17
3.35	**3.27**	**3.16**	**3.08**	**3.00**	**2.92**	**2.86**	**2.79**	**2.76**	**2.70**	**2.67**	**2.65**	
2.29	2.25	2.19	2.15	2.11	2.07	2.04	2.00	1.98	1.95	1.93	1.92	18
3.27	**3.19**	**3.07**	**3.00**	**2.91**	**2.83**	**2.78**	**2.71**	**2.68**	**2.62**	**2.59**	**2.57**	
2.26	2.21	2.15	2.11	2.07	2.02	2.00	1.96	1.94	1.91	1.90	1.88	19
3.19	**3.12**	**3.00**	**2.92**	**2.84**	**2.76**	**2.70**	**2.63**	**2.60**	**2.54**	**2.51**	**2.49**	
2.23	2.18	2.12	2.08	2.04	1.99	1.96	1.92	1.90	1.87	1.85	1.84	20
3.13	**3.05**	**2.94**	**2.86**	**2.77**	**2.69**	**2.63**	**2.56**	**2.53**	**2.47**	**2.44**	**2.42**	
2.20	2.15	2.09	2.05	2.00	1.96	1.93	1.89	1.87	1.84	1.82	1.81	21
3.07	**2.99**	**2.88**	**2.80**	**2.72**	**2.63**	**2.58**	**2.51**	**2.47**	**2.42**	**2.38**	**2.36**	
2.18	2.13	2.07	2.03	1.98	1.93	1.91	1.87	1.84	1.81	1.80	1.78	22
3.02	**2.94**	**2.83**	**2.75**	**2.67**	**2.58**	**2.53**	**2.46**	**2.42**	**2.37**	**2.33**	**2.31**	
2.14	2.10	2.04	2.00	1.96	1.91	1.88	1.84	1.82	1.79	1.77	1.76	23
2.97	**2.89**	**2.78**	**2.70**	**2.62**	**2.53**	**2.48**	**2.41**	**2.37**	**2.32**	**2.28**	**2.26**	
2.13	2.09	2.02	1.98	1.94	1.89	1.86	1.82	1.80	1.76	1.74	1.73	24
2.93	**2.85**	**2.74**	**2.66**	**2.58**	**2.49**	**2.44**	**2.36**	**2.33**	**2.27**	**2.23**	**2.21**	
2.11	2.06	2.00	1.96	1.92	1.87	1.84	1.80	1.77	1.74	1.72	1.71	25
2.89	**2.81**	**2.70**	**2.62**	**2.54**	**2.45**	**2.40**	**2.32**	**2.29**	**2.23**	**2.19**	**2.17**	
2.10	2.05	1.99	1.95	1.90	1.85	1.82	1.78	1.76	1.72	1.70	1.69	26
2.86	**2.77**	**2.66**	**2.58**	**2.50**	**2.41**	**2.36**	**2.28**	**2.25**	**2.19**	**2.15**	**2.13**	

ν_2 = degrees of freedom for denominator

Table A-5   99th and 95 Percentile Values of the F Distribution (Continued)

95th Percentile in Lightface Type; 99th Percentile in Boldface Type;
ν_1 = Degrees of Freedom for Numerator

ν_2	1	2	3	4	5	6	7	8	9	10	11	12
27	4.21	3.35	2.96	2.73	2.57	2.46	2.37	2.30	2.25	2.20	2.16	2.13
	7.68	**5.49**	**4.60**	**4.11**	**3.79**	**3.56**	**3.39**	**3.26**	**3.14**	**3.06**	**2.98**	**2.93**
28	4.20	3.34	2.95	2.71	2.56	2.44	2.36	2.29	2.24	2.19	2.15	2.12
	7.64	**5.45**	**4.57**	**4.07**	**3.76**	**3.53**	**3.36**	**3.23**	**3.11**	**3.03**	**2.95**	**2.90**
29	4.18	3.33	2.93	2.70	2.54	2.43	2.35	2.28	2.22	2.18	2.14	2.10
	7.60	**5.42**	**4.54**	**4.04**	**3.73**	**3.50**	**3.33**	**3.20**	**3.08**	**3.00**	**2.92**	**2.87**
30	4.17	3.32	2.92	2.69	2.53	2.42	2.34	2.27	2.21	2.16	2.12	2.09
	7.56	**5.39**	**4.51**	**4.02**	**3.70**	**3.47**	**3.30**	**3.17**	**3.06**	**2.98**	**2.90**	**2.84**
32	4.15	3.30	2.90	2.67	2.51	2.40	2.32	2.25	2.19	2.14	2.10	2.07
	7.50	**5.34**	**4.46**	**3.97**	**3.66**	**3.42**	**3.25**	**3.12**	**3.01**	**2.94**	**2.86**	**2.80**
34	4.13	3.28	2.88	2.65	2.49	2.38	2.30	2.23	2.17	2.12	2.08	2.05
	7.44	**5.29**	**4.42**	**3.93**	**3.61**	**3.38**	**3.21**	**3.08**	**2.97**	**2.89**	**2.82**	**2.76**
36	4.11	3.26	2.86	2.63	2.48	2.36	2.28	2.21	2.15	2.10	2.06	2.03
	7.39	**5.25**	**4.38**	**3.89**	**3.58**	**3.35**	**3.18**	**3.04**	**2.94**	**2.86**	**2.78**	**2.72**
38	4.10	3.25	2.85	2.62	2.46	2.35	2.26	2.19	2.14	2.09	2.05	2.02
	7.35	**5.21**	**4.34**	**3.86**	**3.54**	**3.32**	**3.15**	**3.02**	**2.91**	**2.82**	**2.75**	**2.69**
40	4.08	3.23	2.84	2.61	2.45	2.34	2.25	2.18	2.12	2.07	2.04	2.00
	7.31	**5.18**	**4.31**	**3.83**	**3.51**	**3.29**	**3.12**	**2.99**	**2.88**	**2.80**	**2.73**	**2.66**
42	4.07	3.22	2.83	2.59	2.44	2.32	2.24	2.17	2.11	2.06	2.02	1.99
	7.27	**5.15**	**4.29**	**3.80**	**3.49**	**3.26**	**3.10**	**2.96**	**2.86**	**2.77**	**2.70**	**2.64**
44	4.06	3.21	2.82	2.58	2.43	2.31	2.23	2.16	2.10	2.05	2.01	1.98
	7.24	**5.12**	**4.26**	**3.78**	**3.46**	**3.24**	**3.07**	**2.94**	**2.84**	**2.75**	**2.68**	**2.62**
46	4.05	3.20	2.81	2.57	2.42	2.30	2.22	2.14	2.09	2.04	2.00	1.97
	7.21	**5.10**	**4.24**	**3.76**	**3.44**	**3.22**	**3.05**	**2.92**	**2.82**	**2.73**	**2.66**	**2.60**
48	4.04	3.19	2.80	2.56	2.41	2.30	2.21	2.14	2.08	2.03	1.99	1.96
	7.19	**5.08**	**4.22**	**3.74**	**3.42**	**3.20**	**3.04**	**2.90**	**2.80**	**2.71**	**2.64**	**2.58**
50	4.03	3.18	2.79	2.56	2.40	2.29	2.20	2.13	2.07	2.02	1.98	1.95
	7.17	**5.06**	**4.20**	**3.72**	**3.41**	**3.18**	**3.02**	**2.88**	**2.78**	**2.70**	**2.62**	**2.56**
55	4.02	3.17	2.78	2.54	2.38	2.27	2.18	2.11	2.05	2.00	1.97	1.93
	7.12	**5.01**	**4.16**	**3.68**	**3.37**	**3.15**	**2.98**	**2.85**	**2.75**	**2.66**	**2.59**	**2.53**
60	4.00	3.15	2.76	2.52	2.37	2.25	2.17	2.10	2.04	1.99	1.95	1.92
	7.08	**4.98**	**4.13**	**3.65**	**3.34**	**3.12**	**2.95**	**2.82**	**2.72**	**2.63**	**2.56**	**2.50**
65	3.99	3.14	2.75	2.51	2.36	2.24	2.15	2.08	2.02	1.98	1.94	1.90
	7.04	**4.95**	**4.10**	**3.62**	**3.31**	**3.09**	**2.93**	**2.79**	**2.70**	**2.61**	**2.54**	**2.47**
70	3.98	3.13	2.74	2.50	2.35	2.23	2.14	2.07	2.01	1.97	1.93	1.89
	7.01	**4.92**	**4.08**	**3.60**	**3.29**	**3.07**	**2.91**	**2.77**	**2.67**	**2.59**	**2.51**	**2.45**
80	3.96	3.11	2.72	2.48	2.33	2.21	2.12	2.05	1.99	1.95	1.91	1.88
	6.96	**4.88**	**4.04**	**3.56**	**3.25**	**3.04**	**2.87**	**2.74**	**2.64**	**2.55**	**2.48**	**2.41**
100	3.94	3.09	2.70	2.46	2.30	2.19	2.10	2.03	1.97	1.92	1.88	1.85
	6.90	**4.82**	**3.98**	**3.51**	**3.20**	**2.99**	**2.82**	**2.69**	**2.59**	**2.51**	**2.43**	**2.36**
125	3.92	3.07	2.68	2.44	2.29	2.17	2.08	2.01	1.95	1.90	1.86	1.83
	6.84	**4.78**	**3.94**	**3.47**	**3.17**	**2.95**	**2.79**	**2.65**	**2.56**	**2.47**	**2.40**	**2.33**
150	3.91	3.06	2.67	2.43	2.27	2.16	2.07	2.00	1.94	1.89	1.85	1.82
	6.81	**4.75**	**3.91**	**3.44**	**3.14**	**2.92**	**2.76**	**2.62**	**2.53**	**2.44**	**2.37**	**2.30**
200	3.89	3.04	2.65	2.41	2.26	2.14	2.05	1.98	1.92	1.87	1.83	1.80
	6.76	**4.71**	**3.88**	**3.41**	**3.11**	**2.90**	**2.73**	**2.60**	**2.50**	**2.41**	**2.34**	**2.28**
400	3.86	3.02	2.62	2.39	2.23	2.12	2.03	1.96	1.90	1.85	1.81	1.78
	6.70	**4.66**	**3.83**	**3.36**	**3.06**	**2.85**	**2.69**	**2.55**	**2.46**	**2.37**	**2.29**	**2.23**
1,000	3.85	3.00	2.61	2.38	2.22	2.10	2.02	1.95	1.89	1.84	1.80	1.76
	6.66	**4.62**	**3.80**	**3.34**	**3.04**	**2.82**	**2.66**	**2.53**	**2.43**	**2.34**	**2.26**	**2.20**
∞	3.84	2.99	2.60	2.37	2.21	2.09	2.01	1.94	1.88	1.83	1.79	1.75
	6.64	**4.60**	**3.78**	**3.32**	**3.02**	**2.80**	**2.64**	**2.51**	**2.41**	**2.32**	**2.24**	**21.8**

ν_2 = degrees of freedom for denominator

Table A-5   99th and 95 Percentile Values of the F Distribution (Continued)

95th Percentile in Lightface Type; 99th Percentile in Boldface Type;
ν_1 = Degrees of Freedom for Numerator

14	16	20	24	30	40	50	75	100	200	500	∞	ν_2
2.08	2.03	1.97	1.93	1.88	1.84	1.80	1.76	1.74	1.71	1.68	1.67	27
2.83	**2.74**	**2.63**	**2.55**	**2.47**	**2.38**	**2.33**	**2.25**	**2.21**	**2.16**	**2.12**	**2.10**	
2.06	2.02	1.96	1.91	1.87	1.81	1.78	1.75	1.72	1.69	1.67	1.65	28
2.80	**2.71**	**2.60**	**2.52**	**2.44**	**2.35**	**2.30**	**2.22**	**2.18**	**2.13**	**2.09**	**2.06**	
2.05	2.00	1.94	1.90	1.85	1.80	1.77	1.73	1.71	1.68	1.65	1.64	29
2.77	**2.68**	**2.57**	**2.49**	**2.41**	**2.32**	**2.27**	**2.19**	**2.15**	**2.10**	**2.06**	**2.03**	
2.04	1.99	1.93	1.89	1.84	1.79	1.76	1.72	1.69	1.66	1.64	1.62	30
2.74	**2.66**	**2.55**	**2.47**	**2.38**	**2.29**	**2.24**	**2.16**	**2.13**	**2.07**	**2.03**	**2.01**	
2.02	1.97	1.91	1.86	1.82	1.76	1.74	1.69	1.67	1.64	1.61	1.59	32
2.70	**2.62**	**2.51**	**2.42**	**2.34**	**2.25**	**2.20**	**2.12**	**2.08**	**2.02**	**1.98**	**1.96**	
2.00	1.95	1.89	1.84	1.80	1.74	1.71	1.67	1.64	1.61	1.59	1.57	34
2.66	**2.58**	**2.47**	**2.38**	**2.30**	**2.21**	**2.15**	**2.08**	**2.04**	**1.98**	**1.94**	**1.91**	
1.98	1.93	1.87	1.82	1.78	1.72	1.69	1.65	1.62	1.59	1.56	1.55	36
2.62	**2.54**	**2.43**	**2.35**	**2.26**	**2.17**	**2.12**	**2.04**	**2.00**	**1.94**	**1.90**	**1.87**	
1.96	1.92	1.85	1.80	1.76	1.71	1.67	1.63	1.60	1.57	1.54	1.53	38
2.59	**2.51**	**2.40**	**2.32**	**2.22**	**2.14**	**2.08**	**2.00**	**1.97**	**1.90**	**1.86**	**1.84**	
1.95	1.90	1.84	1.79	1.74	1.69	1.66	1.61	1.59	1.55	1.53	1.51	40
2.56	**2.49**	**2.37**	**2.29**	**2.20**	**2.11**	**2.05**	**1.97**	**1.94**	**1.88**	**1.84**	**1.81**	
1.94	1.89	1.82	1.78	1.73	1.68	1.64	1.60	1.57	1.54	1.51	1.49	42
2.54	**2.46**	**2.35**	**2.26**	**2.17**	**2.08**	**2.02**	**1.94**	**1.91**	**1.85**	**1.80**	**1.78**	
1.92	1.88	1.81	1.76	1.72	1.66	1.63	1.58	1.56	1.52	1.50	1.48	44
2.52	**2.44**	**2.32**	**2.24**	**2.15**	**2.06**	**2.00**	**1.92**	**1.88**	**1.82**	**1.78**	**1.75**	
1.91	1.87	1.80	1.75	1.71	1.65	1.62	1.57	1.54	1.51	1.48	1.46	46
2.50	**2.42**	**2.30**	**2.22**	**2.13**	**2.04**	**1.98**	**1.90**	**1.86**	**1.80**	**1.76**	**1.72**	
1.90	1.86	1.79	1.74	1.70	1.64	1.61	1.56	1.53	1.50	1.47	1.45	48
2.48	**2.40**	**2.28**	**2.20**	**2.11**	**2.02**	**1.96**	**1.88**	**1.84**	**1.78**	**1.73**	**1.70**	
1.90	1.85	1.78	1.74	1.69	1.63	1.60	1.55	1.52	1.48	1.46	1.44	50
2.46	**2.39**	**2.26**	**2.18**	**2.10**	**2.00**	**1.94**	**1.86**	**1.82**	**1.76**	**1.71**	**1.68**	
1.88	1.83	1.76	1.72	1.67	1.61	1.58	1.52	1.50	1.46	1.43	1.41	55
2.43	**2.35**	**2.23**	**2.15**	**2.06**	**1.96**	**1.90**	**1.82**	**1.78**	**1.71**	**1.66**	**1.64**	
1.86	1.81	1.75	1.70	1.65	1.59	1.56	1.50	1.48	1.44	1.41	1.39	60
2.40	**2.32**	**2.20**	**2.12**	**2.03**	**1.93**	**1.87**	**1.79**	**1.74**	**1.68**	**1.63**	**1.60**	
1.85	1.80	1.73	1.68	1.63	1.57	1.54	1.49	1.46	1.42	1.39	1.37	65
2.37	**2.30**	**2.18**	**2.09**	**2.00**	**1.90**	**1.84**	**1.76**	**1.71**	**1.64**	**1.60**	**1.56**	
1.84	1.79	1.72	1.67	1.62	1.56	1.53	1.47	1.45	1.40	1.37	1.35	70
2.35	**2.28**	**2.15**	**2.07**	**1.98**	**1.88**	**1.82**	**1.74**	**1.69**	**1.62**	**1.56**	**1.53**	
1.82	1.77	1.70	1.65	1.60	1.54	1.51	1.45	1.42	1.38	1.35	1.32	80
2.32	**2.24**	**2.11**	**2.03**	**1.94**	**1.84**	**1.78**	**1.70**	**1.65**	**1.57**	**1.52**	**1.49**	
1.79	1.75	1.68	1.63	1.57	1.51	1.48	1.42	1.39	1.34	1.30	1.28	100
2.26	**2.19**	**2.06**	**1.98**	**1.89**	**1.79**	**1.73**	**1.64**	**1.59**	**1.51**	**1.46**	**1.43**	
1.77	1.72	1.65	1.60	1.55	1.49	1.45	1.39	1.36	1.31	1.27	1.25	125
2.23	**2.15**	**2.03**	**1.94**	**1.85**	**1.75**	**1.68**	**1.59**	**1.54**	**1.46**	**1.40**	**1.37**	
1.76	1.71	1.64	1.59	1.54	1.47	1.44	1.37	1.34	1.29	1.25	1.22	150
2.20	**2.12**	**2.00**	**1.91**	**1.83**	**1.72**	**1.66**	**1.56**	**1.51**	**1.43**	**1.37**	**1.33**	
1.74	1.69	1.62	1.57	1.52	1.45	1.42	1.35	1.32	1.26	1.22	1.19	200
2.17	**2.09**	**1.97**	**1.88**	**1.79**	**1.69**	**1.62**	**1.53**	**1.48**	**1.39**	**1.33**	**1.28**	
1.72	1.67	1.60	1.54	1.49	1.42	1.38	1.32	1.28	1.22	1.16	1.13	400
2.12	**2.04**	**1.92**	**1.84**	**1.74**	**1.64**	**1.57**	**1.47**	**1.42**	**1.32**	**1.24**	**1.19**	
1.70	1.65	1.58	1.53	1.47	1.41	1.36	1.30	1.26	1.19	1.13	1.08	1,000
2.09	**2.01**	**1.89**	**1.81**	**1.71**	**1.61**	**1.54**	**1.44**	**1.38**	**1.28**	**1.19**	**1.11**	
1.69	1.64	1.57	1.52	1.46	1.40	1.35	1.28	1.24	1.17	1.11	1.00	∞
2.07	**1.99**	**1.87**	**1.79**	**1.69**	**1.59**	**1.52**	**1.41**	**1.36**	**1.25**	**1.15**	**1.00**	

ν_2 = degrees of freedom for denominator

Table A-6 Data Derived From Questionnaire

Table A-6 Data Derived From Questionnaire

NOTES

NOTES

NOTES

NOTES

NOTES

NOTES

NOTES

NOTES

NOTES

NOTES

NOTES

AC A3289

NOTES